The Jeffersonian Dream

Historians of the Frontier and American West

Richard W. Etulain,
Series Editor

Paul W. Gates
(Courtesy Robert Barker, Cornell University Photography.)

The Jeffersonian Dream

Studies in the History
of American Land Policy
and Development

Paul W. Gates

EDITED BY ALLAN G. AND MARGARET BEATTIE BOGUE

Published in cooperation with the
University of New Mexico Center for the American West

University of New Mexico Press
Albuquerque

Library of Congress Cataloging-in-Publication Data
Gates, Paul Wallace, 1901–
The Jeffersonian dream: studies in the history
of American land policy and development /
Paul W. Gates; edited by Allan G. and
Margaret Beattie Bogue. — 1st. ed.

p. cm.

(Historians of the frontier and American West)
Includes bibliographical references (p.   )

ISBN 0-8263-1699-9

1. Land tenure—United States—History.
2. Land use—United States—History.
3. Land settlement—Government policy—United States—History.
4. Land tenure—Law and legislation—United States.

I. Bogue, Allan G., 1921–
II. Bogue, Margaret Beattie, 1924–
III. Title.   IV. Series.

HD191.G37   1996
333.3'0973—dc20   95-44547
CIP

Contents

Introduction
Paul Wallace Gates

Allan G. and Margaret Beattie Bogue

Whether dealing in the 1940s with canine invaders in his Cornell classrooms, awing Wisconsin graduate students with the length of his working days during the late 1960s, or rising on numerous occasions across the years to dispute a point at learned society meetings, Paul Wallace Gates has thoroughly enjoyed the scholar's life through his career. After undergraduate study at Colby College in Maine and initial graduate training at Clark University in Massachusetts, and the University of Wisconsin in Madison, Gates completed the doctorate in history at Harvard University in 1930. He accepted his first full-time teaching position at Bucknell University that same year and, during the next, his first scholarly publications appeared. On these foundations, Gates built a scholarly career that led him briefly to adjunct appointments at the Brookings Institution and the Agricultural Adjustment Administration and thereafter to Cornell University, where he taught until his retirement in 1970. During that time, he served occasionally as a visiting professor at other major institutions. Gates has been an indefatigable researcher; he has authored ten books or monographs, edited four volumes, and written seventy-five articles, chapters and introductions, pamphlets, and other miscellaneous publications.

Although not a student of Frederick Jackson Turner, Gates began his scholarly career within the Turnerian tradition. In prescribing a scholarly agenda for western history, Turner stressed the importance of investigating the disposal of public lands. At Clark University, James B. Hedges, a Turner student, alerted Gates to the opportunities for research in the history of the public domain. During a year of graduate work in Madison, Gates decided to enroll at Harvard, where his brothers also studied and where an able Turner student, Frederick Merk, taught frontier history. Gates would agree with Turner that the development of western America was a very important part of American political, economic, and social growth but, unlike Turner, he downplayed the triumphs of western democracy. Instead, he emphasized how the United States' "scandalous" management of public lands perverted the development of democratic institutions.

Other American historians had contributed significantly to general or scholarly knowledge about public lands, but Gates's article, "The Homestead Law in an Incongruous Land System" (1936) particularly caught the attention of historians.[1] In that seminal piece, Gates challenged the conventional wisdom that the famous statute had democratized the American land system. By mid career he was regarded among historians as the leading authority on the American land-disposal system. He has been particularly interested in the application of land laws and in their specific and long-run impact on the agricultural and general development of the United States and American society.

Gates's dissertation, which won the David A. Wells Prize of Harvard University in 1931–1932, appeared as *The Illinois Central Railroad and Its Colonization Work* in 1934. A broadly conceived book, the first third relates the settlement history of Illinois generally, the railroad's efforts to win a charter, the road's early financial and construction difficulties, and western land speculation in general. The balance of the monograph describes the formulation and administration of Illinois Central land-sale policies, the recruitment of American and foreign buyers, the results of sale policies, and the impact of the Granger Era on the railroad.

Gates realized, however, that the Illinois Central was only one element in a much broader picture. With the assistance of the Social Science Research Council, he began research for "a history of the disposal of the Public Domain." He soon concluded that the first steps in this general project must be the preparation of regional studies of land distribution. For some years he worked actively in laying the ground work for an "intensive study of land-disposal policies in the prairie states." From the late 1930s through the early 1950s, he wrote a number of essays dealing with the significance of large-scale landlords, cattlemen, tenants, and laborers in prairie agricultural development (see Chapters 1 and 2). However research opportunities at Cornell University led him to interrupt the flow of his prairie research during the early 1940s.

During 1865–1866 Ezra Cornell persuaded the Comptroller of New York to sell most of the state's agricultural college land scrip to him to use in developing a college of agricultural and mechanical arts. The Wisconsin pine lands, which Cornell acquired with this scrip, provided a considerable endowment for Cornell University. Using the university land-business records and related manuscript collections, Gates prepared *The Wisconsin Pine Lands of Cornell University: A Study in Land Policy and Absentee Ownership* (1943), the first of the regional monographs that he had envisioned during the mid 1930s (see Chapter 5). In addition to developing the specific details of Cornell's land purchases, and their administration and sale, Gates examined the background of the Morrill Act, state policies for disposing of college scrip, and western land speculation. He also explored the character of the Chippewa lumber industry, the impact of state and local tax policies on large holders of Wisconsin pine lands, and their opposition to the bonding and related taxation that accompanied the development of the state's railroad network.

As early as 1937, Gates published an article on the disposal of the Christian Indian tract in Kansas. Intermittently thereafter he returned to the study of the speculative scramble for the reserves of the intruded Indian tribes relocated to eastern Kansas during the 1830s and 1840s and moved south to Indian territory from 1854 onward. The developing interest of other scholars in this subject inspired Gates to write *Fifty Million Acres: Conflicts over Kansas Land Policy, 1854–1890* (1954). This project, he wrote, was an effort to explain the colorful history of pioneer Kansas, "not in terms of population makeup, the course of immigration, the puritan character, or Freudian psychology, but rather through the functioning of governmental policies, particularly Indian and land policies."[2] Here he describes how a colorful collection of railroad executives, government officers, and agglomerative eastern and southern land speculators victimized powerless Native Americans and angry squatters. The latter struggled to delay federal land sales. Once this battle was lost, the settlers labored under shockingly usurious rates of interest on purchase-money loans or battled to pay no more than preemption prices on the Cherokee or Osage reservation lands acquired by rapacious railroad interests. The land-sale policies of the Democratic party, Gates argues, helped carry Kansas and other midwestern states into the Republican party. Those of Kansas railroads helped produce Granger laws (see Chapter 6).

The relation of land distribution to pioneering and subsequent land-use patterns brought Gates to grips with the history of agriculture. He contributed the volume on agriculture to the multivolume economic history of the United States published by Holt, Rinehart, and Winston. Appearing in 1960, *The Farmer's Age: Agriculture, 1815–1860,* institutional in focus, provides a strong treatment of land policy, frontier agriculture, and the relationships between the various agricultural regions of the United States. The publishing program of the Civil War Centennial Commission offered Gates the opportunity to carry this story through the Civil War era in *Agriculture and the Civil War* (1965).

By the late 1950s, Gates had begun to publish his sporadic investigations of the tortuous history of California land disposal. Perhaps a California regional study would have emerged in the late 1960s, but Milton A. Pearl, director of the Public Land Law Review Commission (PLLRC), invited Gates to write a general survey of land disposal. In Pearl's words, this history "would serve as a background for all those considering future public land policy," one "that would give us insights into the manner in which federal public land laws and policies had influenced—through failures and successes—the sweep of our nation's history." Pearl specified a brutal timetable. The PLLRC authorized the study in late May 1966; the Government Printing Office published *History of Public Land Law Development,* an 828-page book, in November 1968. With the exception of seventy-five pages relating to mineral policies and minor end matter, Gates wrote the entire volume. A *tour de force,* the book showed Gates's continuing willingness to make policy judgments on both ideological and moral grounds. Some of his stalwartly Progressive assertions and *obiter dicta* probably sat poorly with some members of the PLLRC, but Pearl lauded Gates's book as "every bit as important as the report of the commission."[3]

Gates never regarded his earlier pronouncements as final statements on land policy. In 1962 he used the Centennial of the Homestead Act to prepare his important revisionary article, "The Homestead Act: Free Land Policy in Operation, 1862–1935" (see Chapter 3). Published in 1973, the collection of prairie articles, *Landlords and Tenants on the Prairie Frontier: Studies in American Land Policy,* showed his awareness of the debate aroused by the essays as originally published. Thomas Jefferson, he admitted, "would have been convinced that . . . the policy had worked reasonably well." But Gates admitted that his own work had been "largely devoted to the malfunctioning of an intended democratic system of land disposal."

> Many of these flaws, he wrote, might have been prevented by more careful drafting of legislation, by congresses more sensitive to the problems of the pioneers, by administrators and judges more concerned with the intent of the land laws and less willing to recognize every loophole in them, and by land seekers less ready to perjure themselves in their greed.[4]

While the PLLRC study was under way, Gates published the sketches of California agriculture of John Quincy Adams Warren as *California Ranchos and Farms, 1846–1862.* In an extended editorial introduction, the Cornell historian discussed the major characteristics of land disposal and early agriculture in California. By the end of the 1970s, Gates had published more than a dozen articles based on extensive research in California source materials. Thirteen of these pieces appeared as chapters in *Land and Law in Califor-*

nia: Essays on Land Policies (1991) (see Chapter 4). Although his bibliography shows that aspects of federal land policy in the southern United States
attracted his attention on occasion and to good effect, Gates was never to investigate land distribution issues in that region in the kind of depth that he
displayed in his research on the Middle West and California.

As he investigated American land policy, Gates blazed a trail through a
wide variety of essential sources. He used original federal land-office records,
primarily entry and tract books, and surveyor's plats and notes. Other in-
valuable sources included: the manuscript census of agriculture and population, 1850–1880; local newspapers; county biographical compendia; county
courthouse deeds, mortgages, and miscellaneous records; tax assessors's and
collectors's books; and probate and civil court records. Manuscript business
records dealing with land speculation and agriculture proved to be especially
fruitful. He also used more conventional printed federal documents such as
the *Congressional Globe, Congressional Record,* statutes, and legal cases.

Gates has never exemplified the cloistered scholar. He enjoyed his contacts with government social scientists in the years 1933 through 1935 and was
happy to contribute a survey of recent federal land policies to the *Supplementary Report of the Land Planning Committee to the National Resources Board*
(1935). He accepted the invitations of government attorneys to testify as an
expert witness before the Indian Claims Commission in cases involving the
Quapaw Indians and other tribes. This troubled some American historians.
No sympathetic historian, they believed, would aid the government's efforts
to resist Native Americans seeking redress. Gates's position was in effect "let
the truth fall where it may." He has admitted, however, that he was profoundly influenced by the writings of nineteenth-century critics of American
land policy—George Henry Evans, Horace Greeley, George W. Julian, and
Henry George—who espoused a labor theory of value. Following their doctrines, Gates estimated appropriate prices for the transfer of lands from Indian
to federal title at relatively low figures. However he has always maintained
that he would have preferred to serve the tribesmen rather than the government in such matters and he did assist in the preparation of one tribal brief.
Like others involved in the claim cases during his period of activity, he made
his estimates on the basis of assumptions drawn from the dominant culture.

No reader of *Public Land Law Development* would suggest that Gates tai-
lored his findings to appease members of the PLLRC. During the 1960s, he
also helped economist Chandler Morris who advocated the revision of American natural resource policies.

In Gates's hands history has been a policy science, a record laid bare for
future policy makers. In various summative or interpretive articles, Gates

tried to place American land policy within broader perspective. Most notable was his effort to show the changing meaning of liberal and conservative positions on American land policy throughout our national history (see Chapter 7). But in a jointly authored article of the mid 1980s (see Chapter 9), he and Lillian Cowdell Gates compared significant attempts to redirect land policy in Canada and the United States. Gates discussed the influence of pressure groups on natural-resource policies in his 1985 prize-winning essay, "The Intermountain West against Itself." In that article, Gates ventured further and more interpretively into current natural-resource issues than he had at any time since his work in the Agricultural Adjustment Administration (see Chapter 8). One scholar has suggested that Gates "dedicated" his career during the 1970s and 1980s to "saving the natural resources on federal lands from profligate exploitation" and that "the environmental movement received a strong boost from the scholarly papers and publications that ensued."[5] However, did Gates join the environmental movement or did that amorphous force join him?

Most scholars agree that Gates has approached his work from the perspective of a progressive-pluralist. Policy outcomes derive from the interaction of contending interests in American society. He found one nineteenth-century example in the disagreement between the older and newer states over appropriate federal land policies. Although this West-against-East theme has a Turnerian ring, Gates developed the class dimensions of interest group conflict much more sharply than did Turner and his students. Turner contended, "Most important of all has been the fact that an area of free land has continually lain on the western border of the settled area of the United States. . . . These free lands promoted individualism, economic equality, freedom to rise, democracy."[6] Gates, however, places the concept of "free land" under the stern light of the economic realities of farm making. He argues that the federal disposal of cheap public lands encouraged the development of a landed aristocracy on the frontier, encouraged speculation, and demonstrated that the accumulation of real estate was a major way to wealth. In his work, landlords, tenants, and landless agricultural laborers take their place along with Turner's independent, democratic, free-holding small farmers. The activities of these actors and Gates's evaluation of them are recorded in Chapters 1 and 2.

Some readers have detected moral outrage in Gates's rendering of these matters. "He never lost his sense of indignation," wrote one.[7] So irreverent was his view of the "Hoosier Cattle Kings," their aquisitive skills, and their reluctance to pay taxes that a sensitive descendant of these gentry quickly purchased the entire inventory of the *Indiana Magazine of History* issue in which Gates described their activities. Gates, however, did not allow the little man to escape scot free. Squatters stole timber from government lands, they participated in lawless mobs, used intimidatory tactics at federal land sales, and were often as speculatively minded as the large holder. But they were closer to Gates's idea of the Jeffersonian yeoman or his lineal descendant, the family farmer, than the large holders were, and if the small holders were sinners, one infers, they were provoked.

For historians of class, race/ethnicity, and gender, Paul Gates's work is somewhat less than satisfactory. To the historian of class, his work is a treasure trove of information on the relation of agrarianism to class. Gates makes the Indians prime actors in some of his writings, gives some attention to slavery and the needs of the freedmen, and discusses the holders of French and Hispanic land titles in some detail. However, other than acknowledging the eligibility of immigrants to acquire holdings under the land laws and speculating about the prevalence of alien tenants, Gates pays little attention to the foreign born. The status of women within the system did not interest him — and one must admit that, despite their widespread role in the settlement process generally, women emerged only as a significant element among land entrants in the later years of the homestead era. Yet Gates's work is critical to any modern historian interested in American federalism, the government and special interests, policy making, lobbying, regionalism, public corruption, environmentalism, class structure, ethnic issues (particularly in regard to Indians and Hispanics), violence, and rural labor history.

Gates's indictment of American public land policies attracted dissenters as early as the 1950s. As Gates had revised Turner, so his own students and young economic historians expressed some reservations about his work. The public land system, they argued, was more rational than Gates indicated. Although in no sense rejecting the great importance of his contributions, the Bogues suggested modifications of his views on money lenders, speculation, and tenancy. Donald L. Winters insightfully critiqued farm tenancy in the Midwest. Robert Swierenga challenged Gates's interpretation of the influence of land speculation on agricultural development and community growth. Others have also sought to qualify his ideas. Conservative policy analysts have challenged Gates's contention that government management of federal lands, for all of its faults, "is less corrosive of nature and the well-being of man" than is private ownership. But some of Gates's students — Yasuo Okada for example — have continued to endorse their teacher's original positions, and independent scholars such as Reginald Horsman have placed both Gates and the revisionists in objective perspective, sparing none. After assessing the virtues and weaknesses of Paul W. Gates's contributions, Jon Gjerde concluded recently: "Perhaps the work of Gates . . . has much to tell us still" and indeed it does.[8]

Research and publication is only part of the academic historian's contribution to his time. Gates was also classroom teacher and citizen. Bucknell University was primarily an undergraduate school, and the young professor from Harvard found many of the students disinterested and the level of performance somewhat below his expectations. His dean felt required to explain the facts of academic life at Bucknell to him. But Gates discovered some bright and interested students there.

Gates's move to Cornell University in 1936 opened new teaching vistas, especially in directing the work of graduate students. He usually reached his office around eight o'clock in the morning and kept his office door open to students until the late afternoon, unless he was rummaging in the library stacks. Sometimes he returned in the evening to work. On one occasion the central stairway in Boardman Hall was closed to allow for repairs, thus blocking access to the History Department offices. Undeterred, Gates "borrowed" a ladder from the campus maintenance crew to allow workaholics like himself to climb from the building's central foyer to the second floor corridor.

Gates was no avuncular Mr. Chips strolling on the campus with hands clasped behind back. Five feet nine or ten inches in height, with black hair, clipped moustache, regular features, and a firm jaw, he strode, in his early and middle years, from place to place with his shoulders back and the hint of a swagger. In his survey classes he abandoned the dais and lectern and paced across the front of the room, clutching some sheets of paper that sometimes had only a few headings scrawled on them, or (according to some assistants) were completely blank. Unsupported by electronic amplification, his voice boomed from the windows of Boardman Hall across the Cornell campus, its range only exceeded, it was said, by that of Clinton Rossiter, a strong-lunged professor of government.

As a teacher, Gates believed that his obligation was to critique the course of American development. A lively undergraduate lecturer, he never hesitated to flay vested interests in the best Progressive style. Even in the United States survey lectures, he might incorporate information or incidents derived from his research experience to fire the imagination of his listeners or make them understand for the first time the essence of what good historical research involved. But undergraduate lecturing was not his great love, and he sometimes criticized other scholars for putting too much of their time into lecture preparation.

Gates conducted his graduate seminar at his office in Boardman Hall until the building was removed to make way for the Olin Research Library. Lined with books, his office was cluttered. A thick layer of books and papers rested upon his desk, on open shelves, on the floor, on the window sills, even spilling out of the closet beside the office door. For some years in the 1940s and 1950s, a phrenological head perched on the desk or window sill. A bundle of big bluestem, a gift of James C. Malin, stood in one corner. An opaque globe light challenged the sight of even the most keen eyed student or scholar. A rocker, its cane bottom sadly ruptured, sat in one corner, and other chairs, were to be approached with extreme caution.

Seated behind the desk in his swivel chair, Gates presided over the seminar, often casually, at other times with great intensity. Seminarians approached their report days with careful preparation, much thought, and a good deal of foreboding. At times Gates held his questions until the end of the report but, on other occasions, he interspersed pungent remarks or queries. In the enthusiasm of the moment, his questioning could become somewhat inquisitorial. Anticipating her report, at least one nervous seminarian fainted. Occasionally Gates's attention wandered during reports. One seminar group remembered the day when Gates, trying vainly to straighten the bottom edge of the fabric, scissored pieces off the bottom of his plaid tie with his large clipping shears. Distracted on another occasion by his impending departure for a professional meeting, he punctuated the delivery of a student report with salvoes of paper clips directed at the metal wastebasket as he cleaned out his desk drawers. Particularly during the years that he was departmental chairman, telephone calls might interrupt proceedings. One afternoon he listened sympathetically to an extended report from the elderly mother of Professor Wolf Laistner, the dour and somewhat irascible professor of ancient history, remarking loudly for the seminar members to hear, "Oh, Mrs. Laistner, You don't meant it! I'm so sorry to hear that Wolf has the mumps! No, I won't tell a soul."

Although Gates was sometimes an easy mark for an undergraduate with a sob story, he expected graduate students to be made of sterner stuff. Indeed, some of them emerged with bruised feelings after a conference or seminar with Gates. But he was honest and well meaning, and if he discerned some promise in a student's work, he quickly encouraged the budding scholar. His disappointment was real, however, when young scholars failed to mature a promising topic into a publishable essay or thesis. Nor did he believe in accepting doctoral dissertations at the minimal level of quality to allow rapid acquisition of the union card. He understood the significance of early high-quality publication to professional advancement and knew that young scholars have little time during their first several years of teaching to rewrite their theses. A truly satisfactory dissertation, Gates told students, was one that he could recommend to a press for publication immediately after its author defended it. His high standard surely helps to explain why an extremely large proportion of his doctoral students published scholarly work subsequent to their graduation. Although Gates preferred to direct research in his special areas of interest, he accepted a history of major-league baseball from one candidate.

Unlike some of his colleagues, Gates happily worked with women graduate students. He urged them to meet the highest professional standards on the assumption that they would make their mark in a male-dominated profession. Lillian Cowdell Gates, his wife, had done so. Why not others? Over the years, he has taken great delight in the fact that a number of women who took the doctorate under his guidance have enjoyed impressive careers at major universities.

Gates believed strongly that historians should understand the theories and methodologies of other relevant disciplines if those concepts and tools helped them to write a more informed narrative. He had learned, he said, much from the social scientists at the Brookings Institution during 1933 and 1934 and in the Land Policy Section of the Agricultural Adjustment Administration during the next year. Gates urged students to take one or even both of their doctoral minors in related fields.

While at Bucknell University, Gates became active in the Pennsylvania Historical Association and was appointed to the Pennsylvania Historical Commission. As a Cornell professor, he regularly attended meetings of the American Historical Association and the Mississippi Valley Historical Association (MVHA). Active in the committee work of both societies, he was president of the latter. Gates sat on the Executive Board of the MVHA during the changeful 1960s when it became the Organization of American Historians. John Caughey was to write, "He has been gadfly, conscience, and catalyst, questioning the stockpiling of reserves instead of giving support to action programs, and urging the profession to speak out rigorously on issues crucial to scholarship."[9] In broader context Gates wholeheartedly supported the successful efforts of the history associations to eliminate segregation at convention hotels.

Gates served for ten years as the chairman of the Cornell History Department (1946–1956). Although secretary of the faculty for a brief period, he was never a campus politician. But he was a vigorous proponent of programs that, he believed, were beneficial to the department and his area of specialization. At his urging, the Cornell librarians built strong holdings in western American history, and he was a driving force (along with Professor George Sabine) in creating the Cornell Collection of Regional History which, under the dynamic direction of Edith Fox, amassed a treasure trove of manuscripts relating to New York and western economic and social development. This agency provided not only source material for doctoral dissertations but hourly labor for numbers of graduate students in American history.

Gates joked that, as a son of a Baptist minister, he was a member of the most discriminated against element in all American life. He was reared in an atmosphere of extreme domestic piety in which dancing, cards, and playing marbles for keeps were taboo. However, Gates found no time as an adult for organized religion, other than dropping Lillian Gates at the church for religious service. But he was secretary of the Varna Volunteer Fire Department and long involved in the operation of a consumer cooperative in Ithaca. Usually Gates contented himself with casting his ballot as a registered Democrat, but deviated, however, in 1948. That year, he threw himself enthusiastically into the "Henry A. Wallace for President" movement and was named treasurer of its New York state party. But he was frustrated by the degree of influence that, he believed, Communists exercised at the national convention. Steadfastly opposing action that would deprive any Americans of their constitutional rights, he came increasingly thereafter to believe that the Communists were perverting American progressivism to their own ends.

We have tried in the following pages to present representative selections from Paul Gates's writings. Given their great number and length and the restrictions as to pagination under which we labored, we found the process to be very difficult. But the nine pieces that follow show the high quality, the relevance, and the diversity of his work. As editors we were singularly fortunate in being able to persuade him to provide a thumbnail sketch of his early life. We thank him for his cooperation and are most grateful for the opportunity to have worked with him once again. We owe a special debt of gratitude to Dr. Gould Coleman who, as Cornell archivist, made available the fine oral history interview with Professor Gates that he recorded and enthusiastically aided us in various other ways.

Notes

1. The publishing information for all works of Paul Wallace Gates cited in this introduction is to be found in the bibliography that follows Chapter 9. In preparing the introductory essay we have drawn as well on two unpublished sources: Paul W. Gates, "Commentary on Robert W. Fogel and Jack L. Rutner, 'The Efficiency Effects of Federal Land Policy: A Report of Some Provisional Findings,'" delivered at the Conference on The Dimensions of Quantitative Research in History at the University of Chicago, 1969, of which a copy is in the possession of the editors; and the Paul W. Gates "Oral History Interview Transcripts" prepared by Dr. Gould Coleman on the basis of a series of conversations with Gates, extending from November 2, 1979, through October 17, 1980.

2. Gates, *Fifty Million Acres*, xi.

3. Milton A. Pearl in *History of Public Land Law Development*, v, and in Harriet

Nathan, ed., *America's Public Lands: Politics, Economics and Administration* (Berkeley: Institute of Governmental Studies, University of California, Berkeley, 1972), 7.

4. Gates, *Landlords and Tenants on the Prairie Frontier,* 12.

5. Lawrence B. Lee in Gates, *Land and Law in California,* xix, xx.

6. Frederick Jackson Turner, *The Frontier in American History* (New York: Henry Holt and Company, 1920), 259.

7. Robert C. Nesbit, *Wisconsin: A History* (Madison: University of Wisconsin Press, 1973), 145.

8. Frederick Merk, "Foreword," *The Frontier in American Development: Essays in Honor of Paul Wallace Gates,* ed. David M. Ellis *et al.* (Ithaca: Cornell University Press, 1969), ix-xxx; Joseph M. Petulla, "Paul Wallace Gates, Historian of Public Land Policy," *California Historical Quarterly* 56 (Summer 1977): 170-74; Margaret Beattie Bogue and Allan G. Bogue, "Paul W. Gates," *Great Plains Journal* 18 (1979): 22-32; Harry N. Scheiber, "The Economic Historian as Realist and as Keeper of Democratic Ideals: Paul Wallace Gates's Studies of American Land Policy," *Journal of Economic History* 40 (September 1980): 585-93; Lawrence B. Lee, "Introduction," in Gates, *Land and Law in California* (Ames: Iowa State University Press, 1991), xiii-xxiv; Allan G. Bogue, *Money at Interest: The Farm Mortgage on the Middle Border* (Ithaca: Cornell University Press, 1955); Margaret Beattie Bogue, *Patterns from the Sod: Land Use and Tenure in the Grand Prairie, 1850-1900* (Springfield: Illinois State Historical Library, 1959); Allan G. Bogue and Margaret Beattie Bogue, " 'Profits' and the Frontier Land Speculator," *Journal of Economic History* 17 (1957): 1-24; Allan G. Bogue, *From Prairie to Corn Belt: Farming on the Illinois and Iowa Prairies in the Nineteenth Century* (Chicago: University of Chicago Press, 1963); Donald L. Winters, "Agricultural Tenancy in the Nineteenth-Century Middle West: The Historiographical Debate," *Indiana Magazine of History* 78 (June 1982): 128-53; Robert Swierenga, *Pioneers and Profits: Land Speculation on the Iowa Frontier* (Ames: Iowa State University Press, 1968); Sterling Brubaker, ed., *Rethinking the Federal Lands* (Washington, D.C.: Resources for the Future, Inc., 1984), Gates quote from p. 55; Yasuo Okada, *Public Lands and Pioneer Farmers: Gage County, Nebraska, 1850-1900* (Tokyo: Keio Economic Society, 1971); Reginald Horseman, "Changing Images of the Public Domain: Historians and the Shaping of Midwest Frontiers," in *This Land of Ours: The Acquisition and Disposition of the Public Domain: Papers Presented at an Indiana American Revolution Bicentennial Symposium* (Indianapolis: Indiana Historical Society, 1978); Jon Gjerde, " 'Roots of Maladjustment' in the Land: Paul Wallace Gates," *Reviews in American History* 19 (March 1991): 142-53. The Gjerde quote is from p. 152.

9. John W. Caughey, review of *The Frontier in American Development: Essays in Honor of Paul Wallace Gates* edited by David M. Ellis, in *Pacific Historical Review* 39 (November 1970): 533.

Memoir

Paul W. Gates

I was born in Nashua, New Hampshire, December 4, 1901, to the Reverend Edwin Lewis Gates, formerly of Nova Scotia, and Alice Wilder Gates of Gilsum, New Hampshire. Their respective ancestors, oddly enough, had arrived in the New World on the same ship, *The Diligent* in 1638, landing at Hingham, Massachusetts, each fleeing persecution of the established English church. The Gateses eventually made their way to Nova Scotia, enticed by the British effort to outnumber the French settlements there. The Wilders ended up in the Ashuelot Valley of New Hampshire where, by the late 1880s, Lansing Wilder had acquired good agricultural property on which to raise his family of two daughters and a son.

The Gateses had also prospered in Nova Scotia. One boy had become a respected minister—Baptist, I suppose—in the region. The second son, Edwin Lewis, after graduating from Acadia College in Wolfville, Nova Scotia, had obtained a theological degree from Newton Seminary in Massachusetts. His first pastorate was in Fiskdale, Massachusetts, in a new struggling Baptist Church, the only Protestant church in a predominantly Catholic community. Here Alice Wilder came to teach school, having graduated from Salem Normal School. She had already taught with success in the local schools of Gilsum, New Hampshire. She attended the 1893 Chicago World's Fair, a broadening experience for a rural girl.

Alice Wilder was a Congregationalist but, in Fiskdale, the only Protestant church was the Baptist Church, so Alice attended that. The young pastor took note of the new member of the congregation and, at the conclusion of the service, he offered to accompany her home, and was refused! But he found ways to overcome her reluctance, and romance and marriage ensued. After tenure in Warner, Massachusetts, the couple were ensconced in Nashua, New Hampshire, where I entered the world. Two brothers had preceded me, and a sister was to follow.

My father's next pastorate in the early 1900s was in Presque Isle, Maine, a prosperous potato-farming community. During a severe drought in 1909, much of the town was consumed by fire, which spread quickly along the wooden sidewalks. The parsonage was engulfed along with many homes. Few of our possessions could be saved. A kindly farmer took in the homeless parson's family, but there was a summons from Grandfather Wilder: "Come home!" And home we went, Mother and her four youngsters, while Father stayed with his flock.

En route, Mother stopped in Boston to buy clothes and bedding for the family. I do not know where we stayed, perhaps in the YMCA. But we boys got to ride on the open trolley cars, a big deal! Also we were taken to Revere Beach, where the merry-go-round and Ferris wheel were huge attractions, and then to Grandfather's! The farm in Gilsum was a tremendous experience: the team of horses, Fan and Hesekiah; the oxen; the cows; the fields of hay; the grove of maple trees from which sap was boiled down to syrup and sugar; the stand of timber. It is true that in time we found that these good things demanded a degree of labor that was not always to a boy's taste, yet rewarding too. This introduction to farm life was never to leave me, as attested by the following publications: *Fifty Million Acres* (1954), *The Farmer's Age* (1960), *Agriculture and the Civil War* (1965), *Land and Law in California* (1991).

Toward the end of that summer to my delight, word came that Father had accepted a call to the Baptist Church of Dover, Maine, and so Mother packed up and we moved there. The Baptist parsonage was a big one, with ample room for four children. There was also a shed and barn. Since Father's pastoral calls were made by bicycle, no steed except a visitor's needed stabling; so there was that play space also.

Early on the boys were impressed with the desirability of college. We were encouraged to undertake any and all small paying jobs that would further this dream. Thus I was a water boy for an elderly neighbor, delivered papers, was janitor of the Thompson Free Library, cleaned the Blenthen House stables, and had other odd chores too numerous to mention. But they netted up to a tidy sum by the time I entered Colby College.

Before then, alas, both my sister and father had died. Ruth died at about six years of a kidney disease that is curable today but not with the medical care available then. The same was true for my father a few years later. The liver ailment of which he died should not have been fatal.

Mother, of course, had to vacate the parsonage, but she elected to stay in

Dover until the boys had finished Foxcroft Academy, a secondary school that was held in esteem throughout the state and sent many graduates on to college. Gordon, the eldest, had already finished the academy and was at Colby, a college with strong Baptist affiliations. So mother bought a house near the Dover Grammar School, and here we stayed until I finished the academy in 1920. Then she returned to Keene, New Hampshire (where Grandfather lived after retiring from the farm), and it became my home during college vacations until I started my own.

Colby College was not a great challenge for me but, in Professor Curtis H. Morrow, also known as "Eccy" Morrow, I found a mentor. Professor Morrow headed, and was, the Economics and Sociology Department. Through Eccy I came to realize the bearing upon history exerted by sociology and economics. In my junior year, Eccy secured me a summer fellowship at the New York School of Social Work, during which I lived at the Settlement House on Rivington and Delancey Streets. It was a fascinating summer. The courses at the School of Social Work were riveting, and so was the life that flowed around the East Side where I lived. I heard John A. Fitch discuss the Colorado miners' strike against the Rockefeller interests, and Thomas Mott Osborne advocate reform of the New York penal system. Upon my graduation from Colby, I entered Morrow's alma mater, Clark University, for graduate study. Two outstanding influences here were James B. Hedges and William L. Langer. Hedges directed my attention to the work that railroads were doing to promote development. Langer revised my thinking relative to German, Russian, French, and British influence on events during and since World War I.

Another person at Clark who became important to me was a young lady whom I met in the required graduate seminar for history majors. She readily answered many questions, which I flubbed. Lillian Cowdell was a graduate of the University of British Columbia. I tried to make her acquaintance and succeeded only moderately at first, for she made it plain that she was more interested in a career than in romance.

The development of the American West and the part played by the railroads had now become my field of special interest. To pursue it further, I entered the University of Wisconsin, attracted by the presence there of Frederic Paxson and Carl Russell Fish. It was an interesting experience but not wholly stimulating, and I applied to Harvard for an appointment and became a teaching assistant from 1927 to 1929, a tutor in 1930, and received my Ph.D. that year.

Lillian and I had corresponded during my Wisconsin stay, and she expressed pleasure that I would be returning east. She was teaching at a Massachusetts college and also taking courses for her Ph.D. at Harvard. In her economic history course, she corrected Professor Gay on a point covered by me in my dissertation, "The Illinois Central Railroad and Its Settlement Work." When he demanded to know her authority, she produced me. He became a factor in my being awarded the Wells Prize in 1933 and leading to my appointment at Cornell in 1936.

Lillian and I married on August 7, 1929, in Vancouver, returning in the fall to Cambridge. The following summer, I held a teaching appointment at the University of Missouri. An offer from Bucknell was enticing and, the next six years, 1930–1936, were ostensibly spent at Bucknell. We secured a home in Lewisburg, Pennsylvania, and embarked on the production of progeny as well as scholarship (both enterprises have been rewarding). However, it appears that many of my Bucknell years were spent elsewhere. Early on, 1932–1933, I obtained a leave of absence to accept a grant from the Social Science Research Council for a seminar on Agricultural History at the Brookings Institute. This was pertinent to my work on public lands. During 1934–1935 I had a hand in the land policy section of the Agricultural Adjustment Administration (AAA). These were heady years in the turmoil of the New Deal.

In 1936 an offer came from Cornell to join its history department. I served first as an assistant professor, then successively as associate professor, John Stambaugh Professor, chairman for ten years, and became emeritus in 1971. During the Cornell years, I spent several summers in other colleges: summer lecturer at Pennsylvania State University in 1933 (during my Bucknell residence); Western Reserve University, 1937; Duke, 1940; University of California at Los Angeles, 1950; Harvard, 1960; and Utah, 1969. I was visiting professor at Wisconsin in 1968–1969 and at the University of Kansas in 1971–1972. I have been consultant to the United States Department of Justice on Indian Land Claims, to the Public Land Law Review Commission on Public Land History, to the Urban Institute on Agricultural Film History, and to the California Historical Society on the American Farm Project.

My wife, Lillian Cowdell Gates, also obtained her Ph.D. at Harvard. Her dissertation, *Land Policies of Upper Canada,* was published by the University of Toronto Press in 1968. Subsequently she published in numerous Canadian journals and wrote articles for the *Dictionary of Canadian Biography.* A major effort was *After the Rebellion: The Later Years of William Lyon Mackenzie* published by Dundurn Press, Toronto in 1988. I must in all honesty say that Lillian did far more to assist in my work than I did in hers, partly because I had little knowledge of Canadian land policy. She improved much of my writing, managed much of the family responsibility and encouraged me to keep at the research I planned for myself especially by the zeal with which she advanced her own. Lillian died in 1990.

As I have been blessed in conjugal life with a supportive and able wife and four truly wonderful children, so in my teaching career I have enormously benefitted by having outstanding students who have extended my work on public lands and delved into its ramifications far beyond the scope I encompassed. To them I owe much, and in them I take great delight and pride.

Dover-Foxcroft, Maine
August, 1993

1

The Role of the Land Speculator in Western Development*

One of the best known of Paul Wallace Gates's shorter publications, this essay describes and analyzes investment in western public lands, particularly those of the Middle West during the nineteenth century. It was based on fifteen years of research in the records of businessmen and corporations, federal and local land records, congressional publications, and newspapers. The forceful and critical treatment of land speculators found here is typical of Gates's approach during the first thirty years of his scholarly career; they were, he suggests, a major element in frustrating the Jeffersonian dream of a republic of small landholders. Although conceding during the 1970s that investors in western lands did make some positive contributions to western development, Gates has, in general, continued to view the opportunities offered for capitalist activity by the land system as overly generous. Whether readers believe that some qualification is or is not appropriate, they must agree that Gates has provided a picture of land distribution at both national and local levels unmatched previously or thereafter in clarity, detail, and the description of illustrative personalities and incidents.

The land use pattern of the twenty-nine public land states of the South, the Middle West, and the Far West is the result of a long process of development and adaptation in which such factors as speculation, absentee ownership, credit, usury, farm mechanization, transportation, and government controls

*Reprinted from *The Pennsylvania Magazine of History and Biography*, Vol. 66 (July 1942). Used by permission of the publisher, the Historical Society of Pennsylvania. All rights reserved.

have played important roles.[1] Only recently has the United States come to realize the monstrous errors it permitted to develop in this land use pattern. Likewise, only recently has it become apparent that this pattern is the product in part of mistaken land policies which were once thought to be establishing a democratic system of land ownership. Wishful thinking, unwillingness to face the facts, and political oratory combined to obscure the appearance of ominous signs that a democratic pattern of ownership was not being achieved. A few notable spokesmen protested against policies which permitted concentration of land ownership; but Americans, big and little, were too much concerned with the accumulation of wealth through land speculation to listen to their Cassandra-like predictions.

From the seventeenth to the nineteenth centuries European immigrants, many of them from classes to which actual land ownership was denied, brought with them to America a craving for land. Land for a home and a competence was first desired; then land to assure wealth and social position was wanted. This craving for land explains much in American history and is one of its central themes. It was the motivating force which sent hordes of settlers into the expanding frontier and it drew forth large sums of money for investment in America's unsettled areas. Until the modern corporation came to be the dominant factor in American economic life, the principal opportunity for investment was in real estate. All persons seeking land for investment rather than for a farm home have been called land speculators, and the term, loose as it may be, has an important position in our terminology.

The term *land speculator* meant different things to different people and different sections. To a frontiersman it meant an eastern capitalist who bought large quantities of newly offered land in anticipation of settlers to come; or it meant a railroad or canal construction company to which had been given alternate sections of land in a strip ten or twenty miles wide paralleling the line of the improvement; or it meant a pineland baron who acquired 5,000, 10,000, or 50,000 acres of rich timberland. The frontiersman distinguished between resident and absentee speculators. Only nonresident owners of land who were not contributing to the development of the West by making improvements upon their lands were regarded by him as speculators and were the object of his resentment. Land grants for internal improvements were strongly favored by the frontier, which thirsted for connections with the outside world, but the frontiersman expected these lands to be sold promptly and on the preemption system.

To an urban worker the term *speculator* meant someone who laid out towns or additions to them, donated lots for churches and schools, attracted industries or state institutions to the new communities and peddled out building lots at high prices to newcomers. To Horace Greeley the term meant, in addition, the thousands of persons settling the West who sought a stake in the land greater than they could expect to use personally. Greeley also applied it scornfully to those westerners of means who purchased wild lands as an investment, as did their eastern associates. All were speculators; all contributed their share to the pattern of ownership which exists today.

Although frontiersmen, as a rule, possessed little or no capital, they were anxious to own as much land as possible. The first wave of settlers who followed the fur trade squatted upon choice locations, made rude improvements, and, when new arrivals came in, sold their claims and moved on to a new frontier before the government auction took place. These squatters were in a sense speculators. They sought to engross a half section or more and established claim associations to protect their rights. Henceforth these quasi-legal claims were bought and sold just like patent titles.

The second wave of settlers remained on the land until the auction sale on which occasion they borrowed to the hilt to buy as much land as possible. The more successful who had brought considerable money with them, or who had accumulated something from land and barter exchanges on the frontier, might have sufficient credit at the western banks to enable them to purchase 320, 480, or 640 acres. Loose banking policies made credit easy to secure and everyone attempted to borrow for land speculation. Rosy dreams of profits to be made distracted the attention of frontiersmen from the business of making farms in the wilderness. An English observer shrewdly remarked:

> Speculation in real estate . . . has been the ruling idea and occupation of the Western mind. Clerks, labourers, farmers, storekeepers, merely followed their callings for a living, while they were speculating for their fortunes. . . . The people of the West became dealers in land, rather than its cultivators.[2]

Calvin Fletcher, an Indianapolis banker and large landlord, deplored the granting of credit for speculative purchases of land. "The consequence is," he said in 1838, "that for the last 4 years say 6 years there has scarcely been the extension of a farm. No new fields opened & at the same time an enormous increase of consumers—What Son will go to work or what farmer will draw out the energies of his family where they can dress them, clothe them & feed them on the glorious anticipations of a years [sic] accidents which may or may not pay the debt without an effort."[3]

On every frontier the settler-speculator was present. He rarely learned from experience. By claiming 320 acres instead of 160 he separated himself that much more from his neighbor. He had to bear a heavier proportion of the cost of road construction and maintenance; his school costs were increased or the establishment of schools was delayed and his children were denied educational opportunities; the expense of county and state government, in a period when the land tax was the principal source of government income, was burdensome. Other social institutions like churches, granges, and libraries came more slowly because the population was so dispersed. Furthermore, railroads, which all settlers wanted in their vicinity, could not be pushed into sparsely settled areas without large subsidies. State and county subsidies required special assessments upon the already overburdened taxpaying farmers and land grants, whether by federal or state governments, created a near land monopoly. Careful observers like Greeley saw many of these results and urged settlers to be content with smaller tracts which they could conveniently cultivate.

The chance of making a fortune in wild lands or town lots in the rapidly expanding communities of the West was an allurement difficult to resist. Fantastic stories of the profits others had won were printed in the newspapers and retold in letters from the West. Here, in 1818–1819, 1835–1837, or 1850–1857 was the lodestone to quick wealth. Touched by the fever of land speculation, excited people throughout the country borrowed to the extent of their credit for such investments. Men from all walks of life permitted their dreams to overcome their better judgment. Politicians, bankers, writers, ministers, planters and poets, everyone, it seemed, who had any resources at all undertook to invest in western lands. Levi Beardsley, a prominent New Yorker who went West in 1836 to invest some $20,000 in wild land has left an interesting description of the speculative excitement of that year:

> Every one was imbued with a reckless spirit of speculation. The mania, for such it undoubtedly was, did not confine itself to one particular class, but extended to all. Even the reverend clergy doffed their sacerdotals, and eagerly entered into competition with mammon's votaries, for the acquisition of this world's goods, and tested their sagacity against the shrewdness and more practiced skill of the professed sharper.[4]

The existence of a class of professional land agents facilitated land purchases by absentee capitalists. Eastern papers with a wide circulation among the wealthy contained numerous advertisements of these land agents during the years from 1830 to 1857. In every enterprising community on the frontier were found agents who were prepared to buy or enter land for others with cash or warrants.[5] For a commission of five per cent or a share in the transaction, generally from a third to a quarter, they would select land, sometimes by personal investigation, sometimes by a superficial search of the entry books, and make purchases for their principals.

Some of the more important of these land agents were Henry W. Ellsworth of Lafayette, Indiana, Cook and Sargent of Davenport, Iowa, and Henry C. Putnam of Eau Claire, Wisconsin. Ellsworth published a booklet, *Valley of the Upper Wabash*,[6] to attract attention to western Indiana and eastern Illinois, and he and his father, Henry L. Ellsworth, Federal Commissioner of Patents, were able to induce hundreds of easterners, mostly New Englanders, to invest in the West. Cook and Sargent maintained offices in each of the eight land-office towns in Iowa where they entered nearly 200,000 acres.[7] Putnam's entries in Wisconsin exceeded a half million acres.[8]

These western land agents rank with the registers and receivers of the land offices as among the most important people on the frontier. They dealt in land warrants and scrip, ran a local note-shaving business, purchased exchange, sometimes operated a bank of issue with funds provided by eastern capitalists, loaned eastern funds to squatters at frontier rates ranging from twenty to sixty per cent, bought and sold land, paid taxes for absentee owners and undertook to protect their lands against depredations. At a later date, they arranged for renting land, made collections, and sold produce received in payment of rent. Small investors in the East were obliged to work through these agents, to submit to their exactions, and to suffer from their inefficiency and could not effectually protest against their obvious neglect. The agent could take his commission from rents or sales before any money was remitted to the owner, could sell his own land to prospective purchasers, rather than that of the owners he represented, could neglect tax payments and get the title involved, or could pay taxes on the wrong land. In numerous cases western agents took advantage of their clients, used the prestige which their contacts provided for personal interests, and constantly minimized the value of the land they represented in order to increase sales and thereby commissions. In this way absentee investors whose eastern responsibilities did not permit them to give personal attention to their possessions in the West were imposed upon and victimized.

A case in point is that of Senator Henry H. Hubbard of New Hampshire who, in association with Daniel Webster and other Yankees, invested well over $50,000 in western lands. Hubbard sent Moses B. Strong of Vermont to Wisconsin Territory in 1836 to invest a part of this money. Land was acquired and some sales were made by Strong before the crash of 1837 put a stop to the business. Thereafter the investment went from bad to worse. Strong's charges for the slight services he rendered after the actual purchase were so heavy that Hubbard was forced to sell part of the land at distress prices. When sales declined, Strong neglected the business for politics and Hubbard was obliged to supplant him.[9]

An analogous case is that of Cyrus Woodman who represented a group of New England capitalists organized as the Boston and Western Land Company. This company invested $100,000 in 60,000 acres of wild land and in numerous embryo towns in Illinois, Wisconsin, and Missouri in 1835 and 1836. The crash of 1837 broke the market; lands could scarcely be sold at any price, and interest, taxes, and agents' costs further discouraged the Boston promoters. Woodman, who was sent to the West to retrieve something from the wreck of the company's once ambitious scheme, made no effort to put the investment in its best light but, from the first, filled his letters with pessimistic forebodings of ever greater contraction in prices accompanied by rising taxes. It is small wonder then that the owners became discouraged and sold their property to Woodman for a fraction of its cost. The land was that good prairie and timberland which in the fifties was to bring prices that almost justified the optimistic hopes of the thirties; but the original purchasers were not to share in the prosperity.[10]

One of the most successful agent-speculator relationships was that of William A. Woodward and Henry C. Putnam who were natives of New York State. Both were shrewd judges of land values and both knew thoroughly the techniques of the land business. Putnam went to Wisconsin in the fifties where he invested funds of Woodward and other New Yorkers in short term loans to settlers and in timber and prairie land. The fees Putnam received for the numerous services performed for his eastern principals made him a leading businessman in the rising town of Eau Claire. He aided in selecting the university, school and swamp land, became land agent for a land-grant railroad, was elected register of deeds and county surveyor, and appointed deputy United States assessor, and with others founded the leading bank in Eau Claire. When Ezra Cornell was looking for someone to help him locate the million acres in land scrip which New York State had received under the Agricultural College Act, Woodward and Putnam persuaded him to let them make the selections in the Chippewa Valley where, Cornell was assured, Putnam virtually controlled all land entries by means of his position in the United States land office at Eau Claire. Cornell gave them the agency, and from it they both made substantial profits.[11]

A great impetus was given to land speculation in the mid-thirties by federal and state banking policies. The failure to recharter the Second Bank of the United States removed the curbs on state bank policy while the lure of federal deposits led to a scramble for such easy funds and to a mushroomlike growth of new banks in the South and West. Loans on real estate at inflated valuations were easily secured. Rising land values and easy credit attracted unprecedented quantities of capital from the East for investment in wild lands and corner lots. The federal surplus produced by increased land sales was distributed among the states, thereby providing funds for elaborate schemes of interal improvements. Canals, railroads, highways were projected throughout the newer states, regardless of their feasibility. This combination of an easy banking policy with large government expenditures on public works came at a time when emigration to the western country was greatly accelerated. The total purchases of the hordes of immigrants and the speculators who were attempting to anticipate settlers' needs made the public land sales of these years the largest in American history.

Between 1835 and 1837, 38,000,000 acres of public lands were sold, 29,000,000 of which were acquired for speculation. A minimum speculative investment of $36,000,000 — exclusive of agents' costs, interest, and taxes — was thus tied up in unimproved lands. To this figure should be added perhaps as large an amount for investments in town and city lots.

Much of this land purchasing was done by banks or bankers. For example, Isaac Bronson and his sons Frederick and Arthur, prominent bankers of New York, together with Charles Butler, brother of the attorney general of the United States, and a group of New York capitalists, used funds of the New York Life Insurance & Trust Company and other banks with which they had connections to buy a third of a million acres in eight states and territories. The prominence of the promoters and the fact that some of them were closely identified with an administration which favored land reform and denounced land speculators gave the Whigs an opportunity of showing how hollow were the pretensions of some Jacksonians.[12]

Another group whose purchases of land were made with credit of banks it controlled consisted of such well-known Massachusetts financiers as John Tillson, Jr., John Shaw Hayward, Charles Holmes, Jr., Winthrop Gilman, and Griggs, Weld & Company. These men controlled the state bank of Illinois from which they were able to borrow for their extensive land speculations. When the bank itself undertook to loan funds to squatters and to buy large quantities of land it came to be regarded as the great financial octopus of Illinois and Iowa against which numerous antimonopoly tirades were directed.[13]

A group whose operations in banks, land, and railroads was scarcely to be matched consisted of Alvah Buckingham and Solomon Sturges of Zanesville, Ohio, and their numerous children. They acquired or established banks of issue in Ohio, Indiana, and Illinois, some of which received federal deposits. The banks made it possible for them to pyramid their land purchases until they ultimately reached 275,000 acres, or the equivalent of 1,760 quarter section farms. Railroads, grain elevators, and lumber yards were added to this princely estate. Neither the Panic of 1837 nor that of 1857 destroyed the economic power of Buckingham and Sturges, and for a generation their names were widely known from Ohio to Nebraska.[14]

Throughout the East and, indeed, to a somewhat less degree in the old South, other banks, directors, and customers of banks were using the credit to buy public lands. For years thereafter these banks or their receivers were engaged in disposing of quantities of wild land they had bought directly or acquired through mortgage foreclosures.

Squatters upon the public lands did not benefit from the easy banking policies of the thirties. Since they had no property to mortgage, credit was available to them only on the most usurious terms.

When newly surveyed lands were first announced for sale, the squatters had to arrange for the purchase of their lands—made valuable by their improvements—before the opening of the auction or run the risk of losing them to speculators. Claim clubs and special preemption laws gave them protection against speculators only to the date of the sale. Squatters were inclined to put their meager capital into stock, housing, fencing, and clearing which seemed the most essential for the moment and to hope that the land sale would be postponed until they could accumulate money with which to purchase their claims. The sale, although announced in advance by advertisement, seemed always to catch the settlers unprepared and obliged them to borrow from the "loan shark."

These moneylenders were the representatives of western banks and eastern capitalists. Their charges were five per cent for arranging loans and from two and one-half to five per cent for making collections. Such eminent westerners as William B. Ogden,[15] James W. Grimes and Lucius Lyon,[16] later to become respectively president of the Chicago and Northwestern Railroad, and United States Senators from Iowa and Michigan, made their start by lending eastern funds on such a basis.

Loan sharks were present at every public land auction and their agents were stationed in every land-office town, prepared to buy claims for squatters. The ten or twelve per cent allowed by the usury laws did not satisfy these moneylenders who found it possible to evade such restrictions. They would buy claims on which squatters had their improvements, according to previous agreements, and would then resell the land to them for an advance of $30 above cost on a quarter section. The squatter would agree to pay at the end of one or two years the maximum interest allowed by law. If the legal interest was twelve per cent and the debt was paid in one year, the lender would net twenty-eight per cent upon his investment. The loan agents always denied that they

were violating the usury laws but they were exceedingly loath to have cases
involving their transactions taken into the courts. Thousands of desperate
squatters throughout the West snatched at the aid offered by the moneylenders
who personally or through land agents invested many millions of dollars in
this lucrative business. When later the squatters had difficulty in meeting their
obligations, they turned against their creditors and raised the cry of usury.

Jackson's specie circular of 1836 struck squarely at the rapidly expanding
volume of land purchases. It showed that the chief executive, unlike many of
his followers such as Butler, Kendall, Walker, and Ellsworth, did not approve
of the operations of land speculators and moneylenders. The president's purpose in issuing the circular was to "repress alleged frauds, and to withhold
any countenance or facilities in the power of the Government from the monopoly of the public lands in the hands of speculators and capitalists, to the
injury of the actual settlers in the new States, and of emigrants in search of
new homes. . . ." Jackson further explained his purpose in his annual message
of December 1836, wherein he said the circular was intended to "save the new
States from a nonresident proprietorship, one of the greatest obstacles to the
advancement of a new country and the prosperity of an old one." [17] Except for
Jefferson, Jackson was the only American president who seriously deplored
that feature of public land policy which permitted speculators to buy land in
unlimited amounts.

The specie circular required that only gold or silver be accepted from purchasers of land, except actual settlers who were permitted to use bank notes
for the remainder of the year. The order brought down the whole bloated
structure which had been erected by unsound banking practices, the deposit
of federal funds in the state banks, and the elaborate programs of internal improvements undertaken by the states. Land purchases by speculators stopped
immediately; only the business of lending money to squatters remained.

The federal government's need of revenue caused the moneylending business to thrive for a time after the crash of 1837. Quantities of land were
ordered into the market when it was clear that squatters could raise the purchase price of their claims only with the greatest difficulty. Despite pleas for
postponement the sales were held. Western banks were now closed, only gold
or silver was accepted at the sales, and only eastern bankers could furnish it.
In 1838 and 1839 Ogden found it possible to loan eastern funds to squatters
to net thirty per cent a year before the deduction of commissions. Such usurious interest rates continued into the forties and, indeed, were increased in the
fifties when it was possible for brokers to use in place of cash the military land
warrants then in wide circulation at prices ranging downward to fifty cents
an acre. By this means returns of forty, fifty, and even sixty per cent could be
secured from squatters.

Ogden, Grimes, and Lyon had assured their principals that there was no risk in lending money to squatters to buy their claims since their improvements had already raised the value of the land above the government minimum price and since they would make every possible effort to pay their debts and secure title to land on which they had expended years of toil. These men did not foresee the deplorable situation into which the West was plunged after 1837. Squatters, now attempting to meet their payments under the most trying circumstances, fought a losing battle. Payments were delayed and then completely suspended. Many settlers became discouraged and moved on to another frontier to try once more to gain ownership of a piece of land.

Moneylenders, land speculators, and gamblers in town lots now found themselves loaded with financial burdens which they could not carry. Their land was unsaleable, yet their taxes continued to mount as did also the interest on the money they had borrowed. Having invested everything in property not easily liquidated they now were forced to surrender much of their land to the banks when these institutions began to call in their loans. The abstracts of conveyances for the years following the Panic of 1837 show a tremendous volume of mortgage foreclosures of large estates.[18]

These foreclosures, the suspension of most of the wildcat banks, and the bankruptcy of many financial institutions in the East all combined to keep land titles in the West in a state of chaos. Taxes were paid tardily, if at all, tax titles of a dubious nature were annually issued, and the difficulties of an already complex situation were thereby increased. During the period of stress settlers accumulated grievances against the absentee owners which seemed to justify stealing their timber, despoiling their fences and buildings, and using their land for pasture. New settlers moved on the absentee-owned land, sometimes bought a tax title, and set up a claim of ownership by right of possession and the tax deed. Absentee owners were powerless to deal with such a problem unless their property investment was sufficiently large to enable them to maintain a local agent employed on a full-time basis to watch over their interests.

During the bleak years of the early forties the equity of absentees was gradually eaten up by tax titles, agents' costs, interest, and depredations. Ultimately the burden became too great and many sold their holdings for less than the original cost, disregarding interest, fees, and taxes. It was this situation that induced Dr. Joseph Schafer, for years a careful student of land problems and policies, to conclude that land speculation was on the whole an unprofitable business.[19]

The career of Calvin Fletcher, a cautious Hoosier from New England and reared in an atmosphere of conservative finance, sheds much light on this era of unbridled land speculation. The craze for speculation overcame Fletcher's better judgment and with Nicholas McCarty, likewise a Hoosier, he engaged in a joint speculation with $40,000 borrowed from the state bank of Indiana of which Fletcher was a director. The mental torture Fletcher went through during the following years as a result of this "hazardous" investment is recorded in his diary. Unlike the majority of settler-speculators who lost their land when the depression years set in, Fletcher was able to carry his investment until it began to produce returns. In 1846, when the banks had foreclosed many mortgages and thousands of farmers, having lost their homes, had either gone elsewhere to make another attempt at securing ownership of land or had sunk to the position of tenants upon their old claims, Fletcher stated that one third of the voters of Indiana were then "tenants or day laborers or young men who have acquired no property." [20]

On the frontier the fog of depression is quickly dissipated by rising commodity prices, quickened immigration, and a new influx of capital. In the middle forties these factors were again at work and there followed a new era of land speculation in which old residents and new settlers participated equally. The curve of land purchases shot upward as people in all occupations once more neglected their routine work to buy raw prairie land or corner lots in newly platted cities. Eastern capitalists again established banks of issue in the West and South under the lax systems still prevailing there and used the funds to purchase land. Land agents, professional locators, loan sharks, townsite promoters flourished. Few seemed to have learned from experience.

The peak years of speculative purchasing were 1854 to 1858, when a total of 65,000,000 acres of public domain were disposed of to purchasers or holders of land warrants. To this figure should be added an equal or greater amount of land which was granted to the states for canals, railroads, swamp drainage, and education and, by them, sold mostly to speculators, large and small. A comparison of the census figures of land in farms with the land-office figures of land sold shows a tremendous concentration of speculator-owned land in all public land states, especially in the newer states like Iowa, Wisconsin, Illinois, Missouri, and Arkansas.

The speculators' contributions to the present-day pattern of land ownership and land use are most important. For a generation agricultural economists have said that tenancy was an inevitable result of the commercialization of farming and rising land values. This is true, but tenancy got its start in the Middle West as a result of the activities of land speculators and moneylenders. Squatters who could not meet their usurious demands had their contracts cancelled and their equity confiscated. They might, however, remain on their old claims as tenants and pay rent for the land, or they might make a new contract for the land but at a higher valuation. In either case, the farmer found ownership difficult to attain. Elsewhere speculators dismayed at the cost of carrying their projects sought relief by inducing land seekers to settle on their holdings, the sole condition being that they must pay taxes. If land was scarce, it was not difficult to persuade immigrants to settle upon speculators' tracts, perhaps with the understanding that they might be able to buy later. The farmers' improvements raised the value of the property but did not bring in immediate cash income sufficient to enable them to make payments upon the land. As the value went up, the owners' price increased; ownership proved unattainable to many. Tenancy thus had come to stay in the first generation of settlement in Illinois, Indiana, Iowa, Kansas, and Nebraska. Furthermore, owners of small farms had borrowed heavily to secure title, and from their debts many were never to be free. Some were ultimately depressed to the state of tenancy.

Speculator ownership and tenancy did not always result in the best use of the land. It has already been seen that speculator ownership forced widespread dispersion of population and placed heavy tax burdens upon farmers whose improved lands could be more heavily assessed than the speculators' unimproved land. Furthermore, speculators were slow to pay taxes. They resisted increased levies, secured injunctions against expenditures for buildings and roads, and sometimes simply refused to pay taxes. Heavy interest penalties and tax titles did not trouble them particularly since they knew they could later make a compromise settlement with the hardpressed county boards or could have the tax titles set aside by the courts. All of this meant that the tillers of the soil, if they were to enjoy the benefits of schools, roads, and local railroads had to dig down into their own jeans more deeply because the speculators were not carrying their share of the burden. Taxes continued to climb and rarely or never declined, even in a period of depression. They are one of the rigid costs which trouble the farmers deeply when their own income is sharply declining. Heavy tax burdens forced farm practices which depleted the soil, produced erosion, and diminished land values.

Speculators left their mark on the West in other ways than in land ownership. The nationalizing influence of their investments in western lands should not be neglected. Speculators were naturally inclined to favor internal improvements in the vicinity of their land. The Wabash Canal, the Illinois and Michigan Canal, the Des Moines River Navigation and Improvement Company, and the Fox and Wisconsin Canal were all the work of speculators who sought to increase the value of their holdings by bringing transportation facilities to them at government expense. The investments of Daniel Webster of Massachusetts and John Rockwell of Connecticut in central Illinois made them keenly aware of the need for internal improvements in the prairie state and led them to support the movement for railroad land grants for that area.[21]

The land and town lot speculators were also influential in securing state, county, and municipal subsidies for local railroads. Many railroad enterprises were in themselves as much land speculations as transportation developments. The pinery railroads of northern Wisconsin promised few or no profits from operations, but the land grants included valuable stands of white pine from which large returns might be secured. Some of the other railroads for which there now seems little justification were doubtless chartered for the sake of the land grant.

Land and town lot speculators had much to do with railroad strategy in the West. During the territorial period of Kansas and in the first decade of statehood the struggle between the supporters of rival routes for land grants for their railroad enterprises is one of the chief issues, transcending in importance the slavery and union issues. Out of the melee certain groups emerged triumphant such as that which revolved around one of the most notorious corruptionists in American history, Samuel C. Pomeroy. Two railroads of which he was an officer and stockholder received land grants, one was permitted to buy a valuable ceded Indian reservation for less than its current value, and three were required to converge on his own town of Atchison. The struggle over the location of the eastern terminus of the Union Pacific Railroad, the efforts of Cairo, Illinois, promoters to require the Illinois Central to locate its southern terminus at that point, the desire of the Northern Pacific to build up its own town on Puget Sound are illustrations of how speculators, whether operating within or without the railroad companies, have influenced the location of railroad routes and their terminal points. Another factor which tended to prevent railroads from selecting the shortest line between two points was the desire of their promoters to secure the largest possible land grants.

The petty fights over the location of county seats, territorial and state capitals, land offices, state universities, agricultural colleges and normal schools, and institutions for the insane, the blind and the criminal comprise no small part of the political controversies of the time. That some of these institutions were located in remote, inaccessible places wholly unsuited to the functions they were to perform may be blamed upon speculators who succeeded in having them established in the vicinity of their lands.

Westerners were united in their demand that the federal government should donate to the states the land within their boundaries. This demand was never attained in full but it was achieved in part through a piece-meal system of securing special grants for education, canals, river improvements, and the drainage of swamp lands. As successive states entered the union they were given larger proportions of their land, the proportion running as high as one third in the case of Arkansas, Louisiana, Michigan, and Minnesota, to two thirds in the case of Florida. The states were expected to sell these lands for the best possible price and the proceeds, if derived from education grants, were to provide endowments. Speculator influence in the state capitals and county seats tended to break down the effective utilization of these grants.

Numerous scandals marked the sale of state lands and indicate that state and local governments were even more subject to speculator influence than was Congress and the General Land Office. The two-township grant for state universities brought in little return, the common school sections were in many cases wastefully administered, the agricultural college lands or their scrip equivalent were sold for a pittance by Rhode Island, Massachusetts, Indiana, Ohio, and other states, and the river improvement grants were wasted away. Worst managed of all were the swamp lands, of which 64,000,000 acres were patented to the states. Some were sold for as low as ten cents an acre; others were given to railroad companies to aid in construction; still others were granted to drainage companies for the improvements they contracted to make. Little or no security was ever required by the local officials for the performance of the contracts, and in few cases were the improvements actually made. One prairie county of Illinois permitted its judge to contract 47,000 acres to a Utica, New York, resident on the understanding that he would drain the lands. The latter were conveyed but no improvements were made; later it was found that the judge had an interest in the business.[22]

Indian lands were fair game for speculators who used both legal and illegal means to secure them. Traders and speculators devised a method by which treaties of cession would include 640 acre allotments of the choicer lands to chiefs and half-breeds. They could easily be induced to sign away their allotments for an extra portion of whisky. By this means most of the desirable land along the upper Wabash Valley in Indiana and other valuable tracts in Illinois, Mississippi, Alabama, and Wisconsin passed into the hands of speculators including the great trading firm of W. G. & G. W. Ewing of Fort Wayne, Senator John Tipton of Indiana, and Simon Cameron of Pennsylvania.[23]

In Kansas speculator influence carried this method of land acquisition even farther. Here Indian tribes such as the Potawatomi (whose members had already been victimized by the Wabash traders), the Kickapoo, the Delawares, the Cherokees, and the Osage were induced to cede over 9,000,000 acres of land in trust, to be sold for their benefit. Such lands were not to become part of the public domain and were, therefore, not subject to the general land laws. Until Congress woke up to what was going on, these tracts were being rapidly conveyed to groups and individuals close to the Indian Office for distinctly less than their actual market value at the time.

Speculators pressed for the general allotment system which was adopted in 1887. They also cooperated with the lumbermen of Wisconsin and Min-

nesota in securing the opening of reservations containing valuable stands of
white pine.

To gain their objectives the speculators were forced to enter politics.
Whether from the East or West, they opposed a free homestead policy which,
they feared, would reduce the value of their holdings. They favored grants
for railroads and measures to make easier land accumulation. They were
influential in local and state governments which they warped to suit their
interests. Thus one sees Wisconsin in the seventies and eighties controlled by
a tight little group of lumbermen-speculators including Cadwallader Wash-
burn, Jim Thorp, Nelson Luddington, Philetus Sawyer, William Price, and
Isaac Stephenson. Elsewhere the story is the same. These men opposed land
reform, fought other agrarian legislation, championed protective tariff duties,
and condemned monetary heresies. They represented the creditor, the large
property owners, the railroads, and the rising industrialists. Not until 1888
and 1889, by which time the best of the public land was gone, were they ready
to abandon their long struggle to prevent the public domain from being reserved for actual settlers only, a recommendation long since made by Jefferson
and Jackson.

The successful land dealer of one generation became the banker, the local
political oracle, and office holder or the country squire of the next. Scarcely
a city or country town in the West but had its first family whose fortune had
been made by shrewd selection of lands and their subsequent sale or rental to
later comers. Wealth which had come easily to them through their speculations had become a vested interest which they sought to protect against the
demagogues who demanded the ten-hour day in the saw mills, or the imposi-
tion of an income tax, or the regulation of railroads.

The influence of the speculator may also be noted in the cultural field. The
owners of western lands were not only responsible for a flood of pamphlets,
booklets, guidebooks and emigrant gazettes advertising their projects, but
also for many travel books published for the same purpose. It is well known
that Samuel Augustus Mitchell's *Illinois in 1837,* was published to aid the
sale of the 124,000 acres of land purchased in 1836 and 1837 by John Grigg,
Mitchell, and other Philadelphians. Similarly, none can doubt that Henry W.
Ellsworth's *Valley of the Upper Wabash,* is a real-estate advertisement and not
a careful appraisal of the Grand Prairie of Indiana and Illinois. William Ferguson, J. G. Kohl, and Richard Cobden also wrote accounts primarily to aid the
sale of lands in Illinois. James Caird, an English agricultural journalist, on the
other hand, disguised his land promotion propaganda so effectively that repu-
table historians have continued to borrow from his *Prairie Farming in America,*
little realizing how prejudiced and distorted it is. Even Charles Dickens,

whose investment in Cairo real estate proved disastrous to him, was attracted to America, in part, out of curiosity to see the investment which had repaid him so poorly.[24] The productions of numerous other writers who were interested in western lands were widely read at the time of their publication and for years were drawn upon by subsequent travelers and compilers of guide books.

For better or for worse the speculator, whether absentee or resident, squatter or banker, local politician or eastern senator, was present on every frontier. He affected every phase of western development and left in all places his indelible mark. His motives and his deeds one may deplore but so characteristically American was he, so dynamic a part did he play in shaping land and cultural patterns that it is difficult to imagine an American frontier without him.

Notes

1. This paper is, in part, a synthesis of a number of articles previously published, as follows: "The Homestead Law in an Incongruous Land System," *American Historical Review* 41 (1936), 652–81; "Land Policy and Tenancy in the Prairie Counties of Indiana," *Indiana Magazine of History* 35 (1939), 1–26; "Land Policy and Tenancy in the Prairie States," *Journal of Economic History* 1 (1941), 60–82. The data concerning land entries was compiled from the abstracts of land entries in the General Land Office, now in The National Archives. Acknowledgment is made to the Social Science Research Council and Cornell University for financial assistance which made possible the research embodied in this article.

2. D. W. Mitchell, *Ten Years in the United States: Being an Englishman's Views of Men and Things in the North and South* (London, 1862), 325–28.

3. Entry of August 22, 1838, manuscript diary of Calvin Fletcher, Indiana Historical Society, Indiana State Library.

4. Levi Beardsley, *Reminiscences: Personal and other Incidents* . . . (New York, 1852), 252.

5. A writer in Janesville, Wisconsin, in 1855, speaks of the "hundreds of land agents and dealers watching to show some new comer . . . and all manner of tricks to gull the unsuspicious." *Rutland* (Vermont) *Herald*, Nov. 16, 1855.

6. New York, 1838.

7. For advertisements of Cook and Sargent, see *Iowa Sun* (Davenport), May 16, 1840; *Davenport Democratic Banner*, Feb. 10, May 5, 1854; *Davenport Democrat and News*, Nov. 2, 1859. Circulars of Cook and Sargent dated Oct. 15, 1847, October 15, 1850, are in the Corcoran and Riggs papers, Library of Congress.

8. The Woodward-Putnam letters are in the Prudence Risley vault, Cornell University.

9. The papers of Moses Strong in the Wisconsin Historical Society Library contain the story of the Hubbard-Strong land business. Joseph Schafer used them in the preparation of an article entitled "A Yankee Land Speculator in Wisconsin," *Wisconsin Magazine of History* 8 (1925), 377–92.

10. Cyrus Woodman was a methodical businessman who kept his papers, including impression copies of letters he wrote. They are now in the Wisconsin Historical Society Library and comprise one of the most valuable extant collections on the land business.

11. See note 8.

12. Aside from the publications and advertisements of the American Land Company and the numerous attacks upon it which may be found in the *United States Telegraph,* quoted in the *Indiana* (Indianapolis) *Journal,* July 23, 1836; *Havanna Republican* (New York), Nov. 27, July 31, 1839; and *Chicago American,* Aug. 12, 1839, the William B. Ogden papers in the Chicago Historical Society Library, and the Butler papers in the Library of Congress are important.

13. *Iowa News* (Dubuque), May 18, Sept. 7, 14, Nov. 23, 1839; *Iowa Territorial Gazette and Burlington Advertiser,* May 4, Jan. 26, Feb. 2, 1839, Nov. 21, 1838; *Burlington Hawkeye and Iowa Patriot,* Aug. 12, 1841.

14. *Prairie Farmer,* May 20, 1858; *History of Muskingum County, Ohio* (Columbus, 1882), two pages and photograph inserted after p. 72.

15. Ogden Manuscripts, Chicago Historical Society Library.

16. There are many Lyon letters in the Ogden collection; others are published in Michigan Pioneer and Historical Society, *Historical Collections* 27 (Lansing, 1897), 414–604.

17. *American State Papers, Public Lands,* vol. 8, 910. James D. Richardson, ed., *Compilation of the Messages and Papers of the Presidents, 1789-1902* (1907) vol. 3, 249–50.

18. The conveyance records of the following counties have been used: Vermillion, Champaign, Iroquois, McLean, Logan, Sangamon, and Christian, Illinois; and Benton, Newton, White, and Carroll, Indiana; and Iowa, LaFayette, and Sauk, Wisconsin.

19. Joseph Schafer, *Wisconsin Domesday Book, Town Studies* (Madison, 1924) vol. 1, 10 and note; *idem, The Wisconsin Lead Region, Wisconsin Domesday Book, General Studies* (Madison, 1932); vol. 3, 153.

20. Diary of Calvin Fletcher, entry of March 23, 1846.

21. Webster and Rockwell were both warm supporters of the measure to grant land for the aid of the Illinois Central Railroad. Rockwell is said to have received for his share in securing the land grant two and a half per cent of the land or its equivalent. Fitz Henry Warner, Washington, D.C., Dec. 1, 1852, to Charles Mason, Burlington, Iowa, Mason MSS., Iowa State Department of History and Archives, Des Moines.

22. H. H. Beckwith, *History of Iroquois County* . . . (Chicago, 1880), 375 *passim;* Iroquois County Deeds, 27:37.

23. I have described this method of land disposal in the introduction to the forthcoming Papers of Senator John Tipton, to be published by the Indiana Historical Bureau in June, 1942.

24. For Ferguson, Cobden, Caird, and Dickens, see Paul Wallace Gates, *Illinois Central Railroad and Its Colonization Work* (Cambridge, 1934), *passim.*

2

Frontier Estate Builders and Farm Laborers*

In this article Gates develops further dimensions of frontier land acquisition and development. Qualifying Turner's view of frontier society, he describes the prevalence of farm laborers, of tenants, and of landholders who wished to develop large agricultural operations under their own management or by renting to considerable numbers of tenants. Referring specifically to Turnerian thought, Gates concluded, "Concepts of the homogeneity of frontier society, similarity of frontier outlook, common addiction to democratic principles, may well be questioned." This piece is also notable for its emphasis on the importance of the midwestern cattle kings — a topic that he would expand at a later time in a notable essay — and for his methodological suggestion on identifying tenants from the manuscript federal censuses prior to that of 1880 when the enumerators specifically listed them. Developed systematically by later researchers, the method has been a standard tool in research on nineteenth-century American tenancy. Here too Gates links the developing social structure of the Midwest to the land system and attributes the "increasingly conservative character of agrarian politics in Illinois and Iowa" to the departure of "disillusioned and frequently angry tenants who emigrated farther west."

To the simple democratic society of the American frontier consisting mostly of small farmers, as Frederick Jackson Turner described it, should be added two types, the one common, the other small in numbers but profoundly important in shaping landownership patterns, political action, and the beginnings of a cultured society. The first of these types includes the farm laborers,

*From Walker D. Wyman and Clifton B. Kroeber, eds., *The Frontier in Perspective* (Madison: University of Wisconsin Press, 1957), 144–63. Used by permission of the publisher, the University of Wisconsin Press. All rights reserved.

some of whom became farm tenants. The other type is the capitalist estate builder who took with him a "seemingly endless appetite for power and for land," as Arthur Moore put it.[1] It was these capitalist estate builders, whether cattle barons, land speculators turned developers, or men who went west with the set purpose of creating great plantations operated by tenants or hired hands, who made possible the employment of thousands of laborers.

The capitalist developer, big and little, was first revealed indirectly in 1860 when the Bureau of the Census presented statistics showing the number of farm laborers—statistics as noteworthy in their way as those showing the extent of farm tenancy in 1880 or the statement of the superintendent of the census in 1890 that the frontier was gone. Notwithstanding America's much-boasted opportunities, its seemingly limitless supply of public lands, its ever-expanding and newly opening frontier, the farm laborer, ordinarily a landless person whose economic status was less secure than that of the European peasant, was shown to exist in large numbers, not only in the older and well-developed communities, but in the new states and middle border territories.

Consider for a moment Iowa, only fourteen years a state, still but lightly touched by settlement, not able to boast two people to the square mile, with less than a third of its land in farms but the bulk of its public lands already in private ownership. Despite the slight development of this state, largely concentrated in the eastern counties, its obvious frontier status, its abundance of raw unimproved prairie, Iowa in 1860 reported 40,827 farm laborers—6 per cent of its population. More to the point, out of every hundred persons engaged in agriculture, twenty-three were farm laborers. Or look at Kansas, which had neither attained the dignity of statehood nor acquired anything but a thin veneer of settlement along its eastern border in the six years since it had become a territory. Census enumerators found here 10,400 farms and, surprisingly, 3,660 farm laborers. Nineteen out of every hundred persons engaged in agriculture were farm laborers. For the states of the Old Northwest the percentage of farm laborers among the total number of people engaged in agriculture ranged from 20 to 28.

Throughout the rest of the century, the number of farm laborers grew rapidly in the newer states of the Upper Mississippi Valley, while in the older states it fluctuated up and down and took a violent upward turn in the last decade. In proportion to the total number of persons engaged in agriculture, the number of farm laborers reached a high point in 1870. The census for that year shows that the percentage of farm laborers in the total number of persons engaged in agriculture was 30 in Minnesota, 32 in Nebraska, 33 in Wisconsin, 34 in Kansas, and 37 in Iowa. All these states had fairly stable and well-developed areas by 1870; but all except Iowa also had portions not yet out of the frontier stage. With so many farm laborers in new as well as old communities, no picture of the West can be considered complete without attention to their social and economic background, the reasons why they existed in such numbers. But western historians have not been concerned about them. The stereotype of the mortgaged farmer is familiar to all students of western lore, but the farm laborer has not been the subject of rowdy ballads, he does not appear in the fiction of the frontier, nor is he to be found in the works of Turner, Paxson, Riegel, or Billington.

Statistics of farm labor for these years in new states and territories are so startling that it seems desirable to look into their compilation to determine just who in the opinion of the census enumerators fitted into this category. Analysis of the original census schedules shows that older boys of farm families who were over fifteen years of age and were living at home were not infrequently listed as farm laborers. Undoubtedly they performed heavy routine work on the farm, but I have not thought of them as laborers, since they rarely drew wages and since they could expect to inherit a share of the farm some time in the future. Offsetting this factor was the exclusion of migratory workers who were employed for the harvest season but were not at the time of enumeration living with the farmers who had previously engaged them or were thereafter to do so. Clearly, the timing of the census was important in the matter of enumerating farm laborers. The first of June, the date for which information was collected, was not the busiest time for farmers in the Corn Belt, because crops were already in, haying had not begun, and wheat was not yet ready for harvest. A month or six weeks later, enumerators would have found greater numbers of hired hands to list.[2]

By 1870 the census takers were collecting information respecting the value of compensation, including board paid hired hands the previous year. True, this information was not processed and published, but a sample study of Poweshiek County in central Iowa shows that of 1,634 farmers owning land, 932 paid out for labor the previous year sums ranging from $5 to $2,000, the average being over $150. In nine townships in this county, payments to farm laborers, including the value of their board, amounted to $234,000.[3]

The census schedules also furnish information on the emergence of farm tenancy, a midway step from laborer to farm owner, which is particularly valuable since we have no specific data on tenancy as such until 1880. Some years ago in a colloquy on land speculation at a meeting of the American Historical Association, this writer ventured to suggest to Dr. Joseph Schafer, superintendent of the State Historical Society of Wisconsin, that in his examination of the profits and losses in speculation, he may have underestimated the rents speculators collected; this suggestion was scoffed at for intimating that tenancy existed on the frontier or that rents could have been collected for land use.[4] Dr. Schafer was a tartar in argument, but the fact remains that tenancy did exist on the frontier, it was not uncommon in Wisconsin in the fifties, and it does have to be taken into account in any consideration of the frontier process. In the absence of detailed census compilations, we can learn much about tenancy from earlier census schedules, the county deed records, local newspaper advertisements, and correspondence of land dealers and landlords.[5]

The censuses of 1850, 1860, and 1870 show a sharp increase in the number of farms in excess of five hundred acres, the expanding volume of hired hands previously alluded to, and numerous "farmers" and farm laborers who owned no real or landed property but did have personal property such as horses, mules, oxen, milch or beef cattle, and hogs. Some of these "farmers" and farm laborers may have been attempting to buy farms they were operating, but whether they were or not, they were at the time tenants. Analysis of the 1870 census listings of farmers and farm laborers in two lightly developed western Iowa townships and one well-settled central Iowa township shows that of 184 persons (excluding children) listed as engaged in agriculture, ninety-six owned land and eighty-eight owned no real property, but fifty-seven of these latter owned personal property and were presumably tenants. Thirty-one "farmers" and farm laborers listed no property of any kind. Of the agricultural population of these three townships (Belvedere, Ashton, and Shiloh), 53 per cent owned farms and 47 per cent owned no land.

Farm land was being rented to tenants in Ohio, Indiana, and Illinois as early as the 1820's, but the practice did not become common for nearly a generation.[6] After the frenzy of land speculation in the thirties, many investors, caught with heavy obligations in a falling market, with interest and tax costs growing, offered to rent their land to squatters or newly arriving immigrants too poor to buy, partly to protect their property but also to get at least the taxes out of them.[7] As early as 1842, Solon Robinson, the well-known agricultural writer, in describing the attractions of the flat lands of northwestern Indiana to immigrants, said: "No matter if you have no money, you can rent land very low, and will soon be in a condition to let land instead of hiring it."[8] By the middle of the century, tenancy was emerging everywhere in the prairies of Indiana, Illinois, and eastern Iowa and a little more slowly in Wisconsin. From northern and eastern Indiana, the Military Tract and the central prairie counties of Illinois, and the eastern counties of Iowa came many reports of persons renting land who lacked the means to buy. Renting was so common in La Salle County, Illinois, that the local newspaper in its price current listed farms as renting from $1.25 to $1.50 an acre. In eastern Iowa, where improved land also was renting at the same prices, a dealer in 1852 advertised thirteen farms for sale or rent. Elsewhere newspapers discussed the growing practice of share renting.[9]

In mid-century Indiana, a move to define the rights of landlords and tenants developed into a major political battle. Bills to give landlords a lien on crops raised by their tenants had the support of legislators from the prairie counties, where landlordism flourished, but were opposed by the Democratic representatives from the small-farm counties of southern Indiana. Opponents, perhaps not aware of how far landlordism had already developed in the richer counties of the north, said that any such measure would stimulate landlords to enlarge their domain, "increase their subordinate tenancies," and strike at "our true policy to encourage every man to become a land owner." It was legislation "in favor of capital, the rich, and against labor, the poor." Another Hoosier opponent of the measure proposed an amendment to give landlords liens on the furniture, the wife, and the children of the tenant! Session after session of the legislature gave consideration to the question from 1857 to 1881, but not until the latter year was action completed.[10]

The growth of tenancy was stimulated by the granting of lands to railroads to aid in their construction. Two early beneficiary railroads—the Illinois Central and the Burlington and Missouri—after making their selections of land, found squatters on them who could not easily be dispossessed without creating ill feeling, but who were not in a position to pay the price asked for their claims. The Burlington officials found that the easiest policy to follow in such cases was to rent the land to the squatters for one to three years at a nominal price of twenty cents an acre with the hope that such improvements as the squatters made would enable the land to bring a good price when the lease expired and legal action might be taken to evict, if necessary. In 1878, the Burlington was renting Nebraska land which had been farmed during the past year for $1 an acre and idle lands for fifty cents an acre; its land in Iowa was then being rented for as much as $1.25 to $2 an acre. Railroad land-grant policy, like the government policy of permitting—and, indeed, encouraging— extensive speculation in Western lands, hastened the coming of tenancy to the West.[11]

The rapid alienation of public land and swiftly rising land values helped to accelerate the renting of land in the sixties and seventies. In 1880, when statistics of tenancy were compiled, the figures for the public-land states, particularly those which still contained land available for homestead, alarmed land reformers. In Illinois 31 per cent and in Iowa 23 per cent of all the farms were tenant operated. The counties of greater land values and higher productivity had tenancy rates ranging into the high 30's and 40's. More surprising was the swift emergence of tenancy in the border counties of Kansas and Nebraska, where the land had been in private ownership no more than twenty-three years, much of it less than fourteen years. Here the tenancy figures ranged from 25 to 40 per cent. In the states of the Upper Mississippi Valley, the percentage of people engaged in agriculture who were either tenants or farm laborers ranged from 32 in Minnesota to 53 in Illinois.[12]

The early appearance of tenancy and agricultural labor in the amount that has been shown in or close to frontier areas, together with their rapid increase, provides convincing evidence that government land policy was not producing the results its defenders claimed. In view of the oft-repeated objective of American land policy—to assure a nation of freeholders—how is it possible to account for the early appearance of farm laborers and tenants in frontier communities?

Paradoxically, the fact that cheap, and finally free, land was to be had in the American West has a direct bearing on the appearance of farm laborers and tenants in that section. Government land prices were progressively reduced from $2 an acre in 1800 ($1.64 for cash) to $1.25 in 1820, to 60¢ to $1 by the use of military bounty land warrants of 1847—55, to as little as 12.5¢ in 1854, until finally, in 1862, free land could be obtained. European peasants and debt-ridden farmers in older sections of America were lured west by the vision of cheap or free farms that they confused with cheap or free raw land.

Nor was it sufficiently noted that the cost of farm making was increasing as settlers moved into the tough-sodded, poorly drained, and timberless prairies, where in competition with construction and railroad building they either had to pay high wages for custom work such as breaking, harvesting, and threshing or buy expensive labor-saving equipment. Custom plowmen, using the heavy breaking plow pulled by a number of yoke of oxen, charged $2 and $3 an acre for breaking prairie. Lumber for the house, fencing, and perhaps a barn could no longer be "hooked" from neighboring government- or absentee-owned tracts and had to be brought in at heavy expense from the Mississippi River mill towns or Chicago. A yoke of oxen, wagon, plow, stove, chains, ax, shovel, grindstone, scythe or cradle, together with seed, funds to maintain the family until the first crop came in, fees for filing land-office papers, or money to make the down payment on a railroad tract, brought the amount needed to start farming to $500 at the minimum; safer estimates were two or three times that much. Land agents and representatives of the land-grant railroads warned prospective emigrants in the East and in Europe that they should bring some capital with them to the West.[13]

Notwithstanding these well-meant warnings, immigrants continued to reach the outer edge of settlement destitute, unable to start farm making. We need not probe their disillusionment when their scant resources proved insufficient to enable them to take advantage of the government's free homestead policy. They could still cherish the dream of owning a farm while they worked for others.

Immigrants newly arriving in the West soon learned that unless they quickly established a claim to land, their chances of making good selections would be minimized, perhaps lost to other more foresighted settlers or to speculators. The settler and the speculator were catching up with the surveyor, especially in Iowa, Kansas, and Nebraska, and land when offered or opened to entry was quickly snatched up. Consequently, a first step toward farm ownership was to select a tract, establish a claim upon it, and hope that it could be held for two or three years without cost even though the claimant was not actually living upon it or abiding by the provision of the pre-emption or homestead acts. Frontiersmen moving early into newly opened communities found they could sell their claims with but slight improvements for $50 to $100 to later comers and then go a little farther west and make another selection. Claim making, a species of land speculation, was indulged in by many who gradually acquired a little livestock and equipment through sales of claims or through outside earnings and were ready in a few years for more permanent farm making. A combination of claim speculation and temporary work on railroad construction jobs or building projects in growing urban centers was common. That many immigrants also took agricultural jobs as hired hands in areas close to, if not right in, the frontier is not as well known.

Some students and readers of fiction relating to western pioneer life have entertained the notion that western farmers never really prospered but were in a more or less chronic state of depression that was aggravated by periods of unusually low prices and near crop failures with resulting acute distress. Perhaps more attention has been directed to the agrarian reaction to such distress and the causes thereof than to periods of favorable prices and bountiful crops that brought early prosperity to many. Certain it is that in no comparable period did such large numbers of immigrants to a new region gain ownership of the farms they were improving and live well upon those farms as in the fifty-year period from 1850 to 1900 in the Mississippi Valley. Boomer literature of the time tells of numerous cases of individuals in Illinois, Kansas, or Nebraska who made enough on one good crop to pay for their land and equipment. That there were such cases cannot be denied, but whether they were typical it is impossible to say. We do know that industrious, skillful farmers blessed by good fortune did succeed not only in subduing the usual 80- to 160-acre tract of wild land to grain production and livestock use, but in many instances in developing even larger farms. This was accomplished not alone by the head of the family and his children, but with the aid of hired men.

The census schedules of 1870 reveal thousands of instances of farmers with no more than 160 acres employing one or two laborers.[14] These farmers did not attract the attention of journalists or travelers of the time, and, consequently, it is more difficult to reconstruct their operations than those of the larger capitalist farmers, whose operations were on a much bigger scale and who individually employed numerous farm hands.

The American West proved attractive not only to poor immigrants but also to men of means interested in developing not single family farms but estates of thousands of acres worked by laborers and tenants. Large capitalistic enterprises in the pioneer West are not unknown to historians, but most attention has been centered on the bonanza wheat farms of the Red River Valley of Minnesota and Dakota and on cattle ranching in the Great Plains. Carried out on a grand scale and with a dramatic flourish, they drew the attention of journalists and other commentators of the time and consequently found their way into most histories of the West.[15] Their day was short, their long-range influence not great, and they deserve a mere footnote in history compared with the quieter, more pervasive, and longer-lasting investments by masterful and aggressive capitalists in the Corn Belt, who came not merely to speculate nor to develop a bonanza farm but to create rent-producing estates composed of numerous farms operated either by hired hands or by tenants.

These estate builders were to be found in practically every portion, one can almost say in every county, of the Corn Belt. Their homes, in highly stereotyped and stilted engravings, the number of acres they owned, and the moral qualities of the owners all are presented in the numerous county atlases and biographical volumes that were the rage in the Gilded Age. Their investments ranged from a few thousand to hundreds of thousands of dollars and, for a score or more, to one or two millions.[16] That is not to say that they brought capital in this amount with them when they first ventured into the West. Much of their capital was made in the West.

The cattle ranchers and drovers who flourished in Indiana and Illinois in the forties, fifties, and sixties and in Iowa and Missouri a little later dominated great areas of the prairies for a time. They built upon their first investments by shrewdly buying the surplus stock of neighbors, fattening them on the prairie bluestem with the addition of a little grain, and then driving them to Chicago, Indianapolis, or the East, wherever they could get favorable prices. Later they brought in cattle from Missouri and Texas. Their profits were invested in land when it could be bought "dirt-cheap" to assure an abundance of grass and grain for their operations. Slowly, they turned to grain feeding and grain production and improved livestock, using meantime an increasing number of hands. By mid-century the operations of the successful cattle kings were being conducted on a huge scale, with herds of cattle numbering in the thousands, fields of corn covering thousands of acres, and scores of hands to carry on the business. Their holdings in land increased to 5,000, 10,000, 20,000, even

40,000 acres.[17] For every giant farm of this size there were a score or more of smaller operators with holdings ranging from one to four thousand acres.[18]

These bonanza farms, located as they were in Corn Belt counties with high land values, soon became as outmoded as the sickle and cradle. Farm workers proved irresponsible when hired at low wages. They were careless with tools, they slighted their tasks, overworked or abused the draft animals, drank heavily, and often engaged in fisticuffs. On slight provocation they quit their jobs, knowing that equally good opportunities were available elsewhere, and they demanded high wages when the peak of employment was reached in the harvest season. Old Isaac Funk, who accumulated a fortune of two million dollars in his land and cattle business in McLean County, Illinois, said in 1861 that no one could afford to hire men to grow and market grain at prices then prevailing. Their wages were too high and they worked too little, thought Funk. Another Illinois landlord, in deploring the wage of two dollars a day being paid to harvest hands in 1862, held that "cheap farm laborers" were essential for the winning of the Civil War.[19] The best agricultural laborers wanted to become tenants or owners and would remain in employment only as long as was necessary for them to accumulate the resources for starting on their own.

Continuing immigration into the prairies with its resulting pressure upon the supply of land, skyrocketing values, taxes, and assessments forced more intensive land use. Ranches with grain as a side issue could no longer be economically justified, and for a time the bonanza farms became grain farms with cattle as a side issue. Before long, central administration of the land was abandoned. The big farms were divided into small holdings and assigned to tenants. Though the workers might prove poor farm hands, it was seen that, given a share in the returns of farming, they were more responsible, more willing to exert themselves, more careful with their tools, horses, and oxen, and with their housing accommodations. In the transition to full tenancy the landlord might provide everything but maintenance for the operator and pay him eight or ten cents a bushel for the corn he produced. In 1870, a tenant who furnished his own team was paid fifteen cents for each bushel of corn, fifty cents for each bushel of wheat, and twenty-five cents for each bushel of oats he produced. A more common practice was for the tenant to pay the landlord one-third to one-half of the crops or a cash rent for each acre of cultivable land.[20]

The day of the Corn Belt cattle kings was short, as was their career as bonanza farmers. As entrepreneurs developing their estates they made jobs available for many workers who later were permitted, if not encouraged, to become tenants. In the tenant stage of land development some of the landlords continued to expend their surplus from rents in additional improvements, so that their constructive period lasted throughout the first generation and, indeed, well into the second. In the process of change, some land was sold; more, through inheritance diffusion, passed to a larger number of landlords. Analysis of the assessment records or the current platbooks of Corn Belt counties reveals a century later how tenaciously third- and fourth-generation descendants of the old cattle kings have clung to their possessions.

Side by side with these modern holdings are other equally large estates which sprang from another type of investment on the frontier, that of the capitalists who came west to create permanent estates like that of the Wadsworth family in the Genesee country of New York by buying and developing extensive areas. Some of these capitalists concentrated their attention entirely upon farm making, while others bought and sold real estate, acted as agents for eastern capitalists wishing to invest in the growing West, or perhaps ran a bank and made loans to squatters. Profits and fees they invested in land improvements. A number took construction contracts on railroads, receiving land instead of cash in payment. They were careful to keep their titles clear, to pay the taxes before liens were issued, and to protect their timber against the prevalent custom of "hooking." With all these side issues, they kept before them the goal of land development.

Extensive improvement of their holdings required these estate builders to seek out workers to break the prairie, fence, erect tenant houses for the families of workers and barracklike constructions for single men, to seed, cultivate, harvest, shuck, thrash, and haul the grain to market. To assure themselves an adequate labor supply, and subsequently to attract tenants, these entrepreneurs had at times to advertise, distribute handbills in eastern communities, and in a number of instances publish pamphlets describing the opportunities their lands provided to immigrants.[21] Workers could not save much from the low wages paid them, but many pioneers did make their start by accumulating small funds from such earnings and investing them, perhaps while still holding the farm job, in nearby land on which they might at the same time make some improvements.

For the Western immigrant who was anxious to have a farm of his own but who lacked the means to acquire it, it was distinctly better to be a tenant than a farm laborer. He could, when he attained this status, feel he was moving toward his goal. Now he shared with the capitalist proprietor the profits from farming, but he also shared the losses. Furthermore, he was usually required by his lease to make capital improvements upon the rented land, and the cost would be deducted from the rent. Every improvement he made raised the value of the land and pushed farther away the possibility of his buying it. If he paid cash rent, continued improvement of the land was certain to be followed by a higher rent charge; if he paid share rent, the landlord might— and in the eighties did—exact a larger portion of the grain. Tenancy was no happy choice to the immigrant looking for the free or cheap land about which he had heard so much, but unless he was willing to go far beyond the railroad into areas lacking social facilities and market opportunities, there was no other alternative.

Some landlords were willing to pay for much of the cost of breaking and fencing, to provide machines and even credit to carry their tenants through harvest. Others insisted on the tenants' making all the improvements, which they then might own or at least have the right to sell to other tenants, subject to the approval of the landlord. Advertisements for tenants were increasingly common in the prairie newspapers, but more ominous from the point of view of the tenant were advertisements of renters looking for land.[22] Eviction for sloth, failure to make required improvements, poor farming, and cheating the landlord increased as hordes of new immigrants looking for land to rent came in from central Europe. The pressure for places to rent made it possible for the landlord to exact more and to allow the tenant less. Farmers of older American stock found the role of tenant increasingly unbearable. Disillusioned by their meager returns and unwilling to compete with the new wave of European immigrants, they abandoned their rented places in Illinois and Iowa by the thousands in the seventies and eighties for a new try at ownership in western Kansas or Nebraska, or perchance in the Dakota country. It was this emigration of older American tenants from the Corn Belt that was responsible for the increasingly conservative character of agrarian politics in Illinois and Iowa. These disillusioned and frequently angry tenants who emigrated farther west carried their resentment with them and made the area in which they settled fertile ground for the Populist agitator.[23]

Meantime, the capitalist estate builders, having divided their holdings into small tenant farms, were emerging as farm managers. Where they had erected tenant homes, set out fences, and established orchards they needed to protect their investment by making certain that proper care and maintenance were provided. They naturally wanted for their tenancies good farmers who would keep the weeds down, get their crops in and harvested at the right time, protect the timber if any, and pay their cash rent promptly or turn in a fair landlord's share of the grain. Good tenants assured better yields and hence more share rent. Both landlords and tenants were driven to exploit the land by their need for high returns to meet costs of farm improvements, new implements, and perhaps livestock. Rotation, the use of alfalfa or clover, prevention of erosion were all subordinated to the production of grain, with declining fertility the natural—though not immediately apparent—result. Much the same thing can be said of farm owners who were struggling to raise funds out of their crops to purchase new equipment, to fence additional land, to drain the low places, or to enlarge their original two- or three-room houses to accommodate growing families. Economic circumstances were largely responsible for a pattern of land use that disregarded the lessons of the past in older states, and was exploitative and destructive of values. In defense of the capitalist estate builders, it should be added that some of them early showed concern for proper land management by insisting upon rotation of crops; the use of alfalfa, clover, and lime; the elimination of weeds; and careful use of pastures.

Elsewhere the operations of capitalist estate builders, whose individual and family holdings ran as high as 60,000 acres and in one case to 200,000 acres, have been described. Few of these "feudal lords," as George Ade called them, would sell unless faced with disaster.[24] They instilled in their children a deep respect for the land they had improved and sought by every possible legal device to restrict the right of alienation. Because of their great success in retaining ownership of their many farms, the names of Scully, Moore, Davis, Vandeveer, Ennis, Funk, Fowler, Wearin, Rankin, and Lawrence-Lowrie are as familiar today to the residents of the prairie states as were the names of the great planters of South Carolina and Georgia to the antebellum residents of those states.

With all the plethora of information the Bureau of the Census had gathered, the problem of multiple ownership of tenant farms received no attention until 1900. Something of the concentration of ownership of tenant farms, the heritage of the capitalist estate builder in the nineteenth century, may be seen in the census data of that year. The figures are not complete and are made less useful by the fact that they are compiled on the basis of residence of owner; but in the absence of anything better we must use them. For the states of the Upper Mississippi Valley, 3,800 landlords appear as owning 32,646 farms. Five hundred and fifty-one of these landlords had an average of 12.8 farms each, and 122 owners had an average of 35.5 farms each. In Illinois 34 landlords are shown owning 1,115 farms, or an average of 32 each.[25]

Ownership of Tenant Farms
by Owners Living in Upper Mississippi Valley, 1900

	Number of Owners	Number of Farms Owned
Owned one farm	419,900	419,900
Owned two farms	39,124	78,248
Owned three to five farms	12,070	39,831
Owned five to ten farms	3,127	21,263
Owned ten to twenty farms	551	7,052
Owned twenty or more farms	122	4,331
Total (plural ownership)	54,994	150,725

Since one landlord owned 322 farms in Illinois and an additional 845 farms in Missouri, Kansas, and Nebraska but had his residence in the District of Columbia, it is easy to see how deceptive, how inadequate, the census data is.

The estate builder brought much-needed funds to the West, developed substantial areas, and provided early employment and housing facilities for many newly arrived immigrants who lacked means to begin on their own. He aided others in getting started by lending them funds to commence farming as a tenant or owner; by furnishing them the necessary farming implements, seed, and food until harvest; and by providing livestock on a partnership basis. Much of the risk in these operations was his. Frequently, he undertook such investments with borrowed capital on which he paid 10 to 15 per cent interest. Taxes bore heavily on him, as the residents of his community seeking better schools and roads raised his assessments on tangibles that could not be hidden. Poor crops or low prices or, worse still, a combination of both might so reduce his income as to make it impossible for him to meet his obligations. One bad year he could take, perhaps two, but a larger combination of bad years was disastrous. The late seventies marked the final defeat of a number of large farm operators, and this was the result of poor prices, unfavorable weather, high interest rates, and perhaps poor management.

This paper may have indicated that society on the frontier and in areas a generation beyond the frontier stage was more complex, had a wider range of economic well-being, than Frederick Jackson Turner thought. The early appearance of farm laborers and tenants, many of whom were never to rise to farm-ownership status, and of great landed estates, whose owners brought wealth with them and added much to it, did not make for a "fundamental unity in its [frontier's] social structure and its democratic ideals. . . ." Concepts of the homogeneity of frontier society, similarity of frontier outlook, common addiction to democratic principles, may well be questioned.

Antebellum Democratic senators of the Upper Mississippi Valley appeared to be more concerned with their own land speculation schemes or the welfare of fur, lumber, mining, and railroad companies than with the fortunes of their farmer constituents; and they did little to loosen the reactionary control southern slave owners had over their party. The land-owning aristocracy early moved into politics via the Whig and Republican parties and fought as vigorously for privilege as did eastern conservatives. It was a combination of prairie landlords—Isaac Funk, Jesse Fell, Asahel Gridley, and David Davis—who had an important share in bringing the Republican nomination to Lincoln in 1860. Their activities contributed to fasten protection, the gold standard, land subsidies to railroads, and an incongruous land system upon the country. When the Democratic party in the Middle West recovered from its debacle, it was in the hands of Bourbons no more liberal in their outlook than the Republican officeholders they sought to displace.

The appearance of the Greenback and Populist parties seemed for a time to offer promise of effective agrarian leadership, but a combination of upper-class landowning families that directed the Greenback and Granger parties and a will-of-the-wisp search for a magic commodity price formula by the Populist party offered no aid to the farm laborer searching for a route to ownership or to tenants struggling to retain their step on the ownership ladder. While western newspapers were bewailing the fate of Irish tenants, they gave no heed to the emergence of the tenant class at home whose rights were less secure, whose plight as serious. The landlords and successful farmers were in the saddle politically, and though they might erupt in condemnation of financial lords of the East, railroad magnates, or tariff-minded manufacturers, they did nothing to assure fixity of tenure, fair rent, and compensation for improvements to tenants; in Illinois they joined together to beat down levels of wages paid to farm workers.[26]

At the close of the nineteenth century the agricultural laborers and tenants outnumbered full owner-operators of farms in five of the states we have studied, and in all the Upper Mississippi Valley the numbers of farm laborers and tenants were fast growing. Agrarian reform movements offered nothing to improve their lot. It was not until the twentieth century that the status of the tenant was substantially bettered with his gradual accumulation of livestock, equipment, and investment in improvements, which has made him a substantial farmer with an equity worth thousands of dollars.

Notes

1. Arthur Moore, *The Farmer and Rest of Us* (Boston, 1945), 131.

2. Information on the use of migratory laborers is meager, but the *Davenport Gazette* (Iowa), published in an important river port, is helpful in its issues of July 13 to 18, 1868. Daily mention is made of the demand for farm hands, for which as much as $3 and $4 per day was being paid. A stampede of city workers was reported which so depleted the community that construction projects could not be carried on. On the 18th, the steamer Dubuque was reported as bringing in 75 field hands, who within thirty minutes after arrival were engaged at $3.50 to $3.75 a day. Later reports of the movement north of wheat harvesters indicate that migratory labor was a major feature of agriculture in Illinois, Iowa, Wisconsin, and Minnesota.

3. The original census schedules of Iowa and Wisconsin are in the Iowa Historical and Art Department, Des Moines, and the State Historical Society of Wisconsin, Madison, where they were used for this paper.

4. For his study of the land speculation of Charles Augustus Murray, who bought

20,000 acres in Grant and LaFayette Counties, Wisconsin, in 1836, Dr. Schafer used the conveyance records at the county seats to determine when the various parcels of land were sold and at what prices. He concluded that Murray had not done as well as if the money had been invested in gilt-edge securities. Since leases ordinarily were not recorded, he had no way of knowing whether any of the land had been rented or what income might have come from rents. In regard to farm tenancy in 1880, these two counties ranked close to the top among Wisconsin counties. The state figure for 1880 is 9 per cent; figures for Grant and LaFayette are 14 and 18 per cent. For Schafer's treatment see his *The Wisconsin Lead Region* (Madison, 1932), 148–54.

5. Notices of Wisconsin farms for rent in the fifties were found in the *Janesville Gazette*, the Janesville *Democratic Standard*, the Baraboo *Sauk County Standard*, and the *Eau Claire Free Press*. The papers of Catlin and Williamson, Cyrus Woodman, and J. Richardson & Co. in the Wisconsin State Historical Society and of Allen Hamilton and George W. Ewing in the Indiana State Library are useful.

6. Solon J. Buck, *Pioneer Letters of Gershom Flagg* (Springfield, Illinois, 1912), 22–46; *Indiana Oracle and Dearborn Gazette* (Lawrence, Indiana), Oct. 4, 1823. Nicholas Longworth had 27 tenants on his farms near Cincinnati in 1850. Ophia D. Smith, *The Life and Times of Giles Richards, 1820-1860* ("Ohio Historical Collections," Vol. 6 [Columbus, 1936]), 45.

7. Paul W. Gates, *Frontier Landlords and Pioneer Tenants* (Ithaca, 1945), 3.

8. Herbert A. Kellar, ed., *Solon Robinson, Pioneer and Agriculturist* ("Indiana Historical Collections," Vol. 21 [Indianapolis, 1936]), I, 351.

9. Letter of J. W. Schreyer, June 22, 1846, in *Indiana Magazine of History* 40 (Sept. 1944), 294; Anon., *A True Picture of Emigration: Of Fourteen Years in the Interior of North America* (London, 1838), 60; Florence E. Janson, *The Background of Swedish Immigration, 1840-1930* (Chicago, 1931), 141–42; Harvey L. Carter, "Rural Indiana in Transition, 1850-1860," *Agricultural History* 20 (April, 1946), 114; La Salle, Illinois, *Independent*, March 4, 1854; G. C. Beman, Croton, Lee Co., Iowa, Jan. 12, 1853, to D. Kilbourne (Kilbourne MSS. in the Iowa Historical and Art Department); *Davenport Gazette* (Iowa), Jan. 29, Nov. 25, 1852; Oct. 6, 1853; March 26, May 5, 1858; *Sioux City Register* (Iowa), March 17, 1860, and March 15, 1862.

10. *Brevier Legislative Reports*, 1852, 1857, 1859, 1861, 1865, 1881; *Laws of Indiana General Assembly*, 1881, p. 565; *Indianapolis State Sentinel*, Jan. 14 and 23, 1857; *Monticello Herald*, April 1, 1875.

11. Peter Daggy, Land Department, Illinois Central Railroad, Nov. 30, 1865, to C. E. Perkins; J. M. King, Clarinda, Iowa, June 21, 1865, to Perkins; J. D. McFarland, Lincoln, Nebraska, Nov. 25, 1868, to A. E. Touzalin; W. W. Baldwin, Land Commissioner, Burlington and Missouri, Aug. 23, 1879, to R. A. Crippen, Burlington Archives, Newberry Library. The correspondence of Edward Hayes of Oak, T. S. Goddard of Hastings, R. A. Crippen of Corning, Iowa, land agents of the B & M, contains allusions to numerous instances of the railroad's leasing to tenants on a cash or share-rent basis.

12. To arrive at these percentages I added the number of tenant farms (presumably farmed each by one tenant) to the number of farm laborers and computed what percentage that total was of the number of people engaged in agriculture. The figures are from the *Tenth Census, Agriculture* (Washington, 1883), *passim*.

13. *Guide to the Lands of the Northern Pacific Railroad in Minnesota* (New York,

1872), 22; Arthur F. Bentley, *The Condition of the Western Farmer as Illustrated by the Economic History of a Nebraska Township* ("Johns Hopkins University Studies in Historical and Political Science," Eleventh Series, No. 7 [July, 1893]), 28; Clarence H. Danhof, "Farm Making Costs and the 'Safety Valve': 1850-1860," *Journal of Political Economy* 46 (June, 1941), 317 ff.; Paul W. Gates, *Fifty Million Acres: Conflicts Over Kansas Land Policy, 1854-1890* (Ithaca, 1954), 223.

14. Paul S. Taylor, "The American Hired Man: His Rise and Decline," *Land Policy Review* 6 (Spring, 1943), 3-17; LaWanda F. Cox, "The American Agricultural Wage Earner, 1865-1900: The Emergence of a Modern Labor Problem," *Agricultural History* 22 (April, 1949), 94-114.

15. Harold E. Briggs, *Frontiers of the Northwest* (New York, 1940), 509-22; and Fred A. Shannon, *The Farmer's Last Frontier, Agriculture, 1860-1897* (*The Economic History of the United States,* David, Faulkner, Hacker, *et. al.* [eds.], Vol. 5 [New York, 1945]), 154-61.

16. In Illinois alone a compiler found in 1892 the following "millionaires" whose wealth was largely made in farm lands: Matthew T. Scott, Orlando Powers, L. B. Casner, Estate of John Shaw Hayward, John C. Proctor, George Pasfield, Horatio M. Vandeveer, William H. Ennis, W. H. Bradley. In Missouri the outstanding millionaire landowners were David Rankin and five heirs of Milton Tootle; in Nebraska, Stephen Miles; in Minnesota, J. A. Willard and A. H. Wilder; in Indiana, William H. English and the Estate of Moses Fowler. Other identifiable millionaires in these states added materially to their wealth through farming operations and land improvement. *American Millionaires. The Tribune's List of Persons Reputed to be Worth a Million or More* (June, 1892), reprinted in Sidney Ratner, *New Light on the History of Great American Fortunes. American Millionaires of 1892 and 1902* (New York, 1953).

17. Gates, *Frontier Landlords and Pioneer Tenants, passim.;* "Hoosier Cattle Kings in the Prairies," *Indiana Magazine of History* 44 (March, 1948), 1-24; "Cattle Kings in the Prairies," *Mississippi Valley Historical Review* 35 (Dec., 1948), 379-412.

18. The Census of 1880 shows 2,916 farms in excess of a thousand acres in the ten states of the Upper Mississippi Valley.

19. *New York Tribune,* July 30, 1861 and Aug. 11, 1861; C. H. Moore to Dr. John Warner, July 21, 1862, Moore-Warner MSS., Clinton, Illinois; *Country Gentleman,* March 10 and May 5, 1864; July, 1865.

20. *Columbus State Journal* (Ohio) in *Davenport Gazette* (Iowa), Aug. 12, 1855; 1 Miscellaneous Record, 434, Logan County Recorder's Office, Lincoln, Illinois; James MacDonald, *Food from the Far West* (London, 1878), 142-48; Appendix, "Agricultural Interests Commission, Reports of the Assistant Commissioner" (London, 1880), *Parliamentary Papers,* 1880, vol. 18, 18, 38-39; *Bloomington Bulletin* (Illinois), March 4, 1887. On the Fowler lands in Indiana, in return for breaking land and putting it in corn, tenants were paid 25¢ a bushel for the corn they raised in the first five crop years. *Benton Review,* June 11, 1885.

21. *Sioux City Register,* Jan. 12, 1861; Margaret Ruth Beattie, "Matthew Scott, Pioneer Landlord-Gentleman Farmer, 1855-1891" (Thesis, Cornell University Library, 1947), 58 ff.; Jacob Van Der Zee, *The British in Iowa* (Iowa City, 1922), 57 ff.

22. The *Champaign Gazette* (Illinois), clipped in the *Bloomington Pantagraph* (Illinois), Jan. 23, 1879, reported "The demand for farms to rent far exceeds the supply, and men are compelled to seek other localities to get places." Monticello, Indiana,

Prairie Chieftain, Nov. 4, 1852; *Bloomington Pantagraph,* Feb. 8, 1854 and Nov. 5, 1856; Watseka, Illinois, *Iroquois County Times,* Oct. 21, 1875; *Malvern Leader* (Iowa), Feb. 8, 1883; Feb. 26 and March 5, 1885.

23. Chester McArthur Destler, "Agricultural Readjustment and Agrarian Unrest in Illinois, 1880–1893," *Agricultural History* 21 (April, 1947), 104–16; Gates, *Fifty Million Acres,* 244 ff.

24. George Ade, "Prairie Kings of Yesterday," *Saturday Evening Post,* July 4, 1931, p. 14.

25. *Census of 1900, Agriculture,* Part 1, lxxxviii; Howard A. Turner, *The Ownership of Tenant Farms in the North Central States* (United States Department of Agriculture *Bulletin,* No. 1433 [Sept., 1926]), 10.

26. A Farmers Union meeting in Mason County, Illinois, in 1885 resolved "not to exceed fifteen dollars per month, by the year, for the best farm labor, . . . that for the limit of six months, the limit of wages be eighteen dollars per month . . . that we pay no more than $1.50 per day for driving header wagon in harvest; $1.50 per day for labor in haying, and from 50¢ to $1.00 for common labor, to be regulated by time and circumstances." *Mason County Democrat,* Jan. 16 and Feb. 6 and 20, 1885.

Selected Readings

Briggs, Harold E. *Frontiers of the Northwest.* . . . New York: D. Appleton-Century, 1940.

Cox, LaWanda F., "The American Agricultural Wage Earner, 1865–1900: The Emergence of a Modern Labor Problem," *Agricultural History* 22 (April, 1948).

Destler, Chester McArthur. "Agricultural Readjustment and Agrarian Unrest in Illinois, 1880–1893," *Agricultural History* 21 (April, 1947).

Gates, Paul W. *Fifty Million Acres: Conflicts Over Kansas Land Policy, 1854–1890.* Ithaca: Cornell University Press, 1954.

──────. *Frontier Landlords and Pioneer Tenants.* Ithaca: Cornell University Press, 1945.

Shannon, Fred Albert. *The Farmer's Last Frontier, Agriculture, 1860–1897. (The Economic History of the United States,* David, Faulkner, Hacker, *et al.* [eds.] Vol. 5.) New York: Rinehart & Co., 1945.

Taylor, Paul S. "The American Hired Man: His Rise and Decline," *Land Policy Review* 6 (Spring, 1943).

3

The Homestead Act
Free Land Policy in Operation, 1862–1935 *

Gates's 1936 essay, "The Homestead Law in an Incongruous Land System," was probably the most influential article that he ever wrote. "Intended to show that the principle of free land to settlers clashed with the revenue principle on which the federal land system was based," this publication was used by dozens of other research scholars and authors of textbooks to support the contention that the Homestead Law of 1862 and its subsequent revisions had been unsuccessful in completing the democratization of American land tenure. A symposium held in 1962 at the University of Nebraska, marking the centennial of the passage of the law, provided Gates with an opportunity to place the Homestead Acts within a broader perspective. Here, he maintained, "their noble purpose and the great part they played in enabling nearly a million and half people to acquire farm land, much of which developed into farm homes, far outweigh the misuse to which they were put." Gates also notes that land acquisition under these laws was greatly affected by homesteaders working within greatly differing natural and institutional environments in the various areas of the West. He later amplified his statements on such matters in several other articles to be found in the listing of his writings included in this volume.

Two generations of agitation by land reformers, including workingmen's advocates, Jeffersonian arcadians, and western agrarians, finally produced the

*From H. W. Ottoson, ed., *Land Use Policy and Problems in the United States* (Lincoln: University of Nebraska Press, 1963), 28–46. Used by permission of the publisher, the University of Nebraska Press. All rights reserved.

Homestead Law of 1862, which offered free a quarter section of public land in the West to citizens or intended citizens who settled upon and improved it. These free-land advocates anticipated Henry George in maintaining that wild, undeveloped land on the frontier had no value until it was improved by the toil of farm makers; the taxes of residents that provided roads and schools; town and county government; subventions that assisted in opening up canals and railroads; and high transportation rates that helped to pay for the railroads. Since it was the investment of the farmer's labor and the public's money that made land valuable, it seemed to the western citizen double taxation to make him pay for government land.[1] The Homestead Act was intended to reward him for his courageous move to the frontier by giving him land, the value of which he and the community would create.

If classical economists found little but sophistry in this reasoning, the western pioneer and the eastern land reformers cared not.[2] Free land, they hoped, would make the life of the pioneer easier, enable him to use his meager capital to purchase farm machinery and livestock, relieve him of debt to the government or to loan sharks (who frequented the land offices to lend their funds at frontier interest rates of 20 to 40 per cent), remove the specter of crushing mortgages, and thereby assure a larger proportion of success among farm makers.

The Homestead Law was the culmination of a series of moves intended to end the policy of using the public lands as a source of revenue for the government. Prior to 1862, the revenue policy had been frequently modified but prices had been reduced only moderately. Now, in one simple act, it seemingly had been replaced by what conservatives regarded as a radical policy of giving land freely to anyone willing to undertake the obligations of farm making.

Not all westerners subscribed to the view that land on the outer fringe of settlement had no value. Some could see that as the western population movement expanded, it shortened the period in which, on successive frontiers land values rose swiftly from little or nothing to a number of dollars an acre. Like speculators from the East, they were prepared to gamble that the land would acquire value with the expected immigration and the improvements the people made. Consequently, they looked for every opportunity to accumulate ownership, whether by one or two quarter sections beyond their needs or acres numbered by the hundreds or thousands. The ambivalence of western attitudes is clear, for with free land established, the West interposed every kind of objection to plans to curb the alienation of homesteads or to provide effective administration of land laws that would prevent accumulation.

The Homestead Law was not without opponents in 1862. Some held it was partial and discriminatory in that the donation would go only to persons who went West. Others held it would drain off population from high-priced land and thereby lower land values in eastern communities; that it would deprive older states of their share in the lands and reduce the value of soldiers' land bounties and railroad grants. But these were the cries of conservatives who feared the elevating effect that free land would have on the propertyless poor, the day laborer, the immigrant.

If conservatives viewed with alarm the social results they foresaw from homesteading, the land reformers were disappointed that the thoroughgoing reconstruction of American land policies they had sought was not achieved. Homesteads were to be alienable, and weak and inadequate safeguards were included to prevent abuse of the law and accumulation of homesteads by capitalists. The privilege of buying public land in unlimited quantities to anticipate settlers' needs was not ended. Huge grants of land were made after the adoption of the Homestead Law to railroads, wagon roads, and states and territories which could make their selections before settlers appeared and thereby acquire the better and more desirable tracts. Indian land, when opened to settlement, was commonly to be sold, not given to settlers, and individual Indian allotments were likewise to be sold. Altogether, between 400 and 500 million acres were selected by states and territories, railroads, and investors and were held for future sales. These were not, therefore, subject to homestead.[3] In fact, the area not open to homestead, though undeveloped, was much greater than the total acreage that homesteaders finally won as free grants. Congress even required in 1889 and 1890 that the 23 million acres it granted the six new states that entered the Union during these years should be sold at a minimum of ten dollars an acre.[4]

Free-land policy as embodied in the Homestead Law was then grafted upon a land system to which it was ill-fitted and incongruous. The two systems existed side by side for the next twenty-eight years, indeed longer, during which time the choicer selections of the railroads, states, and speculators were being sold. Hence the amount of homesteading was smaller than otherwise it surely would have been.[5]

That revenue was not abandoned as a basic feature of government land policy is shown by the fact that homesteaders, desiring to expand their holdings beyond the 160 acres they could acquire by right of development, had the choice of buying additional tracts from railroads, states, or territories — or from the federal government if in areas where land had been proclaimed for sale in unlimited amounts. If the land was in unoffered areas, they might secure a preemption, or take a desert-land entry which would cost them $1.25 an acre, or enter a tree claim with its obligation of setting out trees on forty of the 160 acres. Actually, more government land was sold between 1862 and

1891 than was successfully homesteaded and patented between 1862 and 1899. Or, to put it differently, the government derived from the sale of public land in the sixty years following the adoption of the Homestead Act a far greater sum ($223,000,000) than it did in the first sixty years of its land administration ($186,000,000).

The land reformers had not succeeded, when writing the Homestead Act, in providing that all public lands henceforth should be reserved for actual settlers. Nor had they succeeded in restricting the quantity of land that might be purchased in offered areas. But they did prevail on the government not to offer newly surveyed land at unlimited sale except for timbered land in Michigan, Wisconsin, Minnesota, Colorado, Oregon, and Washington.[6] Henceforth, there were two classes of land in official terminology: offered land which was subject to private entry in unlimited amounts and unoffered lands which could only be acquired through settlement laws: homestead, preemption, timber culture, timber and stone, and their variations. Approximately two-thirds of Kansas, a larger fraction of Nebraska, all of Oklahoma and the Dakotas, and all of the public land farther west except for California and small areas in Colorado, New Mexico, and Washington were not offered. In these states, speculators could not use their cheaply acquired military bounty-land warrants, or their agricultural college scrip that cost them as little as fifty or sixty cents an acre, to build up huge holdings such as the 263,000 acres that the Brown-Ives-Goddard group of Providence, Rhode Island, established mostly in Illinois, Iowa, and Nebraska; the half million acres of pine lands in Wisconsin to which Ezra Cornell acquired the patent; or the huge 650,000 acres of land that William S. Chapman came to own in California.

Yet it is true that in the unoffered areas large estates were created, such as the bonanza farms of the Dakotas, and the equally large cattle ranches of Wyoming and elsewhere. Some of these holdings, like the bonanza farms, were bought partly from the railroads which placed few limitations on the size of tracts they would sell, and partly from the states. And partly they were acquired through the use of dummy entrymen who took advantage of the loopholes in the settler laws.[7] Others, including some of the large cattle ranches, were not ownerships but enclosures, illegally erected on the public lands which, when the order went out for the removal of the fences, became thereafter open to settlement. These large holdings, together with even larger acquisitions of the timber companies (elaborately documented in the report on forest ownership of the Bureau of Corporations of 1913),[8] and the discovery that millions of acres of land have passed into private hands by the fraudulent use of the settlement laws, have led historians to misunderstand and underestimate the role of the Homestead Law and related settlement measures. Recent

textbook writers have declared that the Homestead Law was "not a satisfactory piece of legislation"; it was "a distressing disappointment"; "farmers
only benefited slightly" from it; it ended "in failure and disillusionment"; two-
thirds of all "homestead claimants before 1890 failed." [9]

A reason for the frequency of these misconceptions of homestead is the
continued reiteration in the annual reports of the Commissioners of the General Land Office, of the widespread and indeed common violation of the spirit
and even the letter of the law by land-hungry settlers, land lookers, petty and
large speculators and their agents, and cattle and mining companies. Defec-
tive legislation, insufficient staff, poorly paid personnel in the Washington
office, the low level of people filling the local land offices, and the practical
impossibility of scrutinizing critically the entries made under the various land
laws, all combined to make the commissioners' task of administering the laws
most frustrating.[10] Their comments on the amount of perjury, subornation,
and misuse of the law became increasingly sharp until finally, the commissioner under Cleveland, harassed by the degree of maladministration and the
widespread dishonesty of people trying to take advantage of the government,
took the drastic step of suspending many thousands of land entries moving
toward patent to allow time for examination and the cancellation of fraudulent entries. This action led to swift political pressures by western politicians,
forcing Cleveland to reverse his subordinate, no matter how just his action. So
absorbed were the commissioners in their efforts to make homestead function
as it was intended to, that they devoted the space allowed them for recommendations for future action very largely to the frauds and malfunctionings of the
system. Historians have reflected this jaundiced view, relying upon these continued reiterations, and not finding much in the reports about the hundreds
of thousands of people successfully making farms for themselves.

I must confess that I may have contributed to this misunderstanding some
twenty-six years ago when I wrote a paper, "The Homestead Law in an Incongruous Land System." As the title suggests, the paper was intended to show
that the principle of free lands to settlers clashed with the revenue principle
on which the federal land system was based. My opening sentence might well
do for introduction here, and I quote:

> The Homestead Act of 1862 is one of the most important laws which
> have been enacted in the history of this country, but its significance has
> been distorted and grossly misrepresented.[11]

The article was intended as a corrective for some of the ideas then prevalent
concerning the measure, as, for example, the notion that most of Iowa passed
into private hands through the Homestead Act; that homestead replaced other

methods of land disposal; that cash sales in unlimited amounts ended in 1862; or that the revenue basis of the land system was abandoned.[12] Correction was necessary but, as is often the case, the revision was carried too far, until some writers seem ready to discount the Homestead Law as of little more than minor significance. Such judgment is unsound.

In any attempt to appraise the significance of the Homestead Law, it should be borne in mind that settlers on unoffered land had more protection for their selections and improvements than they did on offered land. Since speculators could not enter or offer to buy their selections or improvements by falsely swearing at the land office that there were no claims against the land, the settler had less fear, once he had filed his original entry, of being dispossessed.

Having filed his original entry (even though he lacked the means with which to develop his claim), the homesteader had an equity that became increasingly valuable and negotiable as population increased the pressure upon the land supply. In the vanguard of settlement on every frontier were land speculators great and small who spied out choice tracts they wished to hold for the expected rise in value that incoming immigration would bring. The extensive speculator might assemble tracts running to tens of thousands of acres. But of equal importance, possibly, was the small man with no capital for the arduous task of farm making who nevertheless took up a piece of land to which he expected to acquire a preemption right. Frontier custom assured that his claim of one hundred to two hundred acres was his to do with as he wished. With patience and little labor he might improve slightly, sell, and then move to another tract and do the same thing. Government conceded only one preemption right, but that right was almost sacrosanct on the frontier and the same person might make a number of fortunate selections in succession and dispose of them profitably. Some contemporaries were not certain whether the first occupation of pioneers was farm making or land speculation. A settler on his homestead claim in central Kansas in 1878, noting how so many of his neighbors were attempting to engross and acquire title to far more land than they could utilize observed:

> The curse of this country is land-grabbing. Few men are satisfied with one claim; they must have a pre-emption, homestead and timber filing, and between the three they have so much work they don't know which end they stand on.[13]

In addition to the three usual claims it was not unknown for different members of a family to file on adjacent tracts, even though they were violating the spirit if not the letter of the law.

Having established a number of claims which they might be doing little or nothing to develop, settlers had the choice of selling relinquishments to others, borrowing to commute and then skipping the country, attempting to make their improvements with loans until they could get the benefit of rising land values, or holding for long range development. The location, sale, and relinquishment of claims became a major business on the frontier as it proceeded into western Kansas, Nebraska, and Dakota.[14] Relinquishments in the middle eighties sold for $25 to $50 in Kansas, for $50 to $400 in South Dakota and for as little as $5 and a shotgun to $700 in North Dakota.[15] Variations in price partly depended upon the nature of improvements. Undoubtedly, the business of selling relinquishments was carried beyond all justification, but it should be emphasized that it permitted persons who lacked the means with which to begin farming to acquire some cash, farm machinery, and stock and after two or three false starts and sale of relinquishments to succeed finally in establishing ownership of a going farm. The process of claim making with the intention of selling was greatly abused, particularly in the eighties, but despite that abuse it provided opportunities for many settlers to reach their goal of farm ownership.

Land office reports, accounts of the cattle and lumber industry, and other government documents are replete with stories of the use of dummy entrymen by individuals and companies eager to get control of large areas of the public lands. The process was fairly simple. Employees of the cattle, mining, or lumber companies would be induced to file claims under one of the settlement laws, possibly make some slight improvements on their claims, take title by commuting their claims and swear before the land officials that their claims were intended for their own use and that they had entered into no agreement to transfer ownership. Funds for their commutation and a fee for their services that ranged from $50 to $200 were provided by the company.[16] As competition for land intensified, compensation to dummy entrymen reached as high as $1,000 for a quarter section.[17]

A third source of income that the weakly administered public land system made possible to westerners was the practice of mortgaging newly entered land with insurance companies at well beyond its going value and then skipping out with the proceeds of the loan and unloading the property on the credit agency. The West had not always been blessed with abundance of capital but in the eighties, attracted by high interest rates, money flowed into the Great Plains in such quantities that agents of eastern insurance companies and petty capitalists vied with each other in pushing their loans on settlers, offering some well beyond the cash value of the land at the time. So marked was this rivalry that agents, eager for their fees, paid little attention to the quality of improvements on the land and only insisted on a mortgageable title. It was reported from northwestern Nebraska in 1886 that it was easy to get an $800 loan on any quarter section of wild land on which a settlement right had been established.[18] In central North Dakota, in 1903, loans to permit commutation of homesteads were being made as high as $1,500.[19] Settlers who had put little effort into their claims could commute their timber claim (before 1891) or homestead, at a cost of $200 for 160 acres, pay all fees and still have left from $600 to $1,300 for a second try under one of the other settlement laws, the privilege of which they had not yet used.

Many western settlers had larceny in their hearts when it came to dealing with the government, and it did not stretch their consciences unduly to take advantage of the insurance companies or other absentee sources of capital. As one insurance adjuster later said, "it became really too easy for settlers to cash in on their western venture and 'go back to their wives' folks.' They borrowed more than the land was worth and fled."[20] An agent for a Kansas bank said of the borrowers in western Kansas: "As soon as their loans are completed they abandon the land, if they can sell it to someone for a nominal sum above the mortgage they do so."[21]

Whether the early settler was defrauding the government, cheating the insurance company, or making the later immigrant buy a relinquishment from him, he was accumulating the means with which he could finally establish himself as a stable farm maker. This is not to say that all persons establishing claims on the public lands were ultimately to become farmers; many had no such intention. They were out for a speculation. But a very considerable portion of the misuse of the public land laws resulted, it appears, from the credit needs of actual settlers.

A common error in appraising the Homestead Law has been the assumption that homesteading was only important in the Great Plains and Interior Basin where the unit of farming characteristic of the more humid regions was not suitable. The fact is that 23 per cent (689,000) of all original homestead entries were filed in the states east of the Mississippi and in the first tier west of that river. Twenty-four per cent of the homestead entries that went to final patent were located in this region. During the first ten years of the operation of the Homestead Law, Minnesota outranked all states in number of final entries of homesteads and was exceeded only by Kansas in the number of original entries. Altogether, 82,845 free homesteads were patented in Minnesota.[22] This constitutes 66 per cent of the farms of Minnesota of 100 acres or more as listed in the census of 1920. It probably would not be far from the truth to say that the abstracts of two-thirds of Minnesota farms trace back to the patent of the homesteader. East of the Mississippi, 143,360 homestead entries for 15,990,533 acres were carried to patent, mostly in Alabama, Florida, Wisconsin, Mississippi, and Michigan.

In all the states around the Great Lakes, in the South, and in the first tier west of the Mississippi, a considerably higher proportion of the original filings were carried to final entry than elsewhere and there were fewer commutations.

In substantial portions of the second tier of states beyond the Mississippi (extending from Dakota to Oklahoma), the 160-acre unit of farming was not altogether unsuited for farm practices in the late Nineteenth Century. The line of 20-inch rainfall begins roughly just west of the Red River of the North and extends in a gentle southwestward direction. East of that line is perhaps a fifth of North Dakota, a third of South Dakota, more than half of Nebraska, and two-thirds of Kansas. The line of 24-inch rainfall leaves, to the east, a small corner of South Dakota, a fifth of Nebraska, and half of Kansas. To and somewhat beyond the 24-inch rainfall line, corn flourished and the 160-acre unit of agriculture seemed reasonably well adapted to farming. I have conservatively estimated that 150,000 homestead applications were filed in the more humid portions of the Great Plains. This means that, together with the 689,000 entries previously mentioned, 839,000 homesteads or 28 per cent of the total number of homesteads were commenced in areas generally suitable in the nineteenth century for 160-acre farm units.

Furthermore, it is important to note that of these early homesteads, established from Kansas north to Dakota territory before 1881, 58 per cent of those in Kansas were successfully carried to final entry, 61 per cent in Nebraska and 52 per cent in Dakota. Sixty-seven per cent of the entries in Dakota made before 1876 were patented by 1880. This is perhaps the best test of the applicability of homestead to these areas. For the country as a whole, slightly less than 50 per cent of the original homesteads were carried to patent.[23]

Doubtless there are other and perhaps smaller areas in the West where the 160-acre homestead unit seemed to work well at the time. One example is in California, where 63 per cent of the original entries made in the years from 1863 to 1875 were carried to completion.

A second error frequently observed in appraisals of the Homestead Act is forgetting that it took five years, later reduced to three (veterans' military service could be counted), for the original entries to mature.[24] Actually, even more than five years was required for many homesteaders who were driven out by drought, grasshoppers, or other misfortunes, and who had to be allowed extensions of time in which to prove up.

In the land selection process many choices were made by settlers and speculators who were misled by the descriptions on the surveyors' plats; by the land lookers who for fees guided settlers to what soon proved to be questionable locations; and by settlers themselves who may have had little knowledge of the quality of land in the vicinity of the 100th meridian. Some settlers, like those who participated in the great rushes into Oklahoma or who desperately tried to get a claim on the Rosebud Reservation in South Dakota, had no time to pick and choose but had perforce to take the first vacant land they could find. Inevitably, mistakes were made. Study of the correspondence of the General Land Office and of western congressmen illustrates the frequency with which errors of location were made from the very outset of the public land system, and the disappointments and frustrations of the land locators who sought the privilege of making exchanges. In the absence of land classification, settlers made many errors that resulted in a high rate of failure on homesteads.

Nebraska well illustrates this tendency to err in the selection of land. When homestead was adopted, or shortly thereafter, the grants to the state for educational purposes, and to railroads for aid to construction had reduced the public domain to less than 37 million acres. Of this amount speculators quickly grabbed up an additional million acres. Yet the records show that settlers filed on nearly 51 million acres either for homesteads or timberculture claims. Some of these filings led to contests between homesteaders and the railroads or between different homesteaders; other filings proved to be unattractive and were abandoned or relinquished, and perhaps the rights transferred to others. For Nebraska, 51 per cent of the homestead entries and 46 per cent of the combined homestead and timber-culture entries were carried to patent as free land. If commuted entries are included, the percentages reaching patent becomes 58 and 53. Those that did not reach patent were either relinquished for a fee to others or simply abandoned for better selections elsewhere. What is important is that ownership of 74 per cent of the land available for homesteading in Nebraska was actually achieved either through the Homestead Act or the Timber Culture Act, with their privilege of commutation. Or, we may go one step farther and say that at least 80 per cent of the land area of Nebraska available for settler location became owned by homesteaders through settler-oriented laws, though some of this ownership was quite unstable and was not acquired by the first owner for farming.

In Kansas, where little more than 24 million acres were available for homesteading when the act was passed, settlers filed for homesteads and timber-culture claims for more than 35 million acres. The business in relinquishments was large in Kansas as in Nebraska: an estimated 93,000 homestead claims were either relinquished or abandoned. Of the land available for homesteading 50 per cent was carried to patent as free land, 14 per cent was patented as commuted homesteads, and 8 per cent was patented to timber-culture claimants.

Since 1607, settlers had been moving westward adapting themselves to different ecological conditions from those to which they were accustomed. The oak openings of Michigan and the rich bluegrass region of Kentucky were as strange to settlers from New York and Virginia as were the prairies of Illinois and Iowa and the Great Plains of Kansas and Nebraska. Adaptation to environment wrought swift changes in methods of farming; those who could not adapt failed. American settlers on whatever frontier were prepared to make these changes and soon did. They did not realize, so general was this process of adaptation, how different their methods—and indeed their whole way of life—had become from those they had followed previously.

Not long after the hungry land seekers crossed the Missouri they came into contact with a region where rainfall was less than they had been accustomed to and the variations greater from year to year; where drought, winter blizzards, and grasshopper plagues were met, and where more extensive farm practices were essential. These conditions made larger farm units necessary. It is interesting to note how the average size of farms in Kansas increased with a certain regularity from east to west as is shown by the census of 1920: 153 acres was the average in Miami County on the eastern Kansas front, 167 in Osage County, 192 in Lyons County, 244 in Morris County, 354 in Ellsworth County, 590 in Ness County, and 900 acres on the western border in Greeley County.[25]

Historians have been troubled that the homestead unit was fixed at 160 acres just when, as they say, settlers were preparing to break into the less humid region of the Great Plains where larger farm units were desirable. Paradoxically, they have also been troubled that the Preemption Law which, with homestead, made possible larger farm units, was kept on the statute books.[26] Following the judgment of the Commissioners of the General Land Office who harped on the amount of fraud involved in preemption, they have given undue emphasis to this aspect and insufficient attention to the fact that preemption was consciously retained by Congress surely because of the greater flexibility it allowed settlers in adapting themselves to farming in the dryer portions of America where land was not offered.[27] There is no mention of repeal of preemption in the discussion leading to the adoption of homestead in 1862 and the law itself carefully provided for saving all preemption rights that may have been established prior to its adoption. Furthermore, just a few days after the adoption of the Homestead Law, Congress, without a word of opposition in either house, enacted a bill that said all lands to which Indian title had been or should thereafter be extinguished should be subject to preemption. We must conclude that Congress had no intention of establishing an inflexible 160-acre unit for settlers in the unoffered areas.[28]

In 1872 and 1873 the two houses of Congress finally came to agreement on a bill to encourage the planting of trees on the Great Plains. An additional quarter section was thereby offered to settlers who would plant and care for forty acres of trees (later reduced to ten acres) for a period of ten years. An effort to limit its benefits to settlers who had not taken up a preemption or home-stead, failed. Timber culture was designed further to adapt the post-1862 land system to farming in sub-humid America. The law was not carefully drafted and as with all other land legislation it quickly became subject to abuse and was repealed in 1891. But it had in the meantime, notwithstanding its abuse, served its purpose. With preemption and homestead it provided a flexibility that after its repeal was to be assured by the more direct method of enlarging the homestead unit to 320 and then 640 acres.

How significant was the Homestead Law in enabling settlers to acquire land and to establish themselves on going farms? It is clear that it was most successful in the period from 1863 to 1880 when the greater proportion of homesteads were being established in the states bordering on the Mississippi River. It was successful also in parts of Kansas and Nebraska well east of the 98th meridian where there was abundance of rain, and where commutations, relinquishments, and abandonments were fewer than they were to be in other areas later. In these eighteen years, homesteaders filed on 469,000 tracts and by 1885 had made their final entries and were in process of getting title on 55 per cent. Doubtless some would complete their residence requirements in later years.

The misuse of the Homestead Law was becoming common between 1880 and 1900. As shown, misuse was by persons not primarily interested in farm making but concerned to sell relinquishments to immigrants or to transfer rights to cattle, timber, and mining companies. But the most glaring abuses occurred later. Between 1880 and 1900, approximately half of the homestead entries were filed in the six states and territories extending from Oklahoma to North Dakota and including Minnesota. These all were major farm states and the Homestead Law was contributing largely to the development of farm ownership, notwithstanding its abuses.

In these states and territories, free government land, advertised by the America letters which earlier immigrants had sent back to their families in the Old World, by the government immigration bureaus, by even the colonization departments of the railroads and land companies, provided the lodestone, the directing force, that set in motion continued waves of settlers in search of free land. It was the prospect of disposing of their lands to these settlers and trans-porting their goods that made possible the financing and construction of the railroads through the Plains, into the Interior Basin, and to the Pacific Coast. Homestead, above all other factors, made possible the fast growth of the West and all the problems this rapid growth brought with it.

Altogether, 1,413,513 original homestead entries were filed between 1863 and 1900, but even more were to be filed in the twentieth century for a substantially larger acreage. The great day of farm making with the material aid of Uncle Sam was over, however. True, some twentieth century entries were made with the enlarged units for small stock-raising farms or ranches or even wheat farms, but the evidence seems strong that the great bulk of the entries filed after 1900 were for large ranching, mining, and lumbering companies. The numbers of original and final homestead entries, when compared with the number of farms in the Rocky Mountain States, provides startling evidence that the homesteads were being assimilated into larger aggregations of land. Using round figures, we find that Idaho had 92,000 original homestead entries, 60,000 final entries and in 1910-1930 its highest number of farms was 42,000. Colorado had 205,000 original, 107,000 final entries, and at its most 59,000 farms. Arizona had 38,000 original, 20,000 final entries, and 9,000 farms. Wyoming had 115,000 original, 67,000 final entries, and 15,000 farms. In six mountain states the original entries came to 848,000, final entries 492,000, and the maximum number of farms 217,000. Thus it seemed to take about four original entries and two final homestead entries to produce a farm, and most of these homesteads were of the enlarged variety.

Major John W. Powell's recommendation of 1879 that the public lands be classified for use and that a 2,560-acre pasturage homestead be established for lands fit only for grazing was somewhat premature, but certainly by 1900, land classification and larger homestead units were essential.[29] Yet the evidence is strong that the enlarged units of 1904, 1909, and 1916 were not altogether wise or successful. The old evils of careless drafting of land legislation, weak and inefficient administrations (inadequately staffed), and the anxiety of interests to take advantage of loopholes in the laws, all brought the Homestead Acts into contempt and censure. But their noble purpose and the great part they played in enabling nearly a million and a half people to acquire farm land, much of which developed into farm homes, far outweigh the misuse to which they were put.

Notes

1. The western point of view concerning the public lands and homestead was perhaps best expressed over and over again in the 1850's by Horace Greeley in the *New York Tribune* when he was vigorously campaigning for the adoption of a homestead law and for drastic curbs on speculative purchasing of public lands. Theodore Roosevelt, no radical as almost everyone would agree, accepted, with his keen understanding of western problems, the traditional western view concerning land values in his *Winning of the West* (4 volumes, New York, 1889-1896), vol. 3, 252-53.

2. Reference should be made to the standard works on public land policy for the period to 1860: George M. Stephenson, *Political History of the Public Lands from 1840-1862* (Boston, 1917); Benjamin F. Hibbard, *History of the Public Land Policies* (New York, 1924); Roy M. Robbins, *Our Landed Heritage, The Public Domain, 1776-1936* (Princeton, 1924); Paul W. Gates, *The Farmers' Age* (New York, 1961).

3. The following statistics of acreage of land and numbers of entries are compiled from the *Annual Reports* of the Commissioner of the General Land Office. Compilations that sometimes differ from data continued in these reports are Thomas Donaldson, *The Public Domain. House Miscellaneous Documents*, 47 Cong., 2 Sess., No. 45, Part 4, 1884, and *Report of the Public Land Commission, Senate Documents*, 58 Cong., 3 Sess., No. 189, 1905.

4. Herbert S. Schell, *History of South Dakota* (Lincoln, 1961), p. 222.

5. Paul W. Gates, *Fifty Million Acres: Conflicts Over Kansas Land Policy, 1854-1890* (Ithaca, N.Y., 1954), p. 237 ff. Also the same author's "The Homestead Law in an Incongruous Land System," *American Historical Review* vol. 41 (July, 1936), 652 ff.

6. Between 1866 and 1876 the public lands of Alabama, Arkansas, Florida, Louisiana, and Mississippi were open only to homesteaders, but in the latter year they were restored to unlimited entry and the best of them were quickly bought up by lumbermen from the North. Paul W. Gates, "Federal Land Policy in the South, 1866-1888," *Journal of Southern History* 6 (Aug., 1940), 303 ff. Elsewhere, lands that had once been offered for unrestricted sale and later withdrawn to permit railroads to select their alternate sections as granted by the United States were restored to the offered and unrestricted status when the selections had been made.

7. Harold E. Briggs, "Early Bonanza Farming in the Red River Valley of the North," *Agricultural History* 6 (Jan., 1932), 20 ff.

8. Bureau of Corporations, Department of Commerce and Labor, *The Lumber Industry*, 3 Parts, 1913-1914 (Washington, 1913-1914), especially Part 1, Chap. 6, "Public-Land Policy a Primary Cause of the Concentration of Timber Ownership," pp. 218 ff.

9. T. Harry Williams, Richard N. Current, and Frank Freidel, *History of the United States* (2 Vols., New York, 1959), vol. 2, 142; Thomas D. Clark, *Frontier America* (New York, 1959), p. 727; Ray A. Billington, *Westward Expansion, A History of the American Frontier* (New York, 1949), pp. 696 ff.; Dumas Malone and Basil Rauch, *Empire for Liberty, The Genesis and Growth of the United States of America* (2 Vols., New York, 1960), vol. 2, 43. Actually 58 per cent of those who homesteaded through 1890 succeeded in gaining title to their land either through final entry or through commutation. James C. Olson, *History of Nebraska* (Lincoln, 1955), p. 166, contemplating the slow alienation of public lands in Nebraska by the homestead route before 1900, asks why did the Homestead Act "fall so short of expectations." Much of western Nebraska was still in public ownership and largely unused save for grazing in 1900 but this was nature's fault, not the fault of the act. In 1900 there were 121,525 farms in Nebraska. It may not be unfair to say that 68,862 of these had been partly or wholly acquired through homesteading for that is the number of homesteads that had gone to patent at that time. In addition, 5,004 homesteaders were to reach the final entry stage in the next five years and should be included in the number of homesteads which were probably a part of the farms of the time.

10. Harold H. Dunham discusses the inadequacies and weaknesses of the person-

nel of the General Land Office in *Government Handout: A Study in the Administration of the Public Lands, 1875–1891* (New York, 1941), pp. 124 ff.

11. *American Historical Review* vol. 41 (July, 1936), 652.

12. Edgar Harlan, director of the Iowa Historical, Memorial, and Art Department assured the writer in 1936 that most of the land of his state was homesteaded and was greatly surprised when he was shown that only 4 per cent went to patent. Congressman Harvey B. Ferguson stated in 1914: "It was great statesmanship that created the homestead laws under which such a State as Iowa developed." *Grazing Homesteads and the Regulation of Grazing on the Public Lands,* Hearings before the Committee on the Public Lands, House of Representatives, 63 Cong., 2 Sess., 1914, Part 1, p. 358. See also Leifur Magnuson, *Disposition of the Public Lands of the United States With Particular Reference to Wage-Earning Labor* (Washington, 1919), p. 29; Theodore L. Nydahl, *Social and Economic Aspects of Pioneers in Goodhue County, Minnesota,* Norwegian-American Historical Association, *Studies and Records,* (Northfield, Minn., 1930), 53.

13. John Ise, ed., *Sod-House Days, Letters from a Kansas Homesteader, 1877–1878* (New York, 1937), p. 212; Francis J. Rowbotham, *A Trip to Prairie-Land* (London, 1885), p. 240.

14. On the basis of careful research in newspapers and in correspondence of the land offices in Kansas, George W. Anderson emphasizes the institutional character of the location of claims by land lookers and the purchase and sale of relinquishments in "The Administration of Federal Land Laws in Western Kansas: A Factor in Adjustment to a New Environment," *Kansas Historical Quarterly* 20 (Nov., 1952), 233 ff. Newspaper proprietors, he found, were deeply involved in this business.

15. Anderson, *ibid.* p. 240; Herbert S. Schell, *History of South Dakota,* p. 173; *North Dakota Historical Collections.* II (1908), 169, 202, 237; and III (1910), 167; *North Dakota History,* XVIII (October, 1951), 242.

16. For the prevalence of the $200 fee, see General Land Office, *Report, 1886,* p. 83. Charles Lowell Green has summarized some of the evidence of frauds in the administration of the public land laws in South Dakota in "The Administration of the Public Domain in South Dakota," *South Dakota Historical Collections,* vol. 20 (1940), 199 ff.

17. *Report of the Public Lands Commission, Senate Documents,* 58 Cong., 3 Sess., 1904, p. 121. This sum was paid for the services of eight dummy entrymen and women in southern Pierce County, by the Prowly & Church Cattle Co.

18. The Aetna Life Insurance Company, which had an average of $8,677,000 invested in western farm mortgages from Ohio to Texas between 1867 and 1890, was forced to take over 812 properties having a book value of $1,877,000. The number of foreclosures was doubtless greater in Kansas, Nebraska, and Dakota than in the region farther east. The figures were kindly provided by Robert H. Pierce, formerly of the Aetna Company. Allan G. Bogue in his *Money at Interest: The Farm Mortgage on the Middle Border* (Ithaca, N.Y., 1955), p. 193, shows that J. B. Watkins of Lawrence, Kansas, and his mortgage company took over 2,500 farms between 1873 and 1893, or between 10 and 20 per cent of the total number of farms on which they made loans.

19. Beatrice *Gage County Democrat,* June 25, 1886; *Report of the Public Lands Commission, Senate Documents,* 58 Cong., 3 Sess., 1904, No. 189, p. 122.

20. Seth K. Humphrey, *Following the Prairie Frontier,* p. 95; General Land Office, *Report, 1885,* p. 54. Humphrey was a claim agent who tried to chase down some of the defaulting mortgagors. His disillusionment with absconding debtors led him to write:

"By far the greater number of landseekers took up government land with the intention of unloading it on somebody else. . . ." *op. cit.*, p. 132.

21. Quoted in Allan G. Bogue, *op. cit.*, p. 146.

22. Since much of Minnesota land had been offered and was therefore subject to purchase in unlimited amounts, there was less resort to the use of dummy entrymen in this state than in areas farther west. The Mesabi Range, partly, and much of the timber land, was open to cash purchase, and well over a million acres of potentially valuable land were acquired through outright purchase in large blocks by capitalists.

23. I have omitted Oklahoma from consideration because its lands came into settlement so much later.

24. Cf. Roy M. Robbins, *Our Landed Heritage, The Public Domain, 1776-1936,* p. 240; Fred A. Shannon, *The Farmers' Last Frontier* (New York, 1945), p. 54.

25. *Fourteenth Census of the United States,* 1920, vol. 6, *Agriculture,* 732-41.

26. Cf. Hibbard, *History of the Public Land Policies,* p. 409; Robbins, *Our National Heritage,* pp. 238, 285-86.

27. In 1870, Joseph Wilson, commissioner of the General Land Office, recommended that persons be allowed to enter only one tract of 160 acres under either the preemption or the homestead laws. His successor, Willis Drummond, urged the repeal of the preemption law in 1871-1873. In 1877, Commissioner J. A. Williamson, and in 1882, Commissioner N. C. McFarland, resumed the attack upon the preemption law with recommendations that it be repealed. Thereafter, until 1891 when the act was repealed, the successive commissioners laid down an increasing barrage against its continuation on the ground that it enabled persons having no intention of developing the land to acquire ownership.

28. *Congressional Globe,* 37 Cong., 2 Sess., April 17, 1862, p. 1711; May 29, 1862, pp. 2432, 2439.

29. The recommendation for the 2,560-acre homestead on "pasturage" lands is made in the Preliminary Report of the Public Lands Commission, *House Ex. Doc.,* 46 Cong., 2 Sess., 1880, Vol. 22, p. lxxvi.

4

California's Embattled Settlers*†

By the 1950s Gates had intensively examined aspects of land disposal and settlement in the midwestern prairie states, the lumbering regions of the upper midwest, the northern plains states, and to a lesser degree, in the public lands states of the lower South. Now he turned to the tangled history of land distribution in California, a state whose historians had been strangely remiss in applying to their state's history the kind of probing, multilevel, and multiarchival research for which Gates was noted. This selection, appearing after Gates was well launched in his California research, emphasizes the response of the California settlers to the peculiar mingling of Hispanic heritage and culture with the American land and legal systems, to bungling and corrupt American politicians, and to rapacious American business interests, but the article also constitutes the best short sketch ever written on evolving land problems in California. The brief acknowledgment of the significance of occupancy laws points to the much longer treatment of such statutes that Gates presented as his presidential address to the Mississippi Valley Historical Association.

Land seekers arriving in California after 1848 — and after the first years of the gold rush most immigrants wanted land — found a most confused complex of seemingly insoluble problems facing them wherever they tried to obtain title to land. From San Diego to Shasta, in the coastal valleys, in the Sacramento and San Joaquin valleys, and in the Bay region there were some eight

* Grateful acknowledgment is made to the Huntington Library for a summer grant that made possible the research for this paper.

†From *California Historical Society Quarterly* 41 (June 1962), 99–130. Used by permission of the publisher, the Historical Society of California. All rights reserved.

hundred private land claims that called for between thirteen million and fourteen million acres of land. A heritage from the Spanish-Mexican period, these claims either had been granted or were alleged to have been granted to government officers, members of their families and supporters, for cattle ranches. Mostly they ranged in size from one to eleven leagues of 4,426 acres to the league. Accumulation of claims or grants had permitted individuals and families to acquire holdings of far greater size. More than half of the eight hundred claims were based on grants made in the years just preceding American control, eighty-seven of them being dated 1846, the year of the transfer. Most of those made in the forties had been given to intimates of officials in anticipation of the rise in land values expected to follow American control. War, the gold rush, and the withdrawal of laborers made improvements impossible for some time after 1846. When the backwash of population from the mines set in and disillusioned Californians turned to the land, not one of the claims had been surveyed—some had not even been located. Few had clearly established boundaries or extensive improvements, and on many there was no indication of use, save for the presence of small herds of cattle or sheep. It was to take years before the claims were adjudicated, their ownership was clearly established, their boundaries were located.[1]

Settlers pouring into California found no fences, no surveyor's corners. Aware of two long held traditions fundamental to American land policies—the right of pre-emption and the right of occupants to their improvements—they felt safe in searching out vacant and undeveloped land, moving upon it, and devoting months, even years, to its improvements. Involved in the right of pre-emption was the right of squatters who settled upon vacant and unimproved land on which there were no other private rights to buy their tracts at the minimum price before the public auction was held. A corollary to the right of pre-emption was the occupancy right of a settler, who had improved land to which he had an imperfect title and who later lost his land when ejectment proceedings were brought against him by someone having a better title, to recover from the successful claimant the value of his improvements as assessed by a local jury, less deductions for damage to the land. Pre-emption is an ancient institution dating from colonial times and was early experimented with by the federal government in special acts. It was made general and prospective in 1841, and applied to unsurveyed land in certain areas in the early fifties. Similarly, occupancy rights were recognized by Virginia in the seventeenth century and despite a hostile Supreme Court decision in 1823 were firmly planted through the newer states by 1851. Rights that had been so generally recognized elsewhere would, American immigrants felt, surely be granted in California by state and federal legislation.[2]

Land for investment and land for improvement into farms was the lode-stone which drew immigrants westward, eager to emulate the life story of affluent men in their home communities whose wealth had come from the rise in the value of landed property which they had had the wisdom to acquire early. It was this scramble for land which sent values up and transformed almost worthless Mexican claims into valuable possessions, particularly in the Bay region and in Santa Clara, Napa, Solano, Sonoma, Sacramento, and San Joaquin counties.[3] Here there were few signs of ownership in the way of im-provements or fences; but, unfortunately, here also were concentrated many large claims. Some original owners were forced to dispose of their claims be-cause of taxes, attorneys' and court fees, and their own extravagance. Other owners clung to their possessions, unwilling to break up the great ranchos, though the titles were becoming involved because of deaths, heirships, and wardships. In the Bay region the Mexican claimants seemed to be most persis-tent in refusing to sell, among them being the Peralta, Estudillo, Soto, Castro, Vallejo, De la Guerra, and Alviso families. They were only willing to lease, it was said.[4] But leasing would not give the tenants a share in the rising land values that everyone expected. Tenancy was rarely a satisfactory position for an American brought up on the assumption that land in the United States was cheap and that everyone should have a piece of it and a share in the prosperity the future was sure to bring.

Settlers swarmed over the slightly used claims of northern California and not finding boundaries, corners, surveyors' posts, or other evidence of owner-ship, assumed that the land would ultimately be surveyed and opened to pre-emption. In the resulting conflict between the landlords attempting to maintain their titles and the settlers hopeful of gaining ownership, bitterness developed that frequently degenerated into outright warfare on a small scale.

By the time the settler issue became one of the most bitterly controverted questions in California politics, the land seekers consisted of two groups: those who had been quite ignorant at the time they made their settlements of any adverse claims; those who, knowing of the possible existence of adverse claims, nevertheless made their settlements willfully, assuming that the claims were either fraudulent or that the United States government would not con-firm grants of such large size without improvements and that the land would therefore become public domain and subject to the public land laws.[5]

Aggravating the problem of land rights was the fact that Congress moved slowly in establishing a board of land commissioners to investigate the claims, to reject those which did not conform to Mexican land law or were fraudu-lent, and to confirm those properly made and on which the conditions had been satisfied. The board in turn was tardy because of the frequent illness of its members, the turnover of the commissioners resulting from the Democratic victory in 1852, and the resignation of some of its members. Also, the frequent long absences of the judges of the district courts seriously slowed the work of adjudication. Furthermore, the government provided a wholly inadequate staff and insufficient funds with which to accomplish the necessary research in the documents in California and in Mexico for the proper defense of cases.[6] Since all the commissioners and the chief agent in charge of the preparation of the defense for the government were at the outset ignorant of the Spanish language and were poorly versed in the problems of claim law with which the United States had been grappling for half a century, it seemed unlikely whether the government's case would be effectively presented.[7] This is the more evident when it is considered that the two men most familiar with Mexican land law—Henry B. Halleck and William Carey Jones—became heads of law firms deeply involved in defending the claims, and indeed had large interests in a number of the most valuable of them. Furthermore, in addition to Halleck and Jones, both extremely able advocates, there were some fifty other attorneys specializing more or less in claim law. Two critics wrote of this situation in 1856:

> The United States Government furnished a law Agent and Assistant, to resist on the part of the Government every claim, and these number 813, with an average of two lawyers to each case in opposition to the two Law Agents.

The agents could do little more, it was brought out, than cross-examine the witnesses of the claimants.[8]

As the land commission and the district and Supreme courts of the United States slowly waded through the piles of documents presented in evidence to prove the validity of the claims, it became apparent that there was a tendency to favor confirming claims even when there were grave questions concerning them. This was particularly true of the two higher courts. Jeremiah S. Black, attorney general of the United States, charged in 1858 that the rights of the government had been placed "in extreme jeopardy" by blatant fraud "so artfully got up" that the tribunals had been "induced to look upon them with a certain degree of allowance and even of favor."[9] Not only did the district court appear to disregard or minimize evidence of fraud and perjury on occasion, but the federal Supreme Court abandoned well-established precedents which required that the utmost vigilance be exercised in determining whether the grantees of incomplete claims had conformed to all the requirements of the law of the governments making the grants.[10]

Settlers learning that their improvements might be within the boundaries of claims became alarmed at the course the law was taking and began a drum-fire of condemnation of the grants. Taking an extreme legalistic position, it was possible for them to argue that the courts were acting too leniently, indeed unwisely, in leaning over backward to concede rights to claimants in dubious cases. They demanded strict interpretation of rights and rigid insistence on complete conformity to the requirements for a legal title to prevent rank injustice and the establishment of a concentration of land ownership not to be found elsewhere in the United States.

With the decisions going against the settlers on many of the claims, it was apparent that help was needed from Congress and from the California legislature, and more funds were essential to secure abler attorneys to combat the skillful defense of the claimants. There was also a question concerning the integrity of the law agents. At least one government attorney defended the government side unsuccessfully when he had a personal interest in securing an adverse decision, and another representative of the government was accused of being largely interested in a number of San Francisco claims.[11]

To accomplish their objectives the settlers, through the few newspapers friendly to them and through representatives in the state legislature and Senator Gwin in Washington, slowly amassed their strength and expressed their will. They wanted settlers whose improvements were found to be on confirmed private claims to be given title to their improvements and the owners of the claims to be granted compensation elsewhere, or in lieu of that they wanted protective measures that would recognize their occupancy rights. Also, they wanted Congress to extend to them the same free land policy it had already given settlers in Oregon, and they wanted restrictions written into the land laws that would reserve land suitable for agriculture for settlers only.

Senator William Gwin in California and Governor John Bigler in California became the chief spokesmen of the settlers in their efforts to gain recognition of what they regarded as their rights. Gwin was much influenced by the 1849 report of Captain Henry W. Halleck on the land claims in which stress had been laid on the doubtful character of many of the claims, particularly those not specifically located and having no clearly established boundaries, no development, and which had been granted in the very closing days of the Mexican regime.[12] Gwin suspected that many of the grants had been antedated or were otherwise based on fraudulent documents. His sympathies seemed to be for the time, whether solely for political reasons is not important, with the "hardy, industrious emigrants" who on their small tracts made intensive improvements which gave them superior equity to their land. His background experience in Kentucky, Mississippi, and Louisiana had acquainted him with the problem of settlers who, after years of toil in improving their tracts, were defeated in ejectment proceedings but, under the occupancy laws, were allowed the value of their improvements minus rents from the time when action was completed. He was familiar with the cases concerning private land claims that had reached the Supreme Court from other states and with the precedents the Court had established in dealing with the many knotty problems, particularly the nature of the title required for confirmation. He had participated in drafting the Land Act of 1851 which provided for the establishment of the land commission and the procedure it was to follow in adjudicating the claims. In drafting the measure he had tried to make sure that care would be taken in judging the "incomplete cattle range concessions," with their "ill-defined, vagrant or floating limits," as he called the claims, to eliminate all that was fraudulent and incomplete. Though not entirely successful in 1851 in securing the protection he deemed necessary for the settlers's interests, for there was keen opposition to his settler oriented views from Benton and others more sympathetic to the claimants of large tracts, he had succeeded in including a provision in the act that confirmation by the commission would "not affect the interests of third parties." In this way he had saved settlers' rights for further adjudication.[13]

The following year Gwin returned to the fray with a bill to confirm settlers's pre-emptions up to eighty acres on the claims where their equities justified it and to grant the claim owners equivalent land elsewhere.[14] Since 1806 Congress in a long series of measures had been giving equivalent land to Spanish, French, and English grantees or their assignees or heirs whose claims had earlier been taken up and mistakenly patented to others. Indeed, at the very time Gwin was speaking, Congress was considering a number of bills to grant scrip to claimants on whose lands in Louisiana and Missouri pre-emptions had been permitted and patents had been issued.[15] Possibly the Gwin bill did not include adequate safeguards against settlers establishing their claims on such land as the claimants themselves had improved, but the scrip legislation then being considered and enacted gave no consideration to the question of improvements or, for that matter, to the quality of the land. There was little that was different in the Gwin bill save that it would assure settlers on claims their small improvements and the claim owners compensation in land elsewhere before any patents had issued to either group. With considerable foresight Gwin warned members of Congress that unless his measure was adopted there would be fierce contests and probably open warfare between the settlers and the claimants.[16]

Although there was nothing particularly radical or new in the Gwin proposal, it ran into strong opposition in California where recent investors in the claims were well prepared to defend their interests. The Whig convention denounced the bill as an attempt to rob citizens of their property. The *Herald*

and the *Alta California* of San Francisco (where owners of lots either unimproved or but slightly developed were having a rough time with squatters
who tore down their fences, destroyed their no-trespassing signs, and erected
shacks upon them for homes) expressed contempt for the settlers and called
them mere highwaymen engaged in "high handed robbery" and a lot of shift-
less speculators who did little or nothing to improve the land on which they
squatted.[17] A blistering attack on Gwin's bill was published by a "Citizen,"
presumably William Carey Jones for the language resembles his hard hitting
rhetoric, his hatred of anyone and anything that retarded or made difficult the
process of confirming the Mexican claims. The author speaks of the "cruelty
and outrage" involved in the bill, of the execrations being rained upon it, and
of "the profoundest depths of infamy to which Gwin had stooped that "be-
grime your political character already sufficiently blackened." [18]

Gwin himself was no mean hand at libelous remarks, but he was no match
for "Citizen." The California reaction to the bill, the fact that his Democratic
colleague from California, John Weller, declared in opposition, and the negative report of the Senate Committee on Public Lands led Gwin to give up the
fight and the bill was tabled.[19]

Two other settler-oriented bills sponsored by Gwin became law on March 3,
1853. The first extended pre-emption to settlers who were then upon, or who
later took up, land on private claims which were subsequently declared invalid
by the Supreme Court. This measure was to give hope unduly and unfortunately to settlers on many California claims. The second measure granted for
one year the privilege of pre-emption to settlers on unsurveyed land in California.[20] Subsequently, in the midst of excitement over the invalidation of the
Occupancy Law in 1857, Gwin was attacked for including a provision in this
act of March 3, 1853, barring pre-emption to settlers on land claimed under
a foreign grant. Possibly the inclusion of this provision was a tactical error,
but there was doubt that a grant of pre-emption on the claims would stand a
court test.[21]

The difficulty of surveying land in the vicinity of Mexican claims was
so great owing to the unsettled boundaries and the slowness with which
the claims were adjudicated and their surveys finally approved (many claims
were not finally surveyed and patented until the 1870's and 1880's) that only
through pre-emption could settlers be protected in their improvements.[22] The
special pre-emption act of 1853 and its extension in 1854 were approved without vocal opposition. After 1853 Gwin contented himself with participation
in the movement for the adoption of a homestead bill which was, however,
unsatisfactory to land reformers, for it did not provide for *free* land. Politics
and Gwin's obligations to the "chivalry" wing of the Democratic party forced

him to oppose homestead by 1859, as did Senators Bright, Fitch, and other administration Democrats from the North.[23]

Meantime, a strong Whig effort was being made to halt the costly and long drawn out litigation over the claims and to make possible the determination of what was and was not public domain subject to pre-emption. William Carey Jones, son-in-law of the redoubtable Thomas Hart Benton and married to a sister of Jessie Benton Frémont, had been appointed by President Polk in 1849 as agent to procure information on California land titles. In that capacity he had argued that the claims or grants of the Spanish-Mexican period were mostly "perfect titles," and those which were not perfect had "the same equity" as those which were perfect. Jones had favored the Frémont method of speedy confirmation of all claims but had been overruled by those more familiar with the history of land claim legislation. The Act of 1851 he thought unduly harsh in its requirements that owners should have to prosecute their claims through the commission, the district court, and possibly the Supreme Court.[24] In 1854 and 1855 Jones was in Washington representing two of the most important claims before the Supreme Court which, with two others, he won.[25] In March, 1855, he revived his efforts to hasten the process of adjudication of the claims. He lobbied for a bill, of which he may have been author, that would have authorized patenting all claims when they were confirmed by any of the four courts, the board of land commissioners, the district courts of northern and southern California, and the Supreme Court of the United States. Like Frémont, Jones had interests in a number of claims, chief of which was the giant twelve league San Luis Rey and Pala grant in San Diego County. Furthermore, as attorney for a large number of claim owners, he was deeply involved in pressing their rights in the courts. When the Supreme Court was leaning strongly in the direction of reinterpreting, and in fact abandoning previous precedents in the litigation of private land claims, Jones published in Washington a *Letter to the Attorney General* in which he attempted to instruct him in the meaning of the Frémont and Ritchie cases and urged that all land claims favorably decided by the land commission should be dropped as decided and that the district court be instructed to reverse cases determined unfavorably, thus ending all further litigation and bringing to a happy end the "groundless litigation and its attendant evils."[26]

The House bill to hasten the process of litigation and patenting the land claims was essentially a revival of the Frémont bill of 1851. It would have excluded Jones's Pala grant of twelve leagues, for it was not to apply to grants in excess of eleven leagues; but Jones at the moment could feel confident that his grant was on the road to final confirmation since it had already passed its first hurdle. Whig advocates of the measure were troubled, fearing that the bill would assure confirmation of the Limantour claim, so notoriously fraudulent that even the most property conscious Californians regarded it as certain to be rejected on appeal from the unwise decision of the commission. There were other claims almost equally certain to be rejected on appeal, as James W. Denver, Democratic representative, well stated.[27] Despite efforts to make the measure more palatable by amendments to exclude the Limantour, Luco, and Iturbide claims, Denver succeeded in puncturing the Whig arguments in behalf of the bill and in defeating it.[28]

While Gwin was abandoning the battle in Washington for settlers's rights on the claims, in California advocates of occupancy laws were beginning their drive to protect settlers in the value of their improvements. The election of 1851 had shown the strength of the settlers, who had supported John Bigler and the Democratic party from which they expected aid—support that had counted significantly in Bigler's victory.[29] A bill to grant occupancy rights was reported back from the Judiciary Committee by Archibald Peachy (member of the law firm of Halleck, Peachy, and Billings, which was to have a major share in the defense of the claims) with the recommendation that it not be passed on the ground that it was in conflict with common law, would be productive of litigation and infringement of the rights of property, and was unconstitutional.[30] Notwithstanding this report the legislature adopted a possessory act, sometimes called a "state pre-emption law," to protect settlers on public lands who made two hundred dollars worth of improvements and filed an affidavit in the recorder's office after which they could be absent from the land for a year without losing their rights.[31] In 1853 Governor Bigler declared his opposition to the inclusion of any mineral lands within private claims and recommended the prompt interposition of the state before the federal courts to prevent confirmation of a decision made by the land commission, presumably in the case of Frémont's claim to Mariposa. To speed up the adjudication of the claims he urged that the land commission be abolished and cases be taken directly into the federal courts. Free land to actual settlers he thought a major need, but he said nothing about an occupancy measure at this time.[32] Such a bill was introduced, however, and elicited considerable discussion in which its opponents found it good tactics to denounce the lawlessness and violence of intruders on the Mexican claims. Such opponents always used the term *squatter* as one of opprobrium, or as we would say as a dirty word, and so it has been ever since in most historical writing in California whereas elsewhere *squatter* has no such connotation. The *Alta California* conceded as much but tried to draw a distinction between settlers who seized privately owned land "to harass the owners into buying them out," and settlers on public land.[33]

Rumblings of settler unrest broke out into bloodshed when claimants resorted to ejectment action to rid large holdings of "squatters." In 1853 a claimant was shot in Sonoma County; a sheriff with a posse and a large cannon was attacked by a group of settlers in Santa Barbara County; one man was killed and the sheriff was knifed; settlers in San Mateo County were angry with the commission for its confirmation of the Pulgas claim and threatened to resist any action to eject them; bitter clashes occurred on the Sutter claim next to Sacramento; and near open warfare developed between thirty-five masked settlers and the sheriff and his posse in Napa County. Elsewhere in Alameda and Santa Clara counties friction between settlers and claimants was common.[34]

The settler movement was becoming a major political issue that no aspiring or incumbent office holder could afford to ignore, and in 1854 Governor Bigler found it desirable to declare in favor of an occupancy law similar to those most states had on their statute books. In line with this recommendation, an assemblyman from Santa Clara County introduced a bill that would concede occupancy rights to settlers claiming no more than 160 acres which, when they entered upon it, was wild and unimproved and appeared to have no title adverse to the government. If ejectment proceedings were brought against such settlers, they would be entitled, if defeated, to have a jury determine the value of their improvements which the successful litigants were to pay, and no man holding a Mexican title was to sit on the jury of evaluation. The *Alta California* of February 14, 1854, thought the bill a well devised scheme of robbery of one class for the benefit of another but agreed that a less one-sided occupancy law was desirable. Need for action was demonstrated by the *Alta* comment of February 11, 1854, on the famous Peralta claim of fifteen leagues in the Oakland-Alameda region. Three hundred people claimed portions of the grant by conveyance from the Peralta family; others held under Castro; and fifteen hundred settlers were said to be on the land, mostly without any title.[35]

Still another factor was complicating an already wildly confused title and settler-claimant controversy. The federal Act of March 3, 1853, extending the pre-emption privilege to settlers on land claimed by Mexican grantees—the title to which was later declared invalid—was given publicity by land officers in 1854.[36] On claims rejected by the Supreme Court, actual or prospective settlers could, if the law meant anything, have their 160-acre improvements patented to them at the price of a dollar and a quarter an acre. Unfortunately, many types of land claims other than pre-emptions had to be considered on the grants that were held invalid—among them state education and swampland selections which might have been sold to speculators—and some of them were entitled to precedence over the claims of settlers. The register's statement was not inaccurate, but American land law was becoming amazingly complex, particularly in California, and the promise of 1853 was to turn to ashes for many settlers.

In 1855 the legislature did make one move toward aiding settlers. Adverse possession laws had long been useful to settlers on land claimed by absentee owners who made no improvements, neglected their taxes, and after years of near abandonment tried through court action to recover possession when their holdings were acquiring value. Settlers who could show continued, actual, and exclusive possession and who had met the taxes on the land for seven to twenty years could at the end of the required time claim absolute title.

In 1850 California had prescribed conditions for bringing action under adverse possession. Settlers having made "substantial enclosures" and "usually cultivated or improved" the land though they had no color of title might be regarded as having good title after five years. An Act of April 11, 1855, seemed to make the statute applicable to Mexican grants.[37]

Delay in determining titles discouraged both owners and settlers from making improvements and seriously retarded the development of the state. The *California Farmer* declared that the entire country was suffering, "families are suffering; emigration is stayed [and what could be worse to a Californian] from our shores, and all stimulus is lost." Failure of the legislature to enact an occupancy law in 1854 and 1855 consequently led that journal to offer its own proposal to deal with title controversies and settlers' rights.[38] The *Farmer* considered itself neutral, as between claimants and settlers, and thought its formula reflected that neutrality, but at the same time it encouraged the making of improvements. The plan called for the election of a board of reference to be composed of the best men of the state who could appraise the improvements made by the occupant in the event the title was confirmed to the claimant, and that the appraisal be paid by the claimant to the occupant. The integrity of the members of the board, the certainty of their fairness, and the knowledge that justice would be done, the *Farmer* thought, would encourage occupants to proceed with their improvements and would enhance the value of the claims. If the claimant's title was rejected, the settler could then enter the land—as settlers elsewhere were doing—and of course have the value of their improvements. Actually, the proposal differed little from the conventional occupancy laws in operation for two hundred years in the United States except that the appraisal of improvements was to be made by the board of reference which might not be a local body and might not therefore be as favorable to the occupants as would a local jury.

Governor Bigler continued to urge the need for legislation on occupancy rights, stressing that other public-land states had long since adopted such measures. In 1856 he held that in California where there was "so much uncertainty as to *lines* and *titles,* errors in location must necessarily often occur, and there certainly should, therefore, be provision made for the security of the *bona fide* settler in such cases." A fully prepared and well-guarded act would produce a feeling of security, "settle existing disputes, and prevent future difficulties and controversies" respecting titles. Persons subject to swift ejectment would not make permanent improvements, and those who had made substantial improvements thinking they were on public land surely deserved to recover the value thereof in ejectment. Bigler took issue with the view advanced by the claimants, their lawyers, and the newspapers reflecting their position that settlers were a disorderly, lawless, rowdy, and drunken people. He believed them to be "the most stable, enterprising and permanent of the population of a new State, and come hither with their families to surround themselves . . . with the manifold blessings and endearments of home." Here he was distinguishing between the squatter element in San Francisco and Sacramento who persisted in removing fences and warning signs on urban lots and putting up their crude shacks as evidence of squatter claims, and settlers who hoped to gain pre-emption rights.[39]

Excitement over settlers's rights reached a high point in 1855 and 1856. A settler convention met in Sacramento for two days in August, 1855, at which threats were made to establish a settler party unless the Democrats and Whigs paid more attention to their needs. The convention resolved that all laws ought to favor the actual possessor who occupied land peaceably and without fraud, that claimants's and settlers's rights should be settled in the courts; and it demanded that settlers if ejected be allowed the value of their improvements. The resolutions were taken back by the members to their communities where signatures were to be secured, and were then to be forwarded to the legislature.[40]

The action of the courts in their generous confirmation of claims, particularly the approval of five debatable claims (Frémont, Cruz Cervantes, Ritchie, Limantour, and Bolton and Barron) aroused great indignation and strengthened the feeling that the entire process of adjudicating the claims was working badly. Influential businessmen in San Francisco, badgered by intrusions upon their speculatively held lots by squatters, whom they found it difficult to eject, looked down their noses at all settlers or squatters until they found themselves virtually in the same position by the decisions in the Bolton and Barron case involving ownership of 10,186 acres and in the Limantour case involving a four-league claim, all in San Francisco County. On announcement of the confirmation of the Bolton and Barron claim, shares in it skyrocketed to $5,000, and persons having improvements on the claim were frightened at the prospect of having to buy their land a second time at the current inflated values. For the moment merchants in San Francisco and settlers on claims in rural areas saw eye to eye. A meeting of owners of improvements on the Bolton and Barron tract voted to raise funds with which to carry the case to the Supreme Court and to join with the Settlers' League throughout the state in elections to secure officers favorable to their position. Auguste Jouan, an associate of Limantour in the fabrication of his giant claim, stated that he was offered $50,000 by San Francisco property holders to provide the evidence that might defeat the city claim to a pueblo grant.[41] When it was rumored that a former member of the commission was seeking the post of United States District Attorney, in which he would have full charge of the defense of the government's case in the land claims, the California assembly urged by a vote of forty-six to three that he not be appointed because he was biased against the government side by previous engagements.[42] The assembly went further in another resolution, pointing out that not only had many farmers settled upon land now claimed under Mexican grants but that entire towns and cities were being built upon lands thus claimed and that to dispute and disarrange rights generally conceded would entail endless confusion, heavy costs, and outright conflict.

Three of these debatable decisions were reversed by Ogden Hoffman, Federal District Judge for Northern California, to whom important questions concerning land claims were carried on appeal. Hoffman was held in high repute as a lawyer and judge, and settlers could take heart from these decisions, for they seemed to assure a more critical examination of the legal base of the claims than the commission was affording.[43] Settlers hopes were soon dashed, for in 1855 the Supreme Court reversed Hoffman in the Frémont and Cruz Cervantes cases and upheld him in the Reading case, thereby establishing broadly liberal precedents that virtually rewrote Mexican law and applied this revision retroactively to California grants.[44] The commission and the Supreme Court, as was implied in the dissenting opinion in the Frémont case and in later decisions of both the state and federal courts, in confirming these large grants, the conditions of which had not been fulfilled, were reversing long-held precedents concerning the need for complete title papers in conformity with the laws of Spain, France, or England.[45] To avoid further effects from this reversal and from the shocking weakness of the government defense, the legislature called for an amendment to the Act of 1851 that would prevent the location of all floating grants, such as Frémont's Mariposa claim, on occupied land and take from the United States surveyors discretion in locating the grants. The resolution also asked that additional and competent counsel be engaged by the government in the defense of its title where antedated, incomplete, spurious, and unimproved grants were up for consideration.[46]

The settlers's agitation gained its major objective with the adoption of a bill on March 26, 1856, for the protection of settlers and to quiet titles. This measure had all the earmarks of occupancy laws which other states had been enacting and strengthening ever since 1797, when Kentucky wrote its first measure; and in addition it had some unique features caused by the chaotic title situation in California. Persons having better titles (Mexican grant) to land on which a settler was established if successful in an action of ejectment were liable for the value of the improvements the settler had made and for the growing crops on the land unless they could maintain that the grant in question had been surveyed, the boundaries distinctly marked, and the field notes of the survey filed in the recorder's office.[47] Thus far the bill met the views of settlers. But the deletion of another section before adoption shows speculator influence in the legislature.

Congress had granted a number of million acres of potentially valuable land to the state as swamp, school, and school lieu lands for the management and sale of which legislation was necessary. There was widespread interest in these lands and their possibilities, and already individuals and groups were moving to acquire large quantities of them. The swamp and overflowed lands, in particular, should have received careful consideration before action was taken concerning them. The record of other states in dealing with similar donations of swamp lands was lamentably bad; and California, having the advantage of this earlier experience, might have profited from it. Such was not to be the case, however. Antimonopoly forces proposed in Section 12 of the settler bill to limit sales of state land to 160 acres to any person, but the provision was struck out. In later legislation loopholes were provided that were to make possible almost unlimited concentration of ownership through acquisition of state lands. One settler uttered a plaintive cry that, having failed to acquire rights on a private claim and having lost his improvements, he had then sought public land outside the claims and had taken up and fenced 160 acres and entered the tract with a military warrant only later to be told that it had been acquired by the state as part of the 500,000 acre grant for internal improvements and in turn sold to another who ordered him off the land.[48]

The occupancy measure, even when shorn of its antimonopoly feature, was still a bitter dose for many members of the legislature to swallow. Objections were made that it was unconstitutional, and the conservative tendencies of many members were revealed by their efforts to weaken it by amendment. Settler influence was too strong, however, and members rushed to be recorded for it on the final vote, which was fifty-one to seventeen in the assembly and sixteen to nine in the senate. Leaders of the opposition were Pablo de la Guerra, whose family had 374,000 acres in claims confirmed to it, and José María Covarrubias, whose Castaic and Catalina Island claims, amounting to 68,000 acres, were confirmed.[49]

The measure was immediately challenged in the state courts and reached the California supreme court in the January term of 1857. Chief Justice Murray, in his search for doctrine to justify striking down the act, reverted to an old, somewhat discredited, and generally abandoned decision of Justice Bushrod Washington of 1823, involving the occupancy laws of Kentucky. Only three out of seven judges had agreed the Kentucky laws were unconstitutional, one had dissented, and three had abstained from participation. Never again had the Supreme Court used this decision as a justification for invalidating the many occupancy laws adopted thereafter, and Kentucky had openly flouted the decision, calling it of no effect in Kentucky courts. Furthermore, in 1873, the United States Congress was to adopt a measure which gave occupants found not to be rightful owners the same privilege in federal courts that local statutes gave them in state and territorial courts. No case decided by the Supreme Court had been so completely overturned by state legislation and state courts, by failure of the federal courts to make use of the case, and finally by the unchallenged act of Congress extending the coverage of federal courts to occupants as *Green v. Biddle*.[50]

The Chief Justice came to the nub of the case by showing that the principal difference between the California statute and those of other states was that most occupancy laws required that a settler should have a color of title in the form of a grant, deed, or tax title to enable him to recover damages in ejectment whereas the California statute assured him damages if the successful claimant had failed to survey and mark out his boundaries clearly and file the survey.[51] The Chief Justice could not see that many California settlers, certainly not the "squatters" who rudely destroyed boundaries in San Francisco, had "entered innocently upon lands" and deserved the protection of the law. Murray was convinced that the California law authorized "one man to intrude upon the lands of another," and he appeared to think it offered "a premium to fraud and violence." He was troubled by the retrospective character of the law, though similar laws throughout American development would have had little significance if they had not been permitted to apply retrospectively. In striking down the measure, the Chief Justice referred sentimentally to the "early pioneers" whose health, welfare, and happiness he was deeply concerned about but made no effort to apply that concern to innocent settlers who had taken up unmarked, unimproved, unsurveyed land, and developed it with years of labor.[52]

Justice David Terry dissented in a well-reasoned opinion that showed familiarity with the history of occupancy legislation and the need in California for such a statute. He emphasized that the majority had found nothing in the Constitution of the United States or in the treaty with Mexico that was in conflict with the statute, offered numerous precedents for upholding it, and deplored the tendency of the court to base its decision on natural justice. The right to enter and establish a pre-emption claim upon unsurveyed federal lands, a right which had been given special protection by the California Possessory Act of 1852, induced many immigrants to settle upon lands which had "never been surveyed or occupied, nor in any manner segregated from the public domain. Nor was there any evidence within their reach to show that such lands were claimed by any private citizen." Terry questioned whether "it would be a greater violation of natural justice to deprive hundreds of citizens and their families of homes . . . without making any compensation for the improvements" than it was to permit them to retain their improvements and pay the claimant for the land.

Settlers had come to expect adverse decisions from the courts; and in 1857, after their defeat at the hands of Chief Justice Murray, they tried to influence judicial nominations to secure friendly candidates.[53] Almost everywhere the judges showed willingness to issue ejectments orders and sheriffs to carry out the orders even though large posses had to be organized at considerable expense, and bloodshed seemed certain. Judges had only to interpret law in relation to constitutional rights; and if they appeared to favor property rights against human rights in the claim disputes, they generally had no alternative because of judicial precedents and the fact that equity jurisdiction was not involved, or could not seemingly be invoked.

Judges could and did protect the interests of settlers, notably in the Luco claim for more than a quarter of a million acres in Solano County. The claim was submitted after the deadline for receiving claims had passed, but the prominence of its supporters induced Congress to make special provision for its late submission.[54] It was then rejected by the land commission and by Judge Hoffman in a stinging decision intimating that practically every official of the Mexican government in California who survived into the American period had perjured himself to support a spurious claim.[55] Settlers on the tract, still fearing that some way might be found to confirm the claim, met and petitioned Congress that if the claim were confirmed, it be located on unsurveyed land since land office officials had first declared the tract open to pre-emption and later reversed that statement only after many equities had been established on the land.[56] The Supreme Court could find no reason to doubt that the Luco claim was "false and forged" and cast doubt on the testimony of the late officers of the government of California in behalf of it.[57] A settler organ, less generous than the Court, called the native Californians, including two former governors, land swindlers and perjurers and suggested that they should be convicted of perjury and sentenced to San Quentin.[58] The relief of the settlers at the final determination of the Luco case in 1859 was doubtless great, but there still remained the question whether the rights of those who had taken up land within the area included in the Luco claim before the commissioner had ordered them withdrawn from entry would now be recognized.

The fact that Congress had been induced to enact special legislation in the Luco case, that the Supreme Court denied settlers the right to bring before it for reconsideration decisions that seemed to them patently wrong, and that the supreme court of California had struck down an occupancy law such as most western states had on their statute books appeared to lend support to the view that government, whether in the hands of Democrats, Americans, or Whigs, was indifferent, if not hostile, to the needs of settlers. The Whiggish Sacramento *Union* and the Democratic Sacramento *Bee* both charged that settlers had been misled into supporting the Democratic party which had promised much over and over again but delivered nothing but an unconstitutional law that was to have no standing in the courts. The *Union* maintained that the author of the bill had submitted it in advance to a member of the supreme court who had assured him that it was in violation of the Constitution and would be struck down in the first case that came before it.[59] The *Union* went on to declare that the entire claim question had been badly handled from the drafting of the Treaty of Guadalupe Hidalgo when the very serious error was committed of including a provision guaranteeing that "property of every kind, now belonging to Mexicans shall be inviolably respected." This virtually made certain that any law designed to protect settlers on the claims would be found in violation of the treaty, if not the Constitution. The second major blunder was in the framing of the federal Pre-emption Act of 1853 for California which excluded the unsurveyed, unlocated, and poorly bounded claims from its provisions. Better might the *Union* have argued, that pre-emption be permitted on unsurveyed and unbounded claims, and that if the claims were confirmed and found to include pre-emption improvements, the owners be given scrip in compensation to be located elsewhere. The *Union* went even further in stating that the best way to have dealt with the claims at the time of the transfer of territory would have been for the United States to have taken over the claims after allowing the grantees a section for homesteads and paying them for their other rights at the going price which was little more than a few cents an acre at the most. This would have avoided all the controversies between settlers and claimants, the *Union* held.

With more foresight from Gwin and less selfish personal interest on the part of Frémont, abetted by Jones and Benton, it might have been possible for Congress to have avoided the worst of the title conflicts in California by providing that only grants fulfilling all obligations of the Mexican land system should be confirmed, that all other claimants should have settlers's rights to land they had improved, and that all the balance of their claims should become public domain. If Congress had rigidly required a strict interpretation of the grants, many of them would have been rejected and at no loss to the owners, for they had made no improvements at all on the grants given in 1845 and 1846. As a further step toward adjusting the Mexican land system to the American economy, the government might have offered to buy the vacant and unimproved land in the claims with good titles at the going price of 1848 or 1850. Such an offer, if accepted, as doubtless it would have been by some of the always impecunious grantees, would have contracted to a small figure the area in confirmed and patented grants. Enlightened congressional leadership combined with abler defense of the government title to the claims in the early fifties and more respect for precedent by the Supreme Court was needed. The worst injustice resulting from the involved California land litigation was not that some claimants were put to great expense in defending their rights and that many lost their inflated and undeveloped claims, but that some persons who *had* made considerable improvements on their claims, but had not succeeded in completing all those required before the final title under Mexican law, and who therefore could not prove title, lost all their improvements without a pre-emption or homestead right. In this respect and in this only the California Land Act of 1851 accorded less generous treatment to Californians than was given residents of other territories at the time they were transferred to American control.

County settler meetings were followed by a state meeting in Sacramento at which it became evident the settlers were not all of one mind. Democratic, Republican, and American party lines crossed; and the Democratic group prevailed, to such an extent that delegations from rural counties, feeling that urban groups and urban settlers or squatters in San Francisco, Alameda, and Sacramento counties were in control and were concerned more with the Democratic party than with settler issues, withdrew. Speakers at the convention opposed land monopoly in swamp tracts as well as in Mexican claims, favored "jumping" or squatting upon the swamp lands whether sold to speculators or still in the hands of the state, and urged legislation to abolish mesne profits in case of ejectment and to give settlers a lien on land on which they had paid taxes but later lost through ejectment. With considerable foresight they denounced Stephen J. Field who was to become the strongest advocate of the Mexican claims on the Supreme Court of the United States.[60]

The attempted Luco and Limantour swindles, which involved 814,000 acres or enough to make 5,000 farms of 160 acres each, together with other doubtful claims as yet unsettled and the growing bitterness between the claim-

ants and the settlers over the question of surveys, pushed the settler movement to greater extremes.[61] Since the Mexican grants had not clearly specified
boundaries, it proved possible for owners, when their claims were confirmed
and the surveys were being run, to have the government surveyors so establish their lines as to exclude the barren, waste, and mountain land from the
allowed acreage and to include the valley land on which their improvements
and those of the settlers had long since been made. Thus settlers on the four-
league Tzabaco Rancho in Sonoma County took violent exception to the way
the surveyors were running jagged lines to include their claims instead of surveying the rancho in a compact form as their instructions were said to pre-
scribe. The surveyors were charged with straddling a mountain to include in
two valley tracts, not one, some of the choicest developed land in the Russian
River valley. Excited by fears of the loss of their homes, settlers mobbed the
surveyors, destroyed their field notes, and roughed up one of the agents of
the claimants. When a federal marshal later appeared in the region to arrest
the participants, it was reported they were all away hunting. There followed
mass meetings, appeals to the land office to order new surveys, and angry de-
nunciation of the "pestilential land thieves" who had no regard for settlers's
interests.[62] With five hundred settlers organized in four land leagues threaten-
ing to prevent the law officers from functioning as long as they appeared to
be on the side of the claimants, further action by the state appeared essential.

Settlers were also harassed by claimants with highly questionable titles who
by threats of ejectment attempted to induce them into buying and making
payments before the final decision on the claims had been made. Two flagrant
cases of this kind occurred in Yolo County. Both claims were ultimately rejected as based on forged documents and perjured testimony, but before they
were struck down a decade of turmoil had retarded improvements on 57,000
acres and done little to encourage respect for claims or for the law.[63]

Settlers were correct in maintaining that many of the claims were fraudulent or incomplete and should be rejected, but their inclination was to maintain that all large claims were of this category. It was difficult for them to
understand why a fully documented claim that had been through all the procedures for a good title and yet was undeveloped, save perhaps for a small
improvement in one corner of the tract, should be confirmed. Improvements
and use were conditions necessary for confirmation, settlers held. Whatever
the conditions for confirmation, they felt that claimants who ejected settlers
and later had their own claims voided deserved severe punishment. In line
with their views Governor J. Neely Johnson recommended in 1858 that steps
be taken to protect the rights of settlers which would avoid the objectionable
features of the Occupancy Act of 1856 but would at the same time assure them

some redress.[64] The resulting law provided that persons ousted from Mexican claims which were later rejected or, if confirmed, did not include the land from which persons had been ejected, could recover possession of the land they had previously lost with the rents and profits from the time they were ejected until they were restored to possession together with all costs and damages they may have sustained.[65] Such a measure might discourage holders of Mexican claims from resorting to the law to eject settlers until the courts had finally determined the validity of the claims and the surveys had been completed and approved.

The grinding of the judicial mills did little to quiet settler unrest, and in the legislative session of 1859 the issues of settlers were again to excite attention. Governor Weller, who had previously not been the most ardent supporter of the demands of settlers, expressed regret at the invalidating of the Occupancy Law of 1856 and urged the importance of protecting settlers' rights on land they had settled upon when it appeared to be public domain but later proved to be included within the boundaries of private claims. He observed that settlers, having learned the boundaries of claims, settled outside them but in their vicinity and that when the official surveys were run, the claimants managed to have settlers's improvements included within the exterior boundaries. To permit the owners of floating claims to extend their boundaries in this way was rank injustice, and the governor urged that the constitutional power of the state be used to remedy the situation.[66] To the lawyers in the legislature the Supreme Court decision must have seemed a difficult barrier to breach, too difficult without a change in the court. Another way was found to show the members's devotion to the settlers's cause in a joint resolution asking Congress to enact a measure that would reopen all land claims where it could be shown that confirmation had been obtained by fraud. The measure was directed at "evidence brokers," "wholesale land pirates and grant manufacturers" who forged claims or otherwise secured confirmation of questionable grants. Most attention in the discussion was given to the Bolton and Barron, Limantour, and Frémont claims. Fear was expressed that any general act providing for the reopening of the claims might further delay an already prolonged and costly litigation, but the Senate rushed the resolution to adoption by a vote of twenty-three to nine. In the Assembly it was amended on motion of a representative of Los Angeles County to exclude the southern counties from the resolution, and was then passed. It may well be questioned whether the members were doing anything more than attempting to show their good will toward the settlers, for the Senate, on the last day of the session, tabled the resolution when it came back from the Assembly.[67]

The same legislature tried to secure relief from the results of its own stupid blundering by rushing into law an ill-planned measure to make possible the speedy sale of the swamp and overflowed land to which the state might be entitled under the Swamp Land Act of 1850. Instead of withholding sales until the land had been segregated and title passed to the state as most other states did, the legislature devised a measure that permitted sale before the state had received title or even the federal government had any knowledge that the lands had been thus selected. When, therefore, federal officials had surveyed the lands in question, sectionized them, and advertised them for sale, the legislature suddenly realized the problems its precipitate action was certain to create for buyers unless emergency steps were taken to prevent the sale. On the very day that the lands were to be auctioned, the legislature adopted a resolution instructing the state land officers to provide lists of swamp lands they had selected and partly sold and urging the local federal officers to withhold them from sale. Such withholding, once the lands were advertised, was beyond the power of the local officers, but the notice of the legislature of the adverse interest of the state may have made potential buyers wary of making a questionable investment.[68]

Other settler-oriented action of the tenth legislature included a resolution urging Congress to restore pre-emption rights to settlers on unsurveyed land —a privilege which had lapsed on March 3, 1856—and resolutions requesting the donation to California of ten million acres for internal improvements, the cession of the desert of southern California and land grants for railroads.[69] State administration of public lands, unfortunately, as it was working out in the new states and particularly in California, offered no improvement over federal policy so far as rights of settlers were concerned.

Meanwhile, greater attention was being given to the defense of government titles in California. As early as December 1854, the district attorney for the northern district had described to a committee of the House of Representatives the crushing burden of work his office had to perform, and the committee in turn advocated increased funds for additional clerks.[70] In the closing days of the Pierce administration, Caleb Cushing, attorney general, instructed the newly appointed district attorney for northern California to stop in Mexico on his way to fill his position for the purpose of securing information and documents that would make possible more effective defense. When Jeremiah S. Black became attorney general in 1857, he gave to the defense of the claims his own remarkable intellectual and physical abilities in Washington before the Supreme Court and named Edwin M. Stanton to proceed to California to provide the same vigorous defense there in the district court. Generous funds were for the first time made available for research in Mexico and in California in records that government attorneys were able to examine but lightly in the past. Black also succeeded in rushing through Congress a measure for the prevention of frauds in California which provided punishment of one to three years in prison at hard labor and up to $10,000 in fines for persons convicted of forging or counterfeiting documents or giving false testimony in the trials of land claims.[71]

Government attorneys were now able to meet the very brilliant California attorneys on equal terms and present their defense with equal effectiveness. In fact, so successful were the new efforts that criticism began to pour into Washington against the activities of Black and Stanton, various charges were hurled at them, and efforts were made in California to secure the removal of the district attorney.[72] Improved presentation of the claims led to the rejection of the Cambustón claim of eleven leagues, the second of the Sutter claims of twenty-two leagues,[73] the Luco and Limantour claims, and the immensely valuable Bolton and Barron claim.[74] In 1859 claims containing close to two and one-half million acres were rejected by the Supreme Court, mostly on the ground of fraud.[75]

Rejection of claims containing such large acreages, some of which were most desirable, might be expected to appease the feelings of settlers, but such was not the case. Settlers on land thus released from the dead hand of the claimants did go ahead with their improvements provided they did not run foul of railroad selections, state selections, scrip and warrants entries by speculators. Elsewhere settler feeling was in no way abated.

Between 1860 and 1862 eleven additional claims containing 317,000 acres were rejected by the Supreme Court on most of which there had been sharp settler-claimant conflict. The reaction to the decisions of the Court on these claims and others on which boundary disputes were producing equally aggravating friction showed that a considerable number of Californians had come to regard large and undeveloped holdings of valley land as immoral, contrary to natural law, and therefore open to settlement by them.

The turmoil in California between settlers and land claimants again attracted attention in Washington and led to the adoption of a remedial act that met some of the settlers's criticisms. Since 1851 the General Land Office, one of the most politically oriented of Washington bureaus, had had final jurisdiction over the survey of claims. When claims were confirmed, the surveyor general for California was instructed to make the surveys. Over and over again settlers had charged that this officer was unduly influenced by the claim owners in so running the lines as to include the settlements which had been made around the periphery of the previously established rough boundaries. As a result settlers who thought they had carefully avoided the claim owners's property found themselves included within the new surveyed lines.

Their protests met with little favor whether forwarded to the surveyor general, the commissioner of the General Land Office, or the secretary of the interior. A judicial trial seemed the answer, and in 1860 Congress provided that settlers were to be notified by public advertisement of the completion of the surveys of nearby claims and were to have the privilege of appealing their case to the district court if they thought their lands and improvements were improperly included. The court was then to hold a public trial and could, if it be found necessary, order a new survey to be made to conform more specifically to the terms of the original grant.[76]

The decade of controversy over titles had wrought much havoc in California and left in its wake bitterness against the Land Act of 1851, which was incorrectly held responsible for the plight of landowners, and contempt for legal institutions which settlers felt leaned heavily on the side of the claimants. Many claim owners had exhausted their resources in litigation instead of using them to develop their properties, and their undeveloped land invited intrusion and settlement. Attorneys's fees, court costs, taxes, and interest on borrowed funds carrying interest rates as high as five and six per cent a month, forced foreclosures and the breakup of many claims, undoubtedly a useful step, but it was achieved in the wrong way. It was far better to come to terms with settlers where possible and use the income from rents or sales to push titles to conclusion as rapidly as possible.[77] Though some critics were coming to recognize the shortsightedness of the large owners in attempting to retain intact their immense holdings, many were to continue to fight to that end for a decade and more to come. The tragedy is that more vision was not displayed in foreseeing some of these difficulties and in devising a means by which all undeveloped and unused land in the claims was made at the outset public lands.

Major and measurable effects of the errors committed in the framing of the Land Act of 1851 that were shown in the Census of 1860 were the great concentration of ownership of agricultural land that has continued into the twentieth century, the high average size and consequent smaller number of farms, and the large number of farmers who owned no land.[78]

Notes

1. Paul W. Gates, "Adjudication of Spanish-Mexican Land Claims in California," *The Huntington Library Quarterly* 21 (May, 1958), 213 ff.

2. Occupancy laws are dealt with in my "Tenants of the Log Cabin," *Mississippi Valley Historical Review* 49 (June, 1961), 3 ff.

3. A map showing the claims as of 1863 is in the Commissioner of the General Land Office, *Annual Report, 1865.*

4. The *Alta California,* Dec. 18, 23, 1857, commenting on the unwillingness to sell of the great landowning families on the eastern side of the Bay region, said they were willing to rent for one-third to one-half of the crops. The writer deplored the selfishness of the landlords, maintaining that they were driving population away from the area by their refusal to sell their unused land in small tracts.

5. The Sacramento *Daily Union,* Aug. 8, 1857, not the most friendly settler organ, distinguished between the two groups of settlers, calling the first "bona fide settlers," and the second mere squatters.

6. San Francisco *Daily Evening Bulletin,* April 29, 1856.

7. Not only was the chief agent ignorant of Spanish, but Senator Gwin charged that he neglected his work, was absent for a visit to Washington, and that all his responsibilities were being carried out by the assistant agent. Senator Weller admitted that the agent, in violation of the law, knew neither Spanish nor French, but insisted that he was absent from his post in California while doing work for the government in Washington. Gwin was a complete spoilsman and wanted to have the agent dropped for his Whig connections, but there was much to his charges. *Cong. Globe,* 32 Cong., 2 Sess., Feb. 26, 1852, pp. 879–82.

8. San Francisco *Daily Evening Bulletin,* Jan. 23, 1856.

9. Letter of Black, *House Ex. Doc.,* 35 Cong., 1 Sess., 1858, no. 10, pp. 1–2.

10. Chief Justice Murray of the California Supreme Court disagreed with the majority of the U.S. Supreme Court on the Fremont case. He took comfort that the "wholesale abandoning of principles, so long and satisfactorily settled, was not unanimous," and welcomed the fact that the justices most familiar with claim law had dissented. *6 California Reports,* 269. Justice Catron, one of the two dissenting justices (a third later expressed his disagreement), said of the Frémont claim, "At law, this claim has no standing; it cannot be set up in an ordinary judicial tribunal. It addresses itself to us as founded on an equity incident to it by mere force of the contract, no part of which was ever performed. The claim is as destitute of merit as it can be, and has no equity in it. . . ." *17 Howard,* 572.

11. Volney E. Howard, law agent for a time, was accused of preparing the defense of a claim then resigning and accepting employment as counsel for the claimant. In defense he maintained that the practice of government attorneys accepting employment on the other side of cases they had previously handled for the government was not uncommon. He was attorney for a number of claims which proved to be based on fraud and perjury. San Francisco *Daily Evening Bulletin,* Apr. 26, Aug. 1, 1856. For the Panoche Grande claim and Pacificus Ord's entanglements in it, see Robert J. Parker, "William McGarrahan's 'Panoche Grande Claim,'" *Pacific Historical Review* 5 (Aug., 1936), 212 ff.

12. For the reports of Henry W. Halleck and William Carey Jones on the California land claims, see Gates, "Adjudication of the Spanish-Mexican Land Claims in California," 220–21.

13. *Cong. Globe,* 32 Cong., 1 Sess., 1851–1852, April 20, 1852, pp. 1129–30, 2033, 2037. There is much on Gwin in William Henry Ellison, "Memoirs of William M. Gwin," in *California Historical Society Quarterly* 19 (Mar., June, Sept., Dec. 1940), 1, 157, 256, 333.

14. A copy of the Gwin bill is in vol. 8 of "Will's California Titles," The Huntington Library.

15. Congress was particularly generous in 1858 and 1859 in giving land scrip (land office money) to owners of private claims in Missouri, Louisiana, and Florida who had not succeeded in pressing their claims to decisions before settlers had taken up most of their lands and secured patents. The amount of scrip thus given was at least 1,409,000 acres. This excludes the scrip given to Indians. Thomas Donaldson, *The Public Domain* (Washington, 1884), pp. 289–90, 1276.

16. *Cong. Globe,* 32 Cong., 1 Sess., 1851–1852, Aug. 2, 1852, p. 2037.

17. San Francisco *Herald,* cited in Josiah Royce, *California* (Boston, 1886), 485; *Alta California,* Feb. 11, Sept. 3, 1851.

18. "Letters to the Hon. Wm. M. Gwin by 'Citizen,' " (San Francisco, 1854), p. 18.

19. *Cong. Globe,* 32 Cong., 1 Sess., July 27, 1852, pp. 1949, 2036–38.

20. *Ibid.,* July 14, 1852, p. 1770; 10 *U.S. Stat.,* 244, 246. Pre-emption on unsurveyed land was sanctioned in California for two additional years by the act of Mar. 1, 1854. 10 *U.S. Stat.,* 268.

21. J. H. Ralston, a Republican candidate for a vacancy on the California Supreme Court, claimed in the midst of the campaign, that this provision was responsible for all the land difficulties in California, a claim that the Sacramento *Daily Union* supported. *Daily Union,* June 24, 1857.

22. A glance at the ownership maps in the Thompson and West atlasses of California counties will illustrate well this difficulty of survey. See especially their *Historical Atlas Map of Santa Clara County, California* (San Francisco, 1876), and *Official and Historical Atlas Map of Alameda County, California* (Oakland, 1878).

23. Sacramento *Daily Union,* Aug. 1, 1859.

24. Gates, "Adjudication of Spanish-Mexican Land Claims in California," 213 ff.

25. The claims were Frémont, Cruz Cervantes, Vaca and Peña and Argüello. John J. Crittendon, Benton, and others were associated with Jones in these cases. See the decisions in *U.S. Reports,* vols. 58 and 59.

26. A copy of this letter is in "*Will's California Titles,*" vol. 17, The Huntington Library.

27. The bill, if enacted, even with the modifying amendments added by the House Committee of the Judiciary would have confirmed perhaps a million acres of land, much of which was based on fraud. Report of Jeremiah S. Black of May 22, 1860, *House Ex. Doc.,* 36 Cong., 1 Sess., 1860, vol. 12, no. 84, pp. 30 ff.

28. Jones's letter of Aug. 5, 1856, written from Washington to Denver, reveals his own part in the matter. The letter appeared in a newspaper from which a cutting was taken and is now found in "*Will's California Titles,*" vol. 13. *See* the *Cong. Globe,* 34 Cong., 1 Sess., May 26, July 30, 1856, pp. 1302, 1842, and Appendix, same Cong., p. 1183.

29. Sacramento *Daily Union,* Oct. 1, 1859.

30. *California Assembly Journal,* third session, 1852, p. 408.

31. Act of April 29, 1852, *Statutes of California,* third session, 1852, p. 158.

32. *California Assembly Journal,* fourth session, 1853, pp. 23–26.

33. *Alta California,* July 26, 1853; Sacramento *Democratic State Journal,* May 11, 1853.

34. San Francisco *Daily Evening Journal,* April 19, May 6, July 26, 1853; Placer *Times and Transcript,* Oct. 27, Nov. 8, 23, 1853; *California Farmer,* 1 (June 15, 1854), 187, quoting the *Herald.*

35. *Alta California,* July 14, 1853, Feb. 11, 1854. A portion of the San Antonio Rancho, amounting to 9,416 acres was patented in 1858, a second portion of 15,206 acres was patented in 1874 and the final portion of 18,848 acres was patented in 1877. Disputes over surveys and the area to be included were responsible for the long delay.

36. *Marysville Daily Herald,* Mar. 4, 1854, quoting the *Shasta Courier.*

37. *Statutes of California,* sixth session, 1855, p. 109.

38. *California Farmer* 4 (July 27, Aug. 3, 17, 1855), 26, 34, 50.

39. *California Senate Journal,* seventh session, 1856, pp. 39–40.

40. *Daily Placer Times and Transcript,* Aug. 11, 21, 1855. This paper fully endorsed the platform of the settlers. One petition from Sacramento carrying 427 signatures is in the *California Senate Journal,* seventh session, 1858, p. 422. See also Sacramento *Daily Union,* Jan. 14, 1856.

41. Los Angeles *Star,* June 23, 1855; San Francisco *Daily Evening Journal,* Jan. 23, April 3, 1858; Philadelphia *Ledger* in Sacramento *Daily Union,* May 25, 1860.

42. R. Augustus Thompson, the former member of the commission, had, it was said, already declared himself favorable to the confirmation of the Bolton and Barron and the Limantour claims. Alpheus Felch of the commission had delivered a favorable opinion on the latter claim in which he said: "The weight of evidence, in our opinion, is decidedly with the claimant. . . ." The case had been badly defended by the government attorney. *Alta California,* Jan. 27, Feb. 4, 1856; San Francisco *Daily Evening Bulletin,* Mar. 11, 17, 18, 19, 1856. Of another U.S. district attorney it was charged that he held an interest in the San Gregorio claim in San Mateo County at the time he was required to defend it before the district court. The court confirmed the claim and further appeal was dismissed. *Daily Evening Bulletin,* April 22, 24, 25, May 5, 1856. *Cf,* note 11.

43. Hoffman reversed the land commission on the Cruz Cervantes, Frémont, and Limantour cases. On the other hand he confirmed a considerable number of claims that were later to be rejected by the Supreme Court, including the dubious Moquelemos claim of Andrés Pico for eleven leagues in Calaveras County and the Lup Yomi claim of Henry F. Teschmaker for sixteen leagues in Napa County. Actually, as events turned out, it was the commission that was to be the most critical of the claims and Hoffman who was to be lenient in confirming. Hoffman's decisions are found in his *Reports of Land Cases Determined in the United States District Court for the Northern District of California* (San Francisco, 1862).

44. I have borrowed my characterization of the Frémont and Cruz Cervantes decisions from my "Adjudication of Spanish-Mexican Land Claims in California," 227. For the Frémont, Reading, and Cruz Cervantes decisions, see 17 *Howard,* 542 and 18 *Howard,* 1 and 554.

45. For the dissenting opinions of Justices Catron, Campbell, and Daniel, see 17 *Howard,* 566 ff., and 18 *Howard,* 11 ff. and 550 ff.

46. Appendix to *Assembly Journal,* seventh session, 1856, unnumbered but presumably no. 18.

47. The bill as introduced is in Sacramento *Daily Union,* Mar. 11, 1856; for the statute, see Act of Mar. 26, 1856, *Statutes of California,* seventh session, 54.

48. *Alta California,* Mar. 3, 1854. At a meeting of settlers and miners at Folsom on the Río de los Americanos claim the participants pledged themselves to resist every effort to eject members from their improvements, protected the survey of the claim,

and urged the adoption of the occupancy measure then before the legislature. San Francisco *Daily Evening Bulletin*, Mar. 14, 1856.

49. Sacramento *Daily Union*, Mar. 20, 21, 1856.

50. Paul W. Gates, "Tenants of the Log Cabin," *Mississippi Valley Historical Review*, 49 (June, 1962), 3 ff.

51. Both Vermont and Tennessee allowed settlers in ejectment suits brought by others to have the value of their improvements, even though they had no color of title to their land other than a settlement or improvement claim. Other states, with their great flow of tax titles made it easy for squatters to gain a color of title for little more than a song and thus come under the occupancy laws. *Laws of Vermont to 1807* (2 vols., 1808), i, 204; *Laws of Tennessee*, 10th Assembly, 1813 (Nashville, 1813), 33-34.

52. Billings v. Hall, *California Reports*, vii, 1-26.

53. Sacramento *Daily Union*, June 5, 1857, quoting the San Jose *Tribune*; Sacramento *Bee*, July 2, 24, 1857. It was not easy for James McClatchey's *Bee* to support a Republican nomination for the Supreme Court but he felt that the Democratic convention had so foully betrayed the settlers by nominating for political offices men who were anti-settler while adopting prosettler resolutions as to merit only contempt. The Democrats must reform to win the confidence of settlers. Sacramento *Bee*, July 20, 1857.

54. Act of July 17, 1854, 10 *U.S. Stat.*, 784.

55. Hoffman, *op. cit.*, 345-73.

56. Stockton *Democrat*, Feb. 7, Mar. 7, 1858.

57. 23 *Howard*, 543.

58. Stockton *Democrat*, July 11, 1858.

59. Murray indiscretely revealed this fact which was promptly denied by the author of the bill. Sacramento *Daily Union*, July 13, 17, 1857.

60. *Ibid.*, July 16, 27, Aug. 4, 5, 1857.

61. The Iturbide claim of 400 leagues was only rejected by the Supreme Court in 1859; the Russian claim which had been purchased by John A. Sutter, amounting to 280 leagues was sold to William Muldrow and others in 1859, but they were not successful in making any headway in securing confirmation. *Ibid.*, May 15, 1860; 22 *Howard*, 290.

62. Stockton *Democrat*, April 25, May 9, 1858; *Alta California*, May 15, 1858.

63. The claims were William Knight's for 44,380 acres and George Swat's for 13,284 acres. For the charges of forgery and perjury, see I *Black*, 228, and Hoffman, *op. cit.*, 230. For the deplorable effects of these fraudulent claims on the growth of Yolo County, see the Sacramento *Bee*, Dec. 3, 1862.

64. *California Assembly Journal*, ninth session, 1858, p. 53.

65. *Statutes of California*, ninth session, Act of April 26, 1858, p. 345.

66. *Journal of the Senate*, 10th session, 1859, p. 37.

67. Sacramento *Daily Union*, Jan. 27, 29, 1859. For the actions in the senate and the assembly, see the *Senate Journal*, 10th session, 142, 180, 815, and *Assembly Journal*, 10th session, pp. 63, 509.

68. Sacramento *Daily Union*, Feb. 15, 1859; *Senate Journal*, 10th session, May 10, 1859, p. 242; *Assembly Journal*, 10th session, Feb. 14, 1859, p. 271. As early as August, 1858, the register of the U. S. land office had told state officials that the sale of the offered land could only be halted by the president. Sacramento *Daily Union*, Aug. 26, 1858. Furthermore, the California surveyor general in his report of 1858, Jan. 8, had

analyzed the problem with great care, showing the need for early action. *Annual Report of the Surveyor General,* 1858, pp. 8 ff.

69. *Statutes of California,* 10th session, 1859, resolutions of April 12 and 15, 1859, pp. 392–96.

70. "California Land Commission," *House Reports,* 33 Cong., 2 Sess., no. 1, 1854, *passim.*

71. *Cong. Globe,* 35 Cong., 1 Sess., May 18, 1858, p. 2212; Act of May 18, 1858, 11 *U.S. Stat.,* 290.

72. Stockton *Democrat,* June 6, 1858. For William Carey Jones' attack upon Jeremiah Black, see *Letters of William Carey Jones in Review of Attorney General Black's Report to the President of the United States on the Subject of Land Titles in California* (San Francisco, 1860), p. 32.

73. It is worthy of note that Justices Daniel and Clifford were convinced that the eleven-league grant of Sutter should not be confirmed for failure to present actual documents showing the grant. 21 *Howard,* 183. Sutter, it should be remembered, had eleven leagues of 48,708 acres, including the site of Sacramento, confirmed to him.

74. The Bolton and Barron claim was rejected by the Supreme Court in 1859, but the many Philadelphians who had invested in it did not easily give up. As late as 1878, maintaining that they had invested $1,300,000 in the purchase of the claim in 1853 and that they had never had a judicial trial, they secured a favorable report from the House Committee on private land claims but nothing came of it. *House Reports,* 45 Cong., 2 Sess., no. 243, Feb. 25, 1878.

75. Compiled from 22, 23 *Howard.*

76. Act of June 14, 1860, 12 *U.S. Stat.,* 33.

77. Horace Greeley, America's ablest contemporary journalist, who visited California in 1859, implored the land claimants and settlers to meet each other half way in efforts to settle their long drawn out litigation. *An Overland Journey from New York to San Francisco, in the Summer of 1859* (N. Y., 1860), 341–42.

78. This latter point is clear from an analysis of the manuscript census schedules of agriculture in the California counties.

5

Conclusion to *The Wisconsin Pine Lands of Cornell University . . .*[*]

This is the first of two brief excerpts designed to introduce the reader to Gates's approach to areas of research in which he has made important contributions that are less well known than are many of his other writings. The story of Ezra Cornell's acquisition of half a million acres of pine lands in Wisconsin on behalf of Cornell University by using much of New York's agricultural college scrip and the subsequent administration and sale of these holdings is a complex one. Gates shows the divergent interests of eastern and western states, the conflict between local interest and nonresident land holders, the implications of local tax policies, the motivations and sometimes nefarious activities of local middlemen who served eastern interests but looked out for themselves as well, the wasteful harvesting that in part reflected institutional imperatives, and the legacy of cutover lands and disadvantaged settlers left behind by the lumber industry. A model case study of regional land disposal and its impact upon subsequent economic development, this book is still one of the best introductions to the history of the lumbering industry in the Great Lakes states.

When the Agricultural-College Act was passed, its opponents predicted that it would not provide adequate endowments for the new colleges and that it would prove a harmful measure to the newly developing states and territories by making it easier and cheaper for speculators to acquire their land. For

[*] From Paul Wallace Gates, *The Wisconsin Pine Lands of Cornell University: A Study in Land Policy and Absentee Ownership* (Ithaca: Cornell University Press, 1943), 245–50. Used by permission of the publisher, Cornell University Press. All rights reserved.

most of the states these predictions were to be amply fulfilled. The application of the Agricultural-College Act to the State of Wisconsin offers an excellent opportunity of testing the wisdom of its framers. This study is largely confined to the timbered section of northern Wisconsin, but, so far as the effect of speculation on the prosperity of new areas, on their local governments, on taxes, and on politics is concerned, there is much similarity between developments in the pineries of northern Wisconsin and in the prairies of Illinois or Iowa.

None of the states received through the Agricultural-College Act sufficient funds to place their agricultural colleges on a sound financial basis at the outset, and with the exception of New York no state east of the Mississippi River ever obtained from land or scrip what might be regarded as an adequate endowment. With two or three exceptions even the public-land states which had previous experience in administering Federal land grants were unable to profit much from their agricultural-college grants, so strong was western opposition to government speculation in lands. For example, the State of Wisconsin received 240,000 acres for its agricultural college which it speedily sold for $300,000. Since the interest on this sum would scarcely pay the salaries of more than six or seven professors, it was hardly sufficient to support a full college program. In consequence, the development of Wisconsin's agricultural college moved slowly in its early days.

If Wisconsin benefited only slightly from the government's bounty, New York State's land-grant college, in contrast, obtained an endowment of $5,000,000 from the land it located in the pineries of the Badger State. Public opinion would never have permitted Wisconsin's officials to withhold its college land from sale for so long, but pressure could not be brought to bear on an absentee institution in the same way. Cornell University acquired an unfavorable reputation because it badgered the tax assessors, fought local levies, and opposed railroad subsidies and large expenditures for county buildings and roads, but discriminatory or confiscatory legislation directed at it was not adopted. Nevertheless residents of Wisconsin could well feel, as many did, that there was a great injustice in permitting Cornell to take such large profits out of the state to which it had contributed nothing.

Over 600,000 acres of land were entered in Wisconsin with agricultural-college scrip in addition to that acquired by Cornell. Much of this was secured by absentee owners like William S. Patrick, David Preston, and Francis Palms of Detroit; Sage, McGraw, and Dwight of Ithaca and Dryden, New York, and William A. Woodward of Vails Gate, New York. Like Cornell University, these men were speculating in timber lands. They paid their taxes reluctantly, if at all, opposed local improvements as did Cornell, and harassed the county and town officials by frequent suits and threats of litigation. When the absentee-owned lands were sold to local residents the pinery counties breathed a sigh of relief.

Resentment engendered by absentee ownership of great blocks of pine land induced the residents of Wisconsin counties and towns in which such holdings were located to vote themselves extravagant and ill-conceived local improvements, the cost of which were levied chiefly on absentee owners by the expedient of assessing their land at disproportionately higher rates. Few early settlers in pinery counties owned much taxable property, and they had little incentive to minimize the costs of local government. This orgy of spending lasted only until homesteaders began to prove up on their claims or to purchase land from settlement companies, but by that time large debts had been accumulated which made heavy taxes necessary for a long time to come.

As the tax burden on timber lands increased, absentee owners as well as many Wisconsin speculators were torn between their desire to withhold their land from sale until higher prices could be secured and the need to sell some of it to reduce the expense of carrying it. Only men and institutions with large capital resources were able to retain their land until the desired price level was reached. Many large owners were forced to sell; others who were interested in lumbering were induced by heavy taxes to cut their timber even though to do so at the time only contributed to an already overstocked market. In the seventies it was the lumbermen's constant lament that high taxes were forcing premature cutting of their timber and were thereby demoralizing the industry.

The rapidly rising tax burden had its share in encouraging abandonment of pine land once it was cut over. Since abandoned land paid no taxes, heavier burdens had to be levied on uncut lands to compensate for the loss of revenue. The vicious circle of increasing expenses, rising taxes, premature cutting, abandonment of land, and narrowing of the tax base continued to harass the holder of timber land in Wisconsin throughout the nineteenth century.

Reckless and prodigal cutting of timber was characteristic of lumbering operations in this period, but in Wisconsin the practice was to some extent made necessary by heavy taxation of timber land. Loggers gave little thought to the future, being concerned solely with immediate profits. The better grades of pine were ruthlessly logged, slash was left on the ground, and the inevitable fires destroyed the growing timber. A writer in the *Eau Claire Free Press* declared in 1880 that it seemed to be the order of the day "to send armies to the woods to slaughter pine by the hundred millions, to get them to market and to convert them to immediate dollars, without regard to any future use or benefit to the country. That's what's the trouble in Maine. They have stripped the state of its great pine forests in the north, and find now only a trouble-some crop of grangers and greenbackers in their place."[1]

When the pine was gone many lumbermen abandoned Wisconsin to con-tinue their destructive practices in the lush pineries of the South or the rich softwood regions of the Pacific Coast states. Isaac Stephenson, for example, transferred his interest to the South, Frederick Weyerhaeuser built giant mills in Minnesota and in Washington, and Henry C. Putnam roamed over Florida, California, and the Canadian provinces in his search for valuable lumber. Not all Wisconsin lumbermen followed their example. Others, like John S. Owen, William A. Rust, James L. Gates, and Henry W. Sage turned to the cutting of Norway pine, then hemlock, finally to the hardwoods and the small stuff used for pulpwood. Secondary industries sprang up to take the place of the great sawmills of the seventies and eighties, and the economy of the section was adjusted to the new conditions. These changes made possible the continued growth of such old mill towns as Eau Claire, Chippewa Falls, and Ashland. The second growth of pine and the inferior grades of trees lasted but a short time, however, and the lumbermen who had stayed to cut them were soon at-tracted to another field.

Around the turn of the century the lumber companies became settlement companies, their attention devoted to lavishing praise upon the north coun-try to induce settlers to buy their cut-over lands. Northern Wisconsin never enjoyed the rush of settlers which made Oklahoma a boom territory in the nineties, but the immigration promotion work of the railroads, the numerous land and colonization companies, Cornell University, and the State Agricul-tural College directed a substantial stream of immigration into the cut-over counties. As the pine disappeared before the ruthless attack of the lumber-men, it was replaced by the settler's tar-paper shack and his small piece of stump-free land cleared at the expense of the heaviest kind of toil.

In northern Wisconsin the struggle for existence was harsh, and there were numerous failures. This could be said of the frontier process elsewhere, but the rate of failure among these new immigrants was high because much of the land on which they were induced to settle was unsuited for farming. Emigra-tion promotion methods had been well tried out before northern Wisconsin was opened to settlement by the removal of the timber barrier. Experience had shown that immigrants could be directed to poor as well as to good land, and although the proportion of buyers who completed their payments on the former was low, efforts continued to be made to settle both classes of land. Settlers were located in remote and out-of-the-way places where roads and schools could be provided only at relatively high costs, and others were colo-nized on sandy and infertile soil unsuited to cultivation. The land companies and railroads were only interested in getting something out of their land and in "developing" the state by bringing in settlers. They gave little thought to the kind of land in which the newcomers were preparing to sink their little capital and years of toil.

A subsequent generation was to regret the destructive cutting practices of the lumbermen, who destroyed irreplaceable resources in a generation, and it was to regret too the zealous work of the land companies which produced many submarginal farms and led to the settlement of areas which have since had to be abandoned. Cornell University had its share of responsibility for both misfortunes. Its insistence on a high price for its timber, together with the high interest charges on its land contracts, forced lumbermen-purchasers to cut the timber quickly and to wrest from the land the utmost profit at the least expense. This of course prevented careful cutting practices. The university, too, long engaged in efforts to settle its cut-over land as the best means of securing additional returns from it. It may be doubted, however, whether the investment of Cornell in Wisconsin was any more harmful to the state than it would have been had it been made by other absentee interests with the New York scrip.

While benefiting to the amount of $5,000,000 from its investment in Wisconsin pine lands, Cornell, like other lumbermen speculators, left the pinery counties nothing to compensate them for the wealth which had been taken away. The project for the establishment of a town at Brunet Falls to be called Cornell was abandoned, although at a later time an ex-employee of the university was influential in having the community built around the new hydroelectric dam at that point named Cornell. Abstracts of titles to half a million acres of land on the Chippewa today all begin with the first transfer from the government to Ezra Cornell. A few local historians have recalled the visit of Ezra Cornell to the Wisconsin pinery; others have written with some bitterness of the part the university played in the pine-land business of northern Wisconsin. Otherwise, the Badger State has forgotten the connection it once had with the institution at Ithaca. Cornell alumni, students, and faculty, on the other hand, should cherish the memory of their founder's wisdom in undertaking the great land venture in Wisconsin; they should be familiar with the part Woodward and Putnam had in selecting the lands; they should never forget the superb management given to the lands by Henry W. Sage; nor should they be unaware of the cost of the investment to the State of Wisconsin.

Notes

1 Quoted in *Northwestern Lumberman,* November 27, 1880, p. 1.

6

Introduction to *Fifty Million Acres . . .*[*]

In his study of American land disposal policies, Gates inevitably dealt with American Indian policy, especially as it related to Indian removal, the creation of reservations, and the efforts of land seekers to appropriate Indian holdings for their own purposes. In Fifty Million Acres, *he developed his most elaborate statement about "the insatiable land-hunger" that drove settler-farmers, speculators, and other investors to push Indians from their legally designated reserves. The setting was eastern Kansas where intruded Indians from Pennsylvania and New York to Wisconsin, Iowa, and Missouri lived on federally created reserves, theirs "as long as the grass grew or water ran." Following the passage of the Kansas-Nebraska Act these immigrant Indians became the victims of the national struggle over slavery in the territories, the aggressive push of settlers and investors into Kansas territory in search of political and economic opportunities, and a vascillating Indian policy. As early as 1937 Gates published an article on Indian land disposal in Kansas. He returned to the Indian lands theme in the introduction to* The John Tipton Papers *in 1942, and he would turn once more to the general question of "Indian Allotments Preceding the Dawes Act" in 1971. The first two chapters in* Fifty Million Acres *stand as his most detailed condemnation of a malfunctioning federal Indian policy.*

"Never in all history, so it would appear, has the insatiable land-hunger of the white man been better illustrated than in the case of the beginnings of the sunflower state."[1] Whether or not Annie Heloise Abel was sufficiently familiar with "all history" to be able to generalize to this degree, few would dispute today that it was "insatiable land-hunger," rather than any idealistic notion of making Kansas a free or a slave state, that drew the bulk of the 100,000 people

[*]From Paul Wallace Gates, *Fifty Million Acres: Conflicts Over Kansas Land Policy, 1854-1890* (Ithaca: Cornell University Press, 1954), 1-10.

who rushed across the Missouri line in the period from 1854 to 1860. True, far larger numbers of people in the same six years were moving for the same reason to Iowa, Illinois, Wisconsin, Michigan, and Texas; but in none of these states was the impact of immigration so explosive in local and national affairs.

In Kansas two kinds of society seemed engaged in conflict, each attempting to establish its pattern of social institutions. That slavery could flourish on Kansas soil few could maintain, and nobody ever claimed that the plantation system, with its emphasis upon a major cash crop demanding a great volume of labor, could exist there.[2] But even though climate, soil, and geography forbade the introduction of slavery to Kansas, proslavery Democrats in Missouri and other southern groups tried desperately to make Kansas a slave state or to secure its assimilation to the southern point of view on slavery.[3] For political reasons which were operative in the 1850's and for many years to come, the struggle was pictured simply as between slavery and freedom—whatever each might connote. More recently attention has been focused upon other causes of conflict, for example the patronage that new territories and states provided to political parties,[4] the pleasures of distributing a rapidly multiplying number of offices paying generous salaries and profitable fees, the desire to control public offices such as territorial and educational institutions, a general hunger for lucrative mail, trucking, Indian, and army procurement contracts, and the granting of lands and loans to railroads. Also of prime importance in the Kansas political struggle was the search for land and for means that would make it valuable. All these issues existed elsewhere, just as in Kansas, and there is nothing unique about them there except perhaps the greater concentration of the people upon them.

The distinguishing features of the Kansas struggle are that the territory was opened to settlement at a time (1) when there was not within it an acre of land that was available for sale, (2) when along the eastern border a formidable array of Indian reserves remained, to which the owners clung tenaciously though unsuccessfully, and (3) when there was emerging the most complex and confusing array of policies affecting the distribution of the public lands and the transfer to white ownership of Indian land-rights that has ever emerged in the continental United States, save perhaps in Oklahoma. This complex and confused character of the land-disposal policies greatly increased the opportunities for administrators to seek plunder and special privilege. Hence land, slavery, plunder, and patronage combined explain the intensity of the political fight in Kansas as compared with that in Minnesota and Nebraska.

The central issues in the Kansas struggle may be summarized as: (1) the slavery question, which motivated federal patronage appointees and Missourians, whether they intended to become residents of Kansas or not; (2) the struggle within Kansas itself over patronage appointments; (3) the scramble for public and Indian land; and (4) the rivalry of railroad groups for land grants and for loans from local and national government bodies. Though the slavery question loomed large at the opening of the territory, it became increasingly blurred, and the sharp division between the proslavery and antislavery factions gradually dissolved. Filibustering, banditry, and personal vendettas continued to flourish under the guise of conflict over slavery, but underlying these activities were struggles over the promotion of towns, over the removal of the Indians and the opening of their reserves to purchase, over the staking of choice claims, and over the selection of railroad routes.

For three-quarters of a century, democratically inclined people had labored to create a system of land distribution that provided easy means to ownership for emigrants willing to undergo the hardships of pioneer life. Settlers had been granted the right to buy land at low prices, the right to enter upon and select the public land before speculative monopolists could anticipate them, and the right to have at least a year of residence and development before they had to pay for their tracts. And by the fifties it had been established that one-eighteenth of the public lands would be given to new states to aid in financing the development of elementary schools. Other extensive grants of land were being given to the states for building canals, river improvements, and railroads, all of which were anxiously sought by residents in isolated frontier communities. By the mid-nineteenth century the government was extending beyond one year the period of grace allowed settlers to raise funds for the purchase of their tracts, and there seemed a good prospect for the adoption of a free-grant measure to provide donations of 160 acres to anyone who would develop them.

Just when settlers' interests were prevailing in legislation and the management of the public lands, the Pierce and Buchanan administrations, under the pressure of southern conservatives and land-jobbing speculators, attempted to turn the clock back a full generation in two notable steps. One of these steps served to throw into discard the land reforms of a generation by blocking the road to further reductions in the price of land, not to mention free homesteads, halting land grants to railroads which the West so ardently wanted, and limiting to a year the period of grace during which one might occupy public lands without paying for them. Large acreages of land on which squatters had resided from one to three years were pushed into market, thus forcing the claimants to borrow at extortionate interest.

By the national administration's action in pushing the public lands into market before settlers had completely invested them, Kansas was saddled with large speculative holdings of absentee capitalists and a mountain of debt.

Nothing conspired to repel Kansas from the Democratic party more than the efforts of Democratic leaders to extract revenue from the lands. When they were first given the opportunity to cast their votes in a presidential election—in 1864—Kansas moved almost *en masse* into the Republican party, whose record on liberal land policies was far better than that of the Democratic party in the past decade.

The second of the Pierce-Buchanan policies was to revive the treaty-making method of disposing of Indian land. The traditional process of divesting the Indians of their right to occupy land was to draw a treaty providing for the sale or cession to the national government of the Indian right; when the treaty was ratified by the Senate, the land thus ceded became public domain and subject to the public-land laws. But in some older states, notably Indiana and Illinois, land was granted by treaty to chiefs and headmen in the form of individual reserves which might be sold directly to whites with the approval of the President.[5] Elsewhere in Mississippi and Alabama a number of million acres were allotted to individual Indians and in turn sold by them to speculators acting singly or in groups. None of these tracts were at any time a part of the public domain or subject to the public-land laws.

Allotment of Indian land by treaty was most frequent in Kansas during the Pierce-Buchanan administrations, though it was also of importance in Nebraska[6] and Minnesota. Eighteen Kansas reserves, ranging from the tiny 2,571-acre tract of the Christian Indians to the great Osage reserve of 8,841,927 acres, were forever barred from becoming a part of the public lands of the United States and subject to such laws as Homestead and Pre-emption.[7] Instead, these reserves became the booty of speculators, land companies, and railroads, with substantial benefits accruing to helpful politicians.

Through the treaty process the reserves were ceded in trust to be sold in large or small tracts for the benefit of the Indians, were allotted to individual Indians, or were held as diminished reserves until some future time when they might either be sold to whites or allotted to Indians. A fourth of the area of Kansas, and by all odds the best fourth, passed by the treaty process from Indian ownership to individuals, land-speculating companies, and railroads without becoming a part of the public domain or becoming subject to Congressional control.

Treaty allotment of those Indian lands which, because of location and soil, were most desirable produced a scramble for the tracts that was accompanied by confusion over titles and assessments and much litigation. None of the ceded trust lands were subject to pre-emption, though squatters were sometimes permitted to buy their tracts, after long delays, at the appraised price, not at the basic western land price of $1.25 an acre. On other occasions great tracts on which individual settlers had already established claims were sold on sealed bids to favored speculators, among them high officers of the government. Most unsatisfactory to Kansans were the acts of land speculating and railroad groups in drawing treaties which provided for the sale to them of entire reserves. Officials of the Indian Office and of the Department of the Interior were induced to approve, and the Senate to ratify, these treaties as a result of generous gratuities in the form of cash and lands. Mark Twain long ago described the boodling career of Senator Samuel C. Pomeroy, but less well known are the activities of Orville Browning, James Harlan, and even Edmund G. Ross in supporting questionable deals for Kansas reserves.

The treaty method of disposing of Indian land gave scant regard to settlers's rights and interests. It permitted speculators and railroads to buy the land before settlers had an opportunity to pre-empt or otherwise acquire them; the speculators and railroad groups thereby became middlemen in the distribution of lands and took the profit which immigration and the demand for land made possible. Disposal of land by treaty denied settlers the benefit of the Homestead Act of 1862, toward which democratically minded reformers had worked for years. It gave paramount influence in shaping Indian relations to the commissioner of Indian affairs and the administration majority in the Senate. The popularly elected House of Representatives, where land-reform sentiment was strongest, was denied any part in policy making. Disposal of land by treaty produced violent antirent wars against the railroads and, combined with resentment against their high rates, led to enactment of radical measures to curb and control the practices of railroad magnates.

Because the railroads were snapping up much of the Indian land, in addition to the great grants of land given to aid in their construction, they were becoming the principal proprietors of the West, gaining all the profit which construction of their lines would assure to owners of land in the way of added value. The more the railroads anticipated the settler in the acquisition of land from Indian tribes or the national government, the more they made a mockery of the Pre-emption and Homestead Laws. Land reformers became increasingly distressed at the proportion of land being acquired by railroads, as well as land companies and other speculating groups and individuals, and at the high cost to settlers of middlemen intruding between them and the government. The reformers sought to halt the use of the treaty-making power in distributing Indian lands; they sought to end the flow of grants to railroads and to stop the unrestricted sale of public lands to large capitalistic interests.

Pioneer settlers moving into the area of public lands were themselves not squeamish about violating the Pre-emption Law, making illegal deals with Indians, and taking advantage of the loopholes in the Homestead Law. They were doubtless as guilty as the large interests of breaking the law and abusing political power. But they were the people, the sovereign citizens, the builders of Kansas, and they demanded the right to share in the rising land values which improvements and settlement assured. The absentee owners, whether James F. Joy and his Boston associates, the members of the "Indian Ring" in Washington, the American Emigrant Company with its charter from Connecticut, or Chick and Northrup of Kansas City, were attempting to rob the Kansas citizen of the right to acquire cheaply a tract of land which he could transform into a valuable investment.

The Kansas conflict between settlers and railroads, first arising in the fifties over the purchase of Indian reserves, flamed anew in the later seventies and eighties over railroad sales and pricing policies, especially over the delay in pushing railroad lands into market and in permitting them to be taxed. These issues and the emotions they engendered kept Kansas in turmoil fairly constantly in the "Gilded Age," and they provide much of the background for the story of agrarian movements. In Topeka and in Washington, Kansans demanded legislative and administrative action that would permit the lands to be settled without too much burden to settlers. They wanted withdrawn and unearned but reserved lands[8] restored to the public domain; they wanted the earned lands made taxable and their price put at a level that would attract buyers and permit their development. They were unhappy over numerous court decisions in which the judges seemed to lean over backward to read into the law rights that Congress had not intended to give the railroads until they had been earned.

At the same time the homestead and land-reform elements were calling for a thorough reorganization of the land system in order to assure settlers and farm makers an easier path to ownership and to prevent cattle, mining, railroad, lumber, and other companies from benefiting by loosely framed and improperly administered laws. To these reform elements should be added the conservationists who wanted to create national forests and the eastern merchants who were shrilly demanding the revival of railroad competition and the establishment of rate regulation to assure low freight rates.

Despite the strength of the "Robber Barons," the fervor of the free enterprisers with their social Darwinism, and the threat of hostile court action, numerous changes, reforms, and radical innovations were actually carried through. Some unearned land grants were forfeited and great areas of withdrawn lands were restored to public entry. Railroad lands were made taxable; the cash-sale law, which permitted unlimited purchase of public lands in certain areas, was repealed. The National Forest Reservation Act was adopted.

The power of aliens to acquire large estates was curbed in the territories and in many of the states. An Interstate Commerce Commission was created and given authority over the country's network of railroads.

In no other state did disillusionment with railroads and clashes with them appear so early and continue so constantly as in Kansas. Representatives of Kansas fathered scores of bills to safeguard settler claims against railroad rights, to require the railroads to take title to their earned lands and to have them placed on the tax roll, to have unearned land grants forfeited, and restored to the public domain. They were in the van of the movement for reform, but not in any way that would restrict the small man's right to take advantage of the land system.

The struggle for land in Kansas brought local issues to the attention of the public elsewhere, produced leaders for the national land-reform movement, and brought about final abolition of the treaty method of land disposal.

Notes

1. Annie Heloise Abel, *The American Indian as a Slaveholder and Secessionist* (3 Vols., Cleveland, 1915–1925), vol. 3, 23–24.

2. Senator George E. Badger, of North Carolina, in arguing for the adoption of the Kansas-Nebraska bill said: "I think . . . it is in the highest degree probable that with regard to these Territories of Nebraska and Kansas, there will never be any slaves in them. I have no more idea of seeing a slave population in either of them than I have of seeing it in Massachusetts; not a whit." *Cong. Globe, Appendix,* 33 Cong., 1 Sess., p. 149.

Similar expressions were made by Edward Everett of Massachusetts, Stephen A. Douglas and James C. Allen of Illinois, Sam Houston of Texas, John Kerr and Andrew P. Butler of North Carolina. Avery Craven summarizes the issue: "The senseless talk of making Kansas a slave state arose, not from any sound hope of slavery expansion, but from a determination to preserve southern equality." "The Price of Union," *Journal of Southern History* 18 (Feb., 1952), 8.

3. The ablest defense of Senator David Atchison and his fellow "Border Ruffians" (to use an expression he constantly employed) is in James C. Malin, "The Proslavery Background of the Kansas Struggle," *Mississippi Valley Historical Review* 10 (Dec., 1923), 285–305.

4. One of the most voracious patronage seekers of the 1850's, George W. Jones, senator from Iowa, in a gossipy letter to Howell Cobb of Feb. 11, 1853, said that the Democrats in Congress were making efforts to create positions for defeated House members of the party. Two bills providing for the division of Oregon and the creation of Nebraska territory were approved by the House which, Jones said, when passed by the Senate, would make available "several fat offices of Governors, Secretaries, Marshalls, Attorneys, Judges, etc., etc., to bestow. I believe all who are going out of

Congress voted for these bills. I said *Nay* to both." Ulrich B. Phillips, ed., "The Correspondence of Robert Toombs, Alexander H. Stephens, and Howell Cobb," American Historical Association, *Annual Report,* vol. 2, 1911 (Washington, 1913), 324.

5. J. P. Kinney has summarized the allotment policy, if it can be called that, for the period before 1887 in *A Continent Lost—A Civilization Won: Indian Land Tenure in America* (Baltimore, 1937), pp. 81 ff. George D. Harmon, in his *Sixty Years of Indian Affairs* (Chapel Hill, 1941), also has useful information on allotments.

6. Addison E. Sheldon provides statistics documenting the sale of 599,018 acres of Indian land in Nebraska in *Land Systems and Land Policies in Nebraska,* Nebraska State Historical Society, *Publications,* vol. 12, (Lincoln, 1936), 204–9, 332–34.

7. Homestead, adopted in 1862, allowed free land to settlers; pre-emption, as of 1854, permitted squatters to buy their claims, prior to public auction, at $1.25 per acre.

8. Withdrawn lands were public lands which had been opened to settlement and later were withdrawn from entry to permit railroads to make their selections of alternate sections. Once the line of the railroad was determined and construction under way, the officers of the companies would select their lands, which were thereafter reserved until construction was completed and the cost of survey paid by the railroad when the patents would issue. Withdrawn and unearned reserved lands as well as earned but unpatented railroad lands all appear prominently in western agrarianism.

7

From Individualism to Collectivism in American Land Policy*

This article presents a broad interpretive view of the evolution of American land policy. Written in the early 1950s, it was delivered at Connecticut College as one in a series of Henry Wells Lawrence Lectures on liberalism as a force in history. Gates took this occasion to demonstrate how the tenets of early nineteenth-century liberalism, the Jeffersonian view, came to dominate American land policy in the 1830s and 1840s, policy geared to creating a nation of small landholders from the public domain. Then followed a confused and conflicting period when mixed policies explicitly assisted both corporate wealth and the small farmer. As principles of individualism, minimal government, and personal freedom became cornerstones in the thinking of America's powerful conservative financial and business interests, a collective, governmentally responsible view became the new liberal position. Given the waste of natural resources under the policies of the nineteenth century, with its emphasis on transferring the public domain to private ownership, the new progressive-liberalism in land policy fostered publically owned and regulated reserves for forest lands, water-power resources, reclamation, mineral and coal lands, and grazing areas. Gates traces these developments in the broad context of America's expansive economy. In the process he adds valuable insights into class conflicts over land ownership and use, and perspectives on the rising concern over wasteful exploitation of natural resources at the turn of the century.

*From Chester McA. Destler, ed., *Liberalism as a Force in History: Lectures on Aspects of the Liberal Tradition*, Henry Wells Lawrence Memorial Lectures, no. 3 (New London: Connecticut College, 1953), 14–35. Used by permission of the publisher, Connecticut College. All rights reserved.

In the course of the nineteenth century, liberalism in America went through profound changes, its early attitudes and meanings being taken over by elements thoroughly conservative in character and its early supporters moving to policies that were quite the reverse of their previous position. In the early years of the century liberalism connoted equality of man, freedom of conscience, of speech, personal liberty, individualism. It also meant *laissez faire* policies on the part of the state, the removal of existing restrictions, class privileges, controls, prohibitions, and monopolies.

Following the Civil War these concepts, which we associate with the Jeffersonian tradition, were assimilated by the rapidly emerging business interests and made to serve their purposes as protection against the new liberalism which was demanding the policing of the corporations, trust busting, even government ownership. By the twentieth century Jefferson and the earlier concepts of liberalism had been taken into camp by the defenders of business ethics who regarded themselves as carrying on the true liberal tradition.[1] On the other hand a combination of western agrarians, labor leaders, middle-class humanitarians and other critics of social institutions, having thrown off their fear of the state, of big government, and of the arbitrary bureaucrat were pushing for ever increasing intervention by government in the affairs of the people. Whatever their labels, the defenders of business were primarily concerned with freedom of opportunity unhampered by government restrictions and aided wherever possible by government subsidies while the reformers, progressives, or new liberals breathed the humanitarian spirit of Jefferson but advocated realistic and forward-looking government action to achieve a better life for the people. The democratic individualism of the nineteenth century was being replaced by the democratic collectivism of the twentieth century.

The history of American land policy reflects this transformation in ideology. What was regarded as liberalism in land policy at the beginning of the nineteenth century was unacceptable to the liberals of 1900, and the restrictions, public ownership, and controlled use and development which the latter advocated would not have found favor with the earlier generation of liberals. It is the object of this paper to trace the changes in the concept of liberalism in land policy and to show that they were the result, not of radical or socialistic theories imported as it were into the field of land policies, although these theories helped to bring about changes, but that fundamentally the new policies were the result of the hard practical experience of the American people.

The objectives of colonial land policies were twofold: those pursued by the mother country and those pursued by influential individuals. Imperial policies as they were finally perfected were intended to permit a slow controlled advance westward and to treat the land as a permanent source of revenue under the quit rent system for the support of the colonial governments. These policies were wiped out by the Revolution. Meantime, prominent and influential individuals in the colonial period had attempted to establish for themselves great baronies over which they might rule, but the abundance of land, the individualism and spirit of independence of the common people, and the comparative ease of squatting upon land without title made their path difficult. Confiscation, abolition of primogeniture and entail and of other relics of medieval tenure, the emergence of a more democratic electorate, the low price and free grant policies of the states after the Revolution shattered their hopes. Nevertheless, the well born, the wealthy, the aggressive, and ambitious did not give up trying to establish large estates.

The new national land system, created to administer the public domain ceded by the states and later acquired from other countries, was framed in an era when liberal principles were not held in high repute. The old imperial policy of using the public land as a source of revenue became the basic principle of the new land system, and the settlement of the West and the welfare of the settlers were subordinated to it. So long as the revenue concept dominated our national land policies, the various regulations adopted to develop that revenue as easily and as quickly as possible gave purchasers of large tracts advantages over the small buyer that for years enabled capitalist groups to act as middlemen in selling land and exacting profits from settlers. To begin with, half the land was to be sold in blocks of 5,120 acres and the other half in the alternate townships was to be divided into 640 acre sections and sold, the minimum price being $2 an acre. Credit was eventually extended but it only helped the capitalist to acquire more land. No restrictions of any kind were placed on the amount of land individuals or groups could buy from the government. Since the units of sale were much too large for him, the pioneer settler was virtually denied an opportunity to acquire public lands and was obliged to go to the middleman who could purchase large tracts and retail them out in small pieces.

In the second, fourth, and sixth decades of the nineteenth century occurred periods of great inflation produced by extravagant public spending on internal improvements with borrowed funds, unsound banking practices, including large emissions of wildcat and shinplaster currency, unusually high commodity prices—cotton in 1818 and wheat in the fifties—war conditions abroad and proliferation of railroad companies at home. Since almost unlimited credit was available for anyone of influence and property, land values were rising rapidly, and there developed a scramble for public lands that reached its greatest excitement in Alabama in 1818, Michigan, Indiana, Illinois, and Mississippi in 1835-1836, and Illinois, Wisconsin, Iowa and Missouri in the fifties. By a conservative estimate it appears that 5 million acres in the second decade, 25 million in the thirties and 40 million in the fifties were bought by land companies and individual capitalists that thus came to control whole townships and large parts of counties.[2]

Some of this speculative ownership was not firm or stable. During the periods of depression that soon followed each era of inflation, many land holders were frozen out by increasing tax and interest costs which they were unable to bear, but others, who had not so overextended, managed to carry their investment for many years in the hope of receiving their anticipated profits. There was thus established in all the better parts of the middle west and Gulf states absentee ownership which contributed nothing to develop either the lands or the communities in which they were located. The owners only waited for the increase in value which settlers on neighboring tracts would create by the labor they performed in making improvements and constructing roads, churches, and schools. By withholding their land from development the speculators retarded growth, kept out settlers who could not pay their price, and gave to areas containing a goodly part of absentee owned land the reputation of being speculators's deserts.

The secondary distribution of wild or unimproved land by these speculators and their resident agents was the biggest business on the frontier. Much of the capital was provided by the East but not infrequently the principal beneficiary was the local agent in Chillicothe, Vincennes, Kaskaskia, Chocchuma, Tuscaloosa, or Chariton who paid the taxes, rented to tenants, made sales and collections, and bought and sold on their own account. Many years later, in 1860, Horace Greeley, commenting on the exactions of the middle men who anticipated settlers's needs and resold to them at high prices on credit with usurious interest, estimated that, for every dollar paid into the public treasury for lands, two and a half or three dollars had gone to the land dealers.[3]

Not all this land that was bought by easterners in large quantities was acquired for mere speculation. A considerable number of easterners like Henry L. Ellsworth of Connecticut, Daniel Webster, James Wadsworth of the Genesee Valley of New York, planned to establish large estates operated by tenants in the midst of whom they would live as country gentry. Ellsworth and others like him moved to their holdings and devoted their energies to improving, developing, and settling them, not always with success, however.[4]

Far the larger part of the 70 million acres acquired in extensive holdings was bought for the expected rise in land values by speculators who had no intention of investing anything more than the cost of the land and management. The intrusion of these speculators between the government and the actual settlers in the primary disposition of its lands won increasing disapproval, both in the West and in the East. Westerners without capital but anxious to own land contemplated with bitterness the extensive tracts owned by absentees who contributed nothing to their development, but insisted on withholding them from sale and use until they would bring a profitable return. In their dislike of absentee owners the westerners took pleasure in stealing their timber, pasturing livestock on their grass, and assessing their land at high valuations. Since the distribution of the public lands in their midst was a government matter, they turned to politics for relief from the unwanted speculator. They petitioned Congress, the president, the General Land Office to grant them the right of preemption which would enable them to get in ahead of the speculator, then to postpone the land sales which would put off the day when they had either to pay for their claims or see them purchased by speculators at the auction, to reduce the price of land, and finally and most important, to grant land without cost to actual settlers. They formed claim or squatter associations to intimidate by mass threat possible buyers of their improved claims. Western representatives and senators took up their pleas and pressed them with increasing vigor in Congress.

It was not only at the speculator with his large holdings that western resentment was directed but increasingly the government was being charged with profiting from the labor of the pioneer in augmenting or creating land values. Long before Henry George shook the foundations of the citadel erected by the industrial barons on the twin doctrines of *laissez faire* and Social Darwinism by calling for the single tax, the West had reached the pragmatic view that unimproved land on the frontier had no value. Only through the coming of the settlers who cleared, fenced, and broke the land, erected their homes and laid out roads, and established schools, churches and local government was value given to land. The government, thought the West, like speculators, gained the unearned increment by charging a high price which came out of the sweat and toil of the pioneers.[5] For his boldness in striking into new and previously untouched territory, his willingness to undergo great hardships and to deprive his family of the amenities of a well-established society, he should be rewarded, not penalized, by being permitted to enjoy the full benefits of his action in developing new communities. He should be given the land, not sold it at high prices.

In the East the organizers of the struggling labor parties took up the cry of land reform in the hope of providing an outlet for the unemployed and a program economically attractive to them. The intellectual leader who framed the reform demands and worked out their philosophical justification was George Henry Evans, borrowing from Thomas Skidmore. As editor of radical weeklies, as lecturer, pamphleteer, and leader in trade union activities, Evans drew attention to the land question as a major issue of the day. He maintained that the use and ownership of land was a natural right as land provided the basis of living. To guarantee that right, the public domain should be distributed freely in small tracts to its users. The right of alienation should not accompany the right of use, argued Evans, for only by preventing the sale or mortgage of homesteads and denying the right of inheritance could land be prevented from accumulating in the hands of a few.[6]

Here then is a combination of western pragmatic reasoning and eastern philosophical support for land reform. Horace Greeley, never one to spurn radical ideas, took over the reform program of Evans and documented it lavishly by accounts in the *New York Tribune* of his experiences and observations gathered on his trips through the west. Contemporaries were shown the harshness of frontier life among settlers who were desperately seeking to make farms for themselves on lands for which they had had to pay outrageously high prices if they had bought from speculators or for which, whether acquired from previous owners or from the government they had used funds borrowed at usury rates that ran as high as 120 and 150 per cent a year.[7]

The reformers's cry for a liberal land policy that would prevent land monopoly and permit the pioneer, the farm maker on the frontier, to acquire ownership of his land without having to pay for the increased value his and neighborhood improvements gave to it gained support in high places. In Congress Thomas Hart Benton, Andrew Johnson, George W. Julian, and others took up the issue, arguing for general preemption, reduction in price, free lands, and restrictions on speculative purchasing. Andrew Jackson was the first and in effect the only president who advocated drastic reform of government land policy so that the public domain would be reserved for actual settlers. In his annual message on the state of the Union in December 1832, he stated his belief that it was the labor of the "adventurous and hardy population of the West" which "gives real value to the land." He urged abandonment of the sales policy with its high minimum price and the substitution of a policy of charging actual settlers a fee just sufficient to cover the cost of survey and management.[8] No legislation followed his recommendation, and in 1836 Jackson returned to the fray, this time with positive action.

The country, particularly the West, was caught up in a frenzy of land speculation in which government sales had skyrocketed from an average of 2 million to 4 million acres a year to 20 million in 1836. In 1835 and 1836 alone probably 22 million to 25 million acres were purchased for speculation.[9] Himself a speculator in public lands in the past, Andrew Jackson knew full well the dangers from such large scale monopolization by a few hundred or thousand speculators. In June 1836, he issued his famous Specie Circular that by requiring the payment of gold or silver instead of bank notes for public lands effectively halted the wild orgy of land speculation.[10] The Circular, Jackson said later, had "measurably cut off the means of speculation and retarded its progress in monopolizing the most valuable of the public lands. It had tended to save the new states from a nonresident proprietorship, one of the greatest obstacles to the advancement of a new country and the prosperity of an old one. It has tended to keep open the public lands for entry by emigrants at government prices instead of their being compelled to purchase of speculators at double or triple prices.[11]

Jackson's vigorous championship of land reform was followed by a strong effort in Congress to halt speculative purchasing and "limit sales to settlers or cultivators" or, as Robert J. Walker, senator from Mississippi put it, "to arrest monopolies of the public lands." With prophetic insight Walker predicted that the accumulation of land by capitalists for speculation would "introduce into the new states, the system of landlord and tenant, by which the occupant will not be the owner of the soil he cultivates, but the tributary of some absentee landlord, who will, in the shape of an annual rent, reap nearly all the profits of the labor of the cultivator." A measure to limit sales to actual settlers was fiercely opposed by eastern conservatives who continued to look upon the public lands as a national treasure which should provide income for the government and thereby reduce the need for taxes. Nothing should be permitted to interfere with the free flow of sales and of resultant income. To these opponents of land reform the Walker-Jackson plan was radical, levelling, and democratic. It would make ownership for the poor and landless too easy, would drain off the laborers from the older areas and reduce land values there, and would accelerate the growth of the West unduly and thereby upset the political balance of power. Against the reform measure was employed every possible parliamentary maneuver and delaying tactic, but almost solid western support carried it through the Senate. In the House, where western influence was weaker, it was defeated.[12] Not for years was another effort to be made to bar speculators from purchasing public lands.

The land reformers welcomed the Specie Circular as a blow to the development of land monopoly but felt let down by Congress, which failed to act upon Jackson's request for protection against speculative purchases. Was not the government the greatest land monopolist and land speculator and a profiteer from the labor of frontiersmen whose painful advances westward gave value to the public lands? Did not a truly liberal land policy call for the abandonment of the revenue concept and the adoption of a free-homestead plan and the rapid transfer of the public domain to private hands? Step by step the country inched nearer these goals, although the revenue concept, while it ceased to be predominant, was never to be completely abandoned. In 1841 the Preemption Law gave settlers the right to move upon and improve surveyed public land from which they might with good luck make the necessary funds to purchase it without competitive bidding for $1.25 an acre. Only 160 acres could be acquired in this way. In 1847–1855 Congress gave enlisted men in the Mexican War and veterans of all previous wars who had not been rewarded with land bounties warrants entitling them to 160 acres of the public lands. These warrants were virtually land office money, but they were issued in such quantities—altogether they covered more than 61 million acres—that they sold at prices ranging from 50 cents to $1.10 per acre. Most entries were made with the warrants since they were available everywhere at quoted rates, and the effect of their issue was to reduce the cost of public land. In 1854 the Graduation Act reduced the price of land not newly brought into market from $1.25 an acre in proportion to the length of time it had been subject to sale, the lower limit being 12½ cents. Only 320 acres could be acquired legally by any individual under this measure. Finally, in 1862, after a bitter struggle with the South, free homesteads of 160 acres were offered to anyone who would settle upon and improve government land.

Greeley's agitation and western yearning for free grants had convinced the Republicans that the issue could win many votes, and it did. During the next decades their stand upon the homestead issue paid the party political dividends. What were then frontier states like Wisconsin, Minnesota, Kansas, Iowa, and later Nebraska were so angered by Democratic President Buchanan's veto of a homestead bill and by the insistence of his administration on forcing lands on the market in the depression days of 1858–1860 as a means of raising revenue to balance the budget, thereby forcing thousands of impoverished settlers to purchase their claims with money borrowed of loan sharks, that they turned to the Republican party with majorities that surpassed the support it had anywhere else.[13]

The philosophy behind the Homestead Act of 1862 was not the natural rights argument of Evans and the land reformers. Few could regard Wade or Chandler or Pomeroy or Morrill as radicals. Yet they pushed to adoption a measure that was comparable to the capitalization and distribution of the national forests, parks, dams, generating plants, mineral reserves, and gold in Fort Knox of today. The free grant policy was based on the assumption that the cost of farm making, of pioneering on the prairies and plains, was so great that few people could succeed in the process if they had to buy the land from the government. The Republicans seem to have come to the view that land itself had no value—that what value it had when made into farms was to be attributed to the labors of the farm maker. To this extent, at least, the land reformers's views prevailed. But the Republicans threw aside all other aspects of Evans's and Greeley's reforms. There were no restrictions on the alienation of homesteads after the title had passed, no limitations on the amount of land that could be acquired from the government, no repeal of the cash-sale law with the right of unrestricted purchase of public lands, no withdrawal of lands from unlimited purchase, no steps taken to confiscate large holdings except the punitive measures directed against the Rebels, and no safeguards to prevent accumulation of new estates.

But free land to the landless was scarcely the great gift that apologists for the homestead measure maintained. A major limitation upon its effectiveness was that at the very time it was adopted Congress was engaged in giving well over 100 thousand acres of the public lands to projected or prospective railroads to aid in their construction. Also Congress continued the practice of granting to the states on their admission into the Union from six to sixteen per cent of their total area to aid in establishing and endowing common schools, universities, asylums, hospitals, and penitentiaries. Both railroads and states were expected to sell their land at the highest price it would bring and at the minimum of $3 to $10 an acre. Such prices brought it about that much of the land was withheld from market and development for years and was ultimately sold on long-term credit which was close to rent. The states thus found themselves dealing with the unpleasant task of collecting from numerous debtors or renting their land. The railroads when they ran into difficulty with their numerous land purchasers over collections were only too glad to shift the debt to local banks which were not quite so vulnerable politically.

Both railroads and states assured, by virtue of the withdrawal of the lands from market for a time until they were in demand at the price they sought, that neighboring settlers through the work they did in farm making, road construction, payment of taxes for the establishment of schools and other government services created a good share of the value these lands acquired. In continuing the donation plan until the admission of Arizona and New Mexico in 1911 Congress not only withdrew 170,000,000 acres from access to homesteaders but assured the continuation of the revenue policy over this large area and contributed to the development of tenancy. Liberal eastern thought and western agrarianism had won a victory over the reactionary forces that wished to retain all the public lands as a major source of revenue, but it was only a partial victory and the campaign for reform in the American pattern continued.[14]

During and immediately after the Civil War the Radical Reconstructionists, who were neither radical nor in the proper sense reconstructionists but on the contrary concerned to further the growth of big business, for a time joined with land reformers in supporting a truly radical program of land reform. The reason for this queer partnership was the hatred entertained by the Wade, Chandler, Morrill, Trumbull group of "Radicals" for the southern planters who had dominated national politics for so long and who were held responsible for the war. To strike at them the "Radicals" proposed to confiscate their plantations and other land holdings and to divide them among the freedmen. Confiscation measures were written into law which, if tolerated by the courts and vigorously enforced, might have brought about a revolution in land ownership in the South. This same group put through Congress the Southern Homestead Act of 1866 restricting the transfer of public lands to private ownership. Under this measure public land in Alabama, Arkansas, Florida, Louisiana, and Mississippi could be acquired by homesteaders only and until 1868 in units no larger than 80 acres. True, there was no restriction on alienability, but with that exception the radical views of Evans seem to have prevailed for the southern states.

Little benefit came to tenants or land seekers in the South from the confiscation acts or the Southern Homestead Act. The former were not vigorously enforced, little land was recovered, and no supplementary legislation was enacted which would have assured its redistribution on a democratic basis. The 47,726,851 acres in the five southern states which were withdrawn from speculative purchasing seem to have been heavily timbered land that would require much capital to improve and for whose principal resources there was but slight demand in the ten years in which the Southern Homestead Act was in operation. The repeal of the act in 1876 ended this venture.[15]

By 1870 the West was repenting of the liberality of the land grants it had advocated and of the ease with which large individual and corporate purchases could be made from the government. All over the newly developing frontier communities were signs that the land system was not working well from the point of view of the poor immigrant searching for land. Large railroad, state, and private holdings were kept out of cultivation and use for years because of the insistence on holding them for high prices. Settlers buying from these holders almost invariably had difficulty in meeting their payments and at the same time buying farm machinery, livestock, constructing their homes, fencing the land, and making other necessary improvements. Mortgage indebtedness was extensive, the interest rates were high, and foreclosures common, especially in periods of poor crops or low prices. Tenancy was appearing everywhere in the corn belt and wheat belt, half the farms in some counties being owned by absentees drawing their rents. Although the statistics of tenancy were not to be collected by the Census Bureau until 1880, no observer could be ignorant of its extent.

It was at this time that Henry George let loose his first blast against the government land system and the means it provided for the accumulation of large estates in the hands of the wealthy. His *Our Land and Land Policy* was no dull esoteric discussion of rent, capital, and labor but was a flaming indictment and by all odds the best contemporary survey of the effect of the federal land system in the distribution of ownership. Railroad land grants were denounced as "reckless prodigality," "land grabbers" were called the curse of the country, the story of the Mexican land claims in California were described as "a history of greed, of perjury, of corruption, of spoliation and high-handed robbery, for which it will be difficult to find a parallel." The land system was declared to enable "speculators to rob settlers." "Was there ever national blunder so great—ever national crime so tremendous as our['s] in dealing with our land?" George asked.[16] His indictment was exaggerated. Small ownerships were being established, and all farmers in the newer areas were not suffering in the clutches of the money monster. George's critique contained much truth; more important, it challenged attention, and contributed mightily to the demand for reform.

For the remainder of the century the land reformers, in harmony with the growing antimonopoly movement in the West, tried to prevent Congress from making additional grants of land to railroads, to secure the forfeiture of unearned land grants, to require the railroads to sell their lands at current market values, rather than to continue withholding them for high prices, to prohibit the accumulation of public land by aliens and to require the breakup of large estates held by them, to end the cash sale law of 1820 which permitted unrestricted purchasing of "offered" land, and to introduce into the General Land Office and the courts a more "settler minded" attitude and to eliminate therefrom the influence of railroad and mining companies and cattle and timber barons.

The reformers, still a combination of eastern laborers and western agrarians, put a halt to further land grants in 1871. Between 1867 and 1894 their pressure led to the forfeiture of 34,530,183 acres previously given railroads but which were unearned. They forced the land-grant railroads to speed up their advertising and sales policy to hasten the transfer of their holdings into private hands, where they would be taxable. In 1916 they were responsible for the recovery of nearly 3 million acres long since given the Oregon and California Railroad but not sold, as the grant provided, for $2.50 an acre. Pressure by the reformers also galvanized the General Land Office into action which should have been taken much earlier to restore to entry lands withdrawn to permit the railroads to make their selections. At least 31 million acres were thus restored to entry.[17] State after state and the federal government placed restrictions on the right of aliens to acquire and hold lands. Finally, in 1891, the cash sale law was repealed, thereby ending the right of unlimited purchase of "offered" lands. To make the General Land Office more "settler minded" was less easy to achieve. In the Cleveland administration there was a definite change of attitude, but it was soon offset by later appointments. Outwardly, at least, the officers deemed it essential to express concern about settler interests and to ask Congress for reform in the laws.

These were notable victories which on the surface looked truly important. They came only after long agitation and continued hard work on the part of men such as George W. Julian, William S. Holman, Henry George, and Terrence V. Powderly. The Grangers, the Greenback party, the Anti-Monopoly party, the Populists, labor organizations, and even the old-line Republican and Democratic parties all had a share in these reforms. But the reforms came late when much of the first-rate land had passed into the hands of speculators and railroads, when the best of the redwood lands of California, the Douglas Fir land of Washington, and the long-leaf-pine land of the South were in the hands of the lumber barons, when the copper, iron, and oil-bearing land were held by capitalistic combinations. Private ownership the West had favored, and steps which hastened the transfer from government hands were continually being pushed by it.

Essentially the reform or liberal position on the land question thus far had been to make the public-land system function in a democratic way by assuring the small man the right to acquire a piece of the national domain. Limitations were put in the Preemption, the Graduation, the Homestead Acts and their variations to make certain that only the small man could take advantage of them until the issue of the patent, but beyond that they had no effect. All such measures were therefore used by large interests acting through "dummy entrymen" to acquire lands they could not legally acquire otherwise. Timber land in Wisconsin, Minnesota, California, and Washington, grazing lands in Colorado, Wyoming, Arizona, and Idaho, wheat lands in Kansas, Nebraska, North and South Dakota passed into the hands of great lumber companies, cattle companies, and bonanza farm groups under laws that were designed to prevent large-scale accumulation. The unwillingness of Congress to experiment with restrictions on alienation made inevitable the concentration of ownership which grieved western agrarians.

Evans, Greeley, George, and other radicals had failed to carry the mass of land reformers with them on the question of alienability. Americans found it easy to be radical or to favor reform when to do so did not impose any self limitation, but few were attracted to any idea that might restrict their right to accumulate property or to sell and gain the unearned increment.

With the larger and more valuable part of the public lands in private hands, the reforms which were being adopted at this late time were both ineffective and to some extent unwise. Since the desirable size for land-use units was increasing as population moved into the arid and semi-arid regions, the 320 acre limitation on the amount of government land persons could acquire compelled either evasion and abuse of the laws to acquire adequately sized units or the establishment of small grain farms in areas unsuited to cultivation. This pattern of evasion and abuse of the land laws and the establishment of small grain farms in areas better planned by nature for grazing carried well into the twentieth century. Not until 1934 were comprehensive and far-reaching reforms initiated to produce a desirable and constructive plan of land use.

The preponderant, almost the universal view of Americans until near the end of the nineteenth century was that the government should get out of the land business as rapidly as possible by selling or giving to settlers, donating for worthy purposes and ceding the lands to the states which should in turn pass them swiftly into private hands. No matter how badly owners abused their holdings through reckless cultivation, destructive and wasteful cutting of the timber, prodigal and careless mining for coal and drilling for oil, few questioned their right to subject their property to any form of use or abuse. An extensive part of the fertile coastal plain and piedmont of the South and of the hill-farming area of the northeast could be cultivated in such a way as to reduce the land to barren, gullied, and eroded tracts no longer able to produce crops, to support families, and to carry their share of community costs, but few denied the right of the owners to do as they wished with their property or, more fundamentally, questioned the system of land distribution that seemed to invite such practices. The shore line of the Atlantic, of bays and inlets, of inland lakes all near congested urban areas could be monopolized by a wealthy few, and still there were few complaints. Rich landlords, speculators, and corporations could buy unlimited amounts of land from the United States, or purchase from other owners who had acquired tracts from the state or federal government and keep their holdings from development for years, thereby blighting whole areas, delaying the introduction of schools and roads and doing immeasurable harm to neighboring residents. The right of private property seemed virtually unlimited, so far had American individualism gone.[18] *Our Landed Heritage,* to borrow Robbins' title, was expendable.[19]

Long before the Civil War agricultural authorities were expressing alarm at the destructive farm practices employed in the tobacco and cotton fields of the South and the wheat land of the North, but their remedy was education through farmers's periodicals, societies, fairs, and the press. Undoubtedly education was helpful[20] but on the frontier where land was cheap and labor scarce, where capital to meet the costs of farm making had usually to be borrowed at high rates, where the most profitable cash crop had to be produced year in and year out, there was no alternative. Soil mining continued from frontier to frontier but, unfortunately, it carried over into later periods when pioneer conditions had passed. Landlordism and tenancy, absentee ownership, and the financial and economic ills into which agriculture fell in the late nineteenth century all contributed to the cropping of tobacco, cotton, corn, and wheat too steadily in areas to which they were adapted. Diminishing yields, the ravages of insects which the continued cultivation of one crop encouraged, and economic necessity forced changes and some improvements, but in many areas the process of exhausting the soil continued. Not from agriculture, despite its ills, was to come the cry for a fundamental change in land use and ownership.[21]

The serious economic losses to the nation resulting from the abuse of the soil were subtle, slow, and cumulative in their effects. The ravaging of our natural resources by the lumber industry was obvious to all. Large-scale commercial lumbering at this time consisted of the cutting and removing of choice white pine in the easiest and cheapest ways possible without regard to protecting remaining trees like Norway, hemlock, spruce, and the hardwoods. Much good timber was destroyed in the cutting, and much when cut was left in the woods to rot. The tops and branches, when dry, easily caught fire which, with right conditions, could easily destroy the standing timber. When lumbermen were finished with an area, its natural beauty had been destroyed and the slash remained to menace surrounding timber and settlements. Persons seeking recreation in forested areas like the Adirondacks of New York, the Alleghanies of Pennsylvania, the White Mountains of New Hampshire watched with increasing dismay the encroachments of the lumbermen on the areas they loved. Early depletion of commercial timber in the more accessible areas forced lumbermen to move into the higher parts of the mountains, the upper reaches of the streams, into the areas where logs could not be floated cheaply to mill by water but had to be hauled on sleds or brought to the mill by expensive logging railroads. The increasing cost of lumber brought home to many people, especially in the older centers where the supply was being exhausted, the desirability of a more conservative and intelligent use of natural resources and the need for the adoption of reforestation policies. Lumbermen with their eye on the balance sheet were not sufficiently concerned to do anything at the time, but an aroused public, working through forestry and science associations, called for a reorganization of our timberland disposal policy as a first step toward conservation and providing for future needs.[22]

Support for a new plan of land administration came not only from the lovers of wildlife, recreation interests, professional forestry people, and university professors but also from business men. Builders, contractors, real-estate agents, even lumbermen and dealers in stumpage were concerned. We know, for example, that one of the largest dealers in timber lands and stumpage in Wisconsin was an ardent supporter of the conservation movement.[23] Those diverse interests center[ed] their attention upon two principal proposals: (1) that the government retain control of its timber land and sell only under careful restrictions the stumpage, that is the right to cut, and not the land; (2) that the government should not only carefully supervise cutting on the forest reserves but should provide for the regeneration of cutover areas and the protection of the forests from fire and disease.

The movement for the permanent withdrawal of timber lands from market and their establishment in organized forest reserves was taken up principally by congressmen from the older states in which the lumber industry was waning or where the higher costs of timber were affecting building development. The most active political support came from John Sherman of Ohio, George F. Edmunds of Vermont, and from other congressmen principally from Ohio, Indiana, Illinois, and New York. For continued and permanent public ownerships of the reserves and public controls, possibly even government lumbering, there was no great support in the Senate, perhaps not in the House. Yet an amendment providing for reservations when attached to an omnibus bill to restrict land entries and repeal the preemption and timber culture acts, was approved by Congress in 1891 without a division in either house. By a series of fortuitous circumstances, including adroit leadership, forest reserves were authorized almost a generation before Congress was "fully converted to the principle" underlying them.[24]

The new forest policies involved a sharp break with the philosophy on which American land policy had thus far rested, that is that the government should not be in the business of purveying land any longer than necessary, that it should provide for the easy and early transfer of the public lands to private ownership, that it should not attempt to make gain from their disposal, that it should not retain from private ownership any part thereof, or attempt to reserve to itself royalty rights, rents, or other benefits.

Although that staunch old advocate of land reform, William S. Holman of Indiana, firmly supported the change, the real impetus for it had not come from the land reformers of the past, nor from farm organizations or trade unions. Neither was this stride toward collectivism the work of single taxers, socialists, or other doctrinaire radicals. True, German intellectuals who were familiar with state forestry in Europe had contributed to the movement but the pressure for the change came out of American experience.[25]

The National Forest Reservation Act of 1891 did not require the establishment of reserves but gave authority to the president to withdraw from the public domain such timbered land as he deemed advisable for permanent government ownership and use. Presidents Harrison, Cleveland, and McKinley withdrew some 50 million acres, but their action touched off opposition in Congress to further withdrawals, and little more was accomplished until Theodore Roosevelt became president. Despite his aristocratic background, Harvard education, and political associations with influential conservatives, Roosevelt, under the tutelage and influence of Gifford Pinchot, espoused and pushed vigorously a program of public land reservation and utilization that makes his administration stand out with that of Franklin D. Roosevelt's as the greatest and most forward looking in matters of planning and conservation. Approximately 100 million acres of public lands were placed under national forest status in Theodore Roosevelt's administration.

Equally important was the establishment of a vigorous National Forest Service that assured adequate protection to the reserves from plundering, trained forces to fight fires and resist the encroachments of insects and disease, controlled cutting, enforced restrictions on grazing in the national forests, and conducted scientific experimentation in forest management and reforestation. As a result of wise leadership, successful public relations work and generous appropriations despite frequent expressions of Congressional disapproval, the National Forest Service quickly became an agency with an ardent following among professional foresters, farmers, and all those persons interested in the preservation of wild life and long-range plans for the development and large-scale expansion of public forestry. No other agency in the growing federal bureaucracy was so advanced in its planning, as collectivist in its thought, as free from doctrinaire conservatism and at the same time free from utopian radicalism as was the National Forest Service under Pinchot, Graves, and successors.[26]

The next major step in forest conservation and the extension of public control was taken in the Taft administration. New Englanders, alarmed by the flood menace and fearful that their mountain areas would be stripped of their splendid timber cover and defaced and forever marred by the advancing lumbermen, pleaded successfully that Congress authorize the purchase and establishment of national forests on the headwaters of the Connecticut and other important rivers of the East. The Weeks Forest Purchase Act has made possible the great forests now being developed by the Federal government along the Appalachian ridge from Maine to Georgia, in the Northern Lake states, and in the older states of the lower Mississippi. Individualism and *laissez faire* were thus given body blows in the citadel of capitalism. The American capacity to adapt its social philosophy to practical necessity has never been better illustrated.[27]

Long after 1891 the public-land states continued hostile to forest conservation, maintaining that other sections had exploited their resources as they wished and that the timber of the West should not be locked up for future generations's use. These states opposed withdrawals and in line with past policy wished the public lands transferred to private hands without reservations. Withdrawing of lands from entry, permanent retention of the land by the Federal government, restrictions on land use, leasing and stumpage fees, the forest purchase program all were condemned as the exercise of unconstitutional power, encroachments upon the rights of the states and of individuals, and filching of public funds.

It became less easy for the West to maintain that attitude, however, as it contemplated the semi-arid land that constituted so much of the region and reflected that in the future the growth of the West in population and political influence depended on filling up that vacant territory. The government had spent millions of dollars in buying the land and sovereignty from Mexico, in exploring and surveying the land and had given rich subsidies to provide it with railroads. Could it now be induced to reclaim these arid wastes by applying to them the funds derived from sales and royalties from minerals? To that end the West came forth with a far-reaching, even breath-taking measure, arguing brazenly that it only involved reinvesting the funds derived from sales within the same states. The East could see little good in a vast effort to reclaim semi-arid America which would bring into competition with its outworn and impoverished soils highly productive but equally highly subsidized land. Withdrawing of lands from entry, other than homestead, the right to condemn land for reservoirs and water use, Federal construction of dams and irrigation ditches, and the appropriation of income from the lands for such schemes were all condemned by eastern congressmen in much the same way that the Weeks Act had been condemned by the West.

Opposition of the East was in sound conservative tradition while the support for government reclamation activity in the West was in line with the changing view that was gradually permeating American thinking that the older individualism of the past could no longer serve in the twentieth-century world. The government in business did not frighten people who foresaw that its result would be growth and economic progress for many areas.

The Reclamation Act of 1902 provided that 95 per cent of the income from the public lands in the thirteen states and three territories containing semi-arid lands was to go into a revolving fund for the construction of dams and reservoirs to impound water for the irrigation of the parched land. Income from water rents was also to feed the fund. Since the remaining five per cent of public-land receipts was already allotted for education, the act of 1902 marked the final abandonment of the notion that the lands should provide any revenue for or even reimburse the Federal government for its large expense in managing them.

Large-scale government subsidies to agriculture thus began in a Republican Roosevelt administration. Some would say that no greater handout to special interests has been given.[28] Since 1902 and through 1949 more than $1,805,000,000 have been appropriated for reclamation projects. The size of the appropriation for 1949—$266,000,000—and the numerous projects that are being pressed upon Congress calling for vastly greater sums indicate that we are closer to the beginning than the end. Not only are giant dams and storage basins, hundreds of miles of canals, vast pumping projects, and huge power developments being undertaken, but the course of major rivers is being reversed, all for the major purpose of providing water for irrigation.

Many of the reclamation projects have not been economically successful, and few could have been financed in any sound way without grafting on them hydroelectric power development.[29] The sale of electric power has provided much of the income and the cost of the various projects. Increasingly, as less and less economically feasible irrigation projects were proposed, power was included to finance and justify them. Long before the inauguration of Franklin D. Roosevelt and even prior to the building of Muscle Shoals Dam on the Tennessee which marked the beginning of the Tennessee Valley development, the Federal power industry, a thoroughly socialistic scheme, was under way, not at the urging of the few theoretical socialists but through the strong administrative leadership of Theodore Roosevelt and Gifford Pinchot, supported by numerous western Republicans and Democrats. Furthermore, Roosevelt, who has recently been characterized as a conservative progressive, and Pinchot were responsible for the withdrawal of water-power sites to assure public control, ownership, utilization, and a fair rate structure when development was undertaken. Today, the United States government is the greatest power-producing agent in the world. Such tremendous structures with their enormous power output as Boulder, Shasta, Grand Coulee, Shoshone, Friant, Arrowrock, and Roosevelt to name only a few are the result of the demand of the West for Federal aid in developing the arid lands.

American individualism, the belief that private interests could best and most usefully exploit the mineral resources of the public domain had been responsible for the transfer of the Calumet and Hecla copper of Michigan, the Anaconda "World's Richest Hill" lode in Montana, the Mesabi iron field in Minnesota, and other valuable deposits to private ownership.[30] Private enterprises rapidly developed these and other natural resources and excited national pride in the growing industrial strength of the United States. Before long, however, the fear was aroused that "monopoly" was being established in the mining industry as in manufacturing, transportation, banking, and in land ownership, and that too much economic power and too much wealth was in too few hands. Again, however, it was from the conservationist that the impetus came for government reservation of mineral land and the practice of leasing.

Exhaustion of natural resources was a widely discussed topic around the turn of the century when predictions were being made that our coal, our oil, other minerals, and forests would soon be depleted as to force dependence on high-cost mines, expensive timber, and importation from abroad.[31] Fearing that the still unplumbed resources on the remaining public lands would soon be acquired by private interests who would be concerned to transform them into wealth at the earliest possible moment, Roosevelt, under the continued guidance of Pinchot, withdrew from entry and private acquisition the sub-soil rights on all remaining public lands suspected of having value for their minerals. These withdrawals gave Congress time over the years to formulate legislation for leasing these lands to mining and oil companies under such conditions as were deemed essential to assure supplies to meet current needs and those of the future and especially to meet the needs of the Navy. Royalties from the mineral development were assigned to the reclamation fund.[32] Not again could a United States Steel Corporation, a Utah Copper Company, or a Standard Oil Company secure ownership of rich deposits which they might exploit and solely profit from without regard to other social interests, future needs, or public welfare.

Conservation, the term popularly used for the changes being introduced into land policy, meant in practice the careful use and management of the natural resources of the public domain. By purely pragmatic reasoning the leaders of the movement had reached the conclusion that the government should not only retain or "reserve" title to ungranted lands but should manage and control their use and exploitation to assure their wise and cautious use with the profits derived therefrom assigned to other worthy objects for expansion. This did not necessarily mean putting the government in business. Where these objectives could be attained under private development government controls would only be used to assure that end. Lumbering has been done within the National Forests only by private enterprise; public power has been sold to private distributing and manufacturing companies; drilling for oil and mining phosphate, coal, and other minerals on public lands has been done by private interests. But no longer may the timber within the National

Forests be wastefully cut or drilling for oil be continued in an overstocked market; no longer may a small part of the coal be extracted once a mine is opened or the power generated at a government plant be sold at excessively high prices to consumers.

After the great withdrawals for National Forests there remained large areas of public domain good for forage. These grass or range lands varied widely in vegetation, capacity to support cattle and sheep, and in economic value to interested groups. Being unfenced and completely unregulated, they were pastured early and with harmful effect in the spring by livestock men anxious to save their own forage. The edible grasses were browsed too closely, were pastured too long, and were trampled badly by too many sheep and cattle. As a result, the more nutritious plants were killed out in a greater or less degree and noxious weeds came in; removal of the binding effect of the plant cover permitted erosion to strip off the soil and cover with silt agricultural lands in the valleys or fill up the reservoirs and ditches. Unregulated and uncontrolled use of the public range lands also produced strife between livestock interests.

In contrast, range land within the National Forests was fenced, the number of animals permitted on it was carefully correlated with the carrying capacity, overgrazing was not permitted, noxious weeds were eliminated, erosion was minimized, seeding and replanting was done, and experiments were conducted in the introduction of new and hardy types of grasses. In this way the National Forest ranges continued to provide well for their users, strife was avoided, and the management and development costs were paid by users on a permittee basis.

The extension of range control within the National Forests was not accomplished without friction and sharp opposition from livestock interests. However, with a decentralized control and local participation in the framing of policies and regulations, this opposition gradually dissolved. It was another matter, however, to secure agreement among the livestock people concerning the best way of bringing order and improved conditions to the public domain range.

A third of a century was spent in discussion and argument as to the need for and best way of obtaining controlled use of grazing on the remaining public lands. Proposals were advanced to turn the land over to the states for their administration, to permit private groups of livestock men to organize grazing districts on the public lands and to maintain controls over their use, to add the public lands to existing National Forests for administrative and regulatory purposes, to sell or transfer the lands in large grazing homesteads to livestock interests, and to establish a new government bureau whose task it should be to introduce controlled use of the range.

Bureaucratic bickerings as well as the opposition of western livestock interests delayed the final solution. The United States Department of Agriculture contended that the grazing of livestock was an agricultural matter and problems relating to it and to land use should be administered by an agency thoroughly integrated with its Bureau of Animal Industry, Soil Conservation Service, National Forest Service, and Bureau of Agricultural Economics. Like every good bureaucratic agent, the Department of the Interior disliked giving up any field of authority and fought vigorously to retain the public lands and, when it saw the growing sentiment in behalf of conservation, to have a new agency created within the department to handle the controlled use of the range.

The break came in 1934 when amidst depression, drought, poor range conditions, and low meat prices the remaining individualists of the grazing states ceased their opposition and joined with others who had long favored the final withdrawal of the remaining lands from private entry and the establishment of government controls in their use. A new agency was created to administer the range lands which has since been consolidated with the old General Land Office into the Bureau of Land Management. It was authorized to withdraw and place under organized control 80 million acres, later 142 million acres or all the public lands then unreserved and ungranted that had or seemed to have any value for forage. For all practical purposes, this ended the transfer of land to private ownership, except for the small five acre residence homesteads and the reclamation lands that are slowly passing into individual hands. True, the various land administering agencies are still racked with jealous struggles to take over or swallow up each other, the old feud between Agriculture and Interior remains unresolved, despite the recommendations of the Hoover Commission on the Reorganization of Government, and western interests struggle to gain control over the administrative agencies that most intimately affect them with the intention of reducing fees, liberalizing use, and perhaps of securing additional handouts from the Treasury. Numerous political problems affecting the public lands remain unsolved.[33]

We have thus seen how beginning with 1891 and continuing until today the old policy of permitting, in fact encouraging the rapid transfer of the public lands with their resources into private ownership, was breached and finally abandoned. No longer did private ownership seem the highest goal. Instead, there was substituted for it public ownership, public controls designed to ensure intelligent use of the resources, distribute their benefits more widely, and safeguard the interests of future generations. In the administration of its public lands America has moved far from the revenue concept, through the free grant and monopoly stage, which only partly met the objectives of the reformers, through the third period in which permanent and public ownership and controls were established. We are now beginning to reap the benefits. We all may enjoy the beauties and scenic wonders of the national parks and forests, thrill at the gigantic dams at Boulder and Grand Coulee, marvel at the way reclamation and water projects have made great desert areas produce rich crops and thriving cities. The liberal and reform position of the nineteenth century might have avoided some of the worst blunders of the past but, because restriction was unacceptable to all but a few, it had to be replaced by a philosophy of use that was more socially minded.

Notes

1. This "capture" of the democratic tradition by the advocates of laissez faire and later supporters of "free enterprise" is lucidly described by Robert Green McCloskey in *American Conservatism and the Age of Enterprise* (Cambridge, 1951).

2. For material on speculative purchases, see Paul W. Gates "Southern Investments in Northern Lands Before the Civil War," *Journal of Southern History* 5 (May, 1939), 155-85; "Land Policy and Tenancy in the Prairie States," *Journal of Economic History* 1 (May, 1941), 60-82; "The Role of the Land Speculator in Western Development," *Pennsylvania Magazine of History and Biography* 66 (July, 1942), pp. 314-33; "Land Policy and Tenancy in the Prairie Counties of Indiana," *Indiana Magazine of History* 35 (March, 1939), 1-26.

3. *New York Semi-Weekly Tribune,* January 31, 1860.

4. For Ellsworth, one of the largest buyers of western land but who ultimately failed in his goal to establish a great and long-lasting estate, see Paul Wallace Gates, "Land Policy and Tenancy in the Prairie Counties of Indiana, *Indiana Magazine of History* 35 (March, 1939), 6 ff. The most successful and largest farming estate in America that was acquired from the United States and developed through tenants, that of William Scully, is described in the same author's *Frontier Landlords and Pioneer Tenants* (Ithaca, 1945), pp. 34-63.

5. Henry C. Carey, an influential political economist, held this same view which he expounded in *The Past, The Present and the Future* (Philadelphia, 1848), pp. 60-61. As a widely read man his views may have contributed to the support for free-land policies that was shown by eastern congressmen.

6. Helene S. Zahler, *Eastern Workingmen and National Land Policy* (New York, 1941), 19 ff.; Joseph Dorfman, *The Economic Mind in American Civilization,* vol. 2 (New York, 1946), 684-85.

7. Roy M. Robbins, "Horace Greeley: Land Reform and Unemployment, 1837-1862," *Agricultural History,* 7 (January, 1933), 18 ff.

8. James D. Richardson, *Messages and Papers of the Presidents,* vol. 2 (1904), 601.

9. My estimate is based on analysis of the sales for early years together with those of 1835 and 1836. Although I have worked through all the land entry books for this period, I have not made a detailed investigation to determine the actual amount of land bought by nonsettlers. Thomas Ewing, senator from Ohio, estimated that about 20

million acres were purchased by speculators in 1835 and 1836. Apparently he thought of speculative purchasing as including only those large tracts bought by men of wealth or by land companies. For Ewing's estimates see *Congressional Globe,* 24 Cong., 2 Sess., Appendix, p. 289.

10. For the Circular which was actually issued by Levi Woodbury, secretary of the treasury, see *American State Papers, Public Lands, VIII,* 910.

11. Annual Message to Congress, December 5, 1836, in Richardson, vol. 3, 249–50. The House of Representatives had previously provided for an investigation of the amount of borrowing by members of Congress and other government officials from deposit banks for speculation in public lands. A comprehensive investigation might have been salutary for there is plenty of evidence of prominent members of Congress buying public lands in large quantities, but the efforts of the House Committee to secure evidence were fruitless. *Congressional Globe,* 24 Cong., 1 Sess., pp. 609-10, July 2, 1836; *House Reports,* 24 Cong., 1 Sess., No. 846, pp. 1-6.

12. Walker's telling speech in behalf of land reform, of January 14, 1837, is in *Congressional Globe,* 24 Cong., 2 Sess., Appendix, pp. 167-70. The measure was under consideration from December 1836 through March 1837 and can be followed in the *Congressional Globe,* 24 Cong., 2 Sess., *passim.*

13. Paul W. Gates, "The Struggle for Land and the 'Irrepressible Conflict,' " *Political Science Quarterly* 66 (June, 1951), 248-71.

14. Paul W. Gates, "The Homestead Law in an Incongruous Land System," *American Historical Review* 41 (July, 1936), 652 ff.

15. Paul W. Gates, "Federal Land Policy in the South, 1866-1888," *Journal of Southern History* 6 (August, 1941), 303-30.

16. George's pamphlet, whose full title was *Our Land and Land Policy, National and State,* was published in San Francisco in 1871. I have used the more accessible reprint under the title *Our Land and Land Policy* (New York, 1901), pp. 21, 39, and 89.

17. David Maldwyn Ellis has told the story of the fight for the forfeiture of unearned grants and for the retrocession of the Oregon and California lands in two admirable articles: "The Forfeiture of Railroad Land Grants, 1867-1894," *Mississippi Valley Historical Review* 33 (June, 1946), 27-60, and "The Oregon and California Railroad Land Grant, 1866-1945," *Pacific Northwest Quarterly* 39 (October, 1948), 253-83. See also John B. Rae, "Commissioner Sparks and the Railroad Land Grants," *Mississippi Valley Historical Review* 25 (September, 1938), 211-30.

18. I should exclude from this generalization urban property which was subject to controls and restrictions.

19. Roy M. Robbins, *Our Landed Heritage. The Public Domain, 1776-1936* (Princeton, 1942).

20. Avery O. Craven, *Soil Exhaustion as a Factor in the Agricultural History of Virginia and Maryland* (Urbana, 1926).

21. None of the major works on agrarian discontent in the late nineteenth century include any critical analysis of government land policies and the part they played in aggravating the farmers' problems. For the fierce resentment at large estates that led to the adoption of anti-alien landowning measures by the United States and a number of middle western states, see Paul W. Gates, *Frontier Landlords and Pioneer Tenants,* 49-61.

22. John Ise, *The United States Forest Policy* (New Haven, 1920), *passim,* is excel-

lent for the beginning of the conservation movement. Richard G. Lillard, *The Great Forest* (New York, 1947), is useful for its account of the monopolistic practices of the lumbermen and the way they brought ruin to areas of superlative natural beauty. Cf. Agnes M. Larson, *History of the White Pine Industry in Minnesota* (Minneapolis, 1949).

23. The allusion is to Henry C. Putnam whose estimates of the remaining commercial stand of white pine in the Lake States as published in the Census of 1880 were so low as to give a big boost to stumpage prices from which he was a major beneficiary. Paul W. Gates, *The Wisconsin Pinelands of Cornell University* (Ithaca, 1943), 226-29.

24. Ise, *op. cit.*, pp. 116-18.

25. Bernhard E. Fernow, *Brief History of Forestry in Europe, The United States and Other Countries* (Toronto, 1907), pp. 406 ff.

26. Gifford Pinchot, *Breaking New Ground* (New York, 1947), is contentious, opinionated, and at times severely prejudiced, but it is a remarkably clear and useful statement and is indispensable for anyone working on the history of conservation and changing land policies.

27. It is true that many New Englanders seem to have regretted the startling step taken in 1911 and in more recent years have supported action to restrict the executive authority embodied in the Weeks Act.

28. Triple A farm relief of 1933 was an emergency measure designed to bring the farmers out of the worst depression we have suffered, though the subsidy program therein established has grown into a different monster whose longevity is appalling. The data on appropriations for the Reclamation Service is computed from the *Annual Report* of the Commissioner Bureau of Reclamation to the Secretary of the Interior, 1949, p. 70. Needless to say the *Annual Reports* of the Secretary of the Interior and of the Reclamation Service, now the Bureau of Reclamation, are most detailed and useful but are slanted, apologetic, uncritical, and tinged with propagandistic fervor.

29. The best critical analysis of government reclamation activity, now somewhat dated but still useful, is R. P. Teele, *The Economics of Land Reclamation in the United States* (Chicago, 1927).

30. The state of Minnesota owns rich ore lands in the Mesabi from which it draws generous royalties but most of the range went into private ownership.

31. Charles R. Van Hise, *The Conservation of Natural Resources in the United States* (New York, 1910), reflects this conservationist fear of early exhaustion more than opposition to monopolistic control of valuable resources.

32. John Ise, *The United States Oil Policy* (New Haven, 1926), is important on mineral reserves.

33. Particularly good on the question of bringing the remaining public range lands under organized control is E. Louise Peffer, *The Closing of the Public Domain. Disposal and Reservation Policies, 1900-1950* (Stanford, 1951). For the recommendations of the Hoover Commission, see *The Hoover Commission Report on Reorganization of the Executive Branch of the Government* (New York, 1949), 253-57.

8

The Intermountain West against Itself *

Published in 1985, "The Intermountain West against Itself" is one example of the broader interpretive articles emphasizing recent developments in American land policy characteristic of Gates's research and thinking in the 1980s. Here he examines major land management policies in the West during the preceding two decades, relating them to their nineteenth- and early-twentieth-century antecedents. The article exemplifies his interpretive skill as a historian of policy. He establishes the linkages between public land and resource policies identified with conservation in the late nineteenth century and the New Deal years with the environmental orientation of resource management in the 1970s and 1980s. The article is rich in the factual content of differences over management of range lands, conflicts over railroad lands, coal slurry pipelines, severance taxes, and reclamation of arid lands, and the battles over water resources. Gates ventured further and more interpretively into current natural resource issues than at any time since his work in the Agricultural Adjustment Administration. The Western History Association awarded him its prize for this article in 1986 in recognition of how his fifty years of research and publication "have enormously broadened our understanding of the western experience in American history."

A consistent theme in American history has been the demand by western states that they be treated equally with the original states in the control and management of the public lands. To appease the region, the federal government shared these lands by making grants for various purposes, and in 1902 decreed that 95 per cent of the income from the sale and disposal of the pub-

* From *Arizona and the West: A Quarterly Journal of History* 27 (Autumn 1985), 205–36. Used by permission of the publisher, the Arizona Historical Society. All rights reserved.

lic domain remaining in the sixteen western states should be devoted to the irrigation of arid lands. As a result of these policies, California has outdistanced New York as the wealthiest and most prosperous commonwealth in the nation, and the older states have lost population and industry to the West. Their farmers have increasingly suffered from the competition with the West's federally subsidized farms and irrigated crops.[1]

This frenetic growth of the West created serious problems both for the West and for the nation. In a series of articles in the 1940s Bernard DeVoto, one of the region's ablest historians and environmentalists, pointed to some of these problems. He said the cattlemen and sheepmen were destroying the grass cover on rangelands by permitting overgrazing; that mining companies were ripping up extensive tracts of the public domain, poisoning streams and wells and filling up the reservoirs; and that timber interests were seeking to gain control of the National Forests. Equally harmful were the land companies and speculative enterprisers who promoted growth, regardless of what it might do to priceless scenic areas and to public opportunities to enjoy wide open space. In a famous article in *Harper's Magazine* (1947), "The West Against Itself," DeVoto warned his section of the country that Theodore Roosevelt's policies for conserving natural resources had been in the West's best interests and should be followed. His warning, supported by the outcries of other environmentalists, helped blunt some of the worst schemes of the 1950s by greedy capitalists to wrest the public lands from federal control.[2]

Nearly forty years later, William K. Wyant in a 1982 indictment of federal land policies, focused on the problem of administering the public land system. "Much damage has been done by the myopic view, rooted deep in our history," he wrote, "that there is something wrong and inappropriate about federal ownership of land. Better that the Devil own it than Uncle Sam, who is seen as a meddlesome interloper. Better the local, regional, state or private interest than the national interest." This antigovernment view has been expressed over and over in congressional hearings concerned with public lands. Added to this deep prejudice (which "real" westerners never seem to shake) is the current view that public ownership smacks of European socialism.[3]

During the past century, Congress appointed a number of land commissions (1879, 1903, 1929, and 1964) to investigate and report on the weaknesses of the land system. Most of their proposals took years to implement; many were discarded. Even the Public Land Law Review Commission (PLLRC), which reported in 1970, waited six years before seeing action on its program. To a large degree, these delays have been caused by westerners who, finding they could not gain their objectives in law, won their way by evasion, neglect, false testimony, and other frauds.[4]

During the early years of the twentieth century, conservationist ideas gained acceptance, but the West, always critical of Washington bureaucracy, increasingly voiced the view that the states might do just as well, if not better, by administering the public lands themselves, especially the grazing, mining, and forest lands. Western leaders lusted after the power and responsibility to be gained through state control, and were vigorously supported by economic users of the lands—the livestock interests, the miners, and, to a lesser degree, the lumber interests. Lumbermen considered federal restrictions as petty and were hopeful that they could deal with state officials much more easily. However, the question of the ability of western states to handle such responsibilities has become a matter of debate.

In recent years, the western states—especially those in the Intermountain West—have had difficulty in standing together on measures that would protect and conserve their natural resources and at the same time guarantee their wise development and use. They have become sharply divided over certain economic issues that have taken on a political color and are deeply involved in federal-state relations. A number of these issues have revolved around range use and management, railroad lands, coal slurry pipeline rights-of-way, severance taxes, reclamation and acreage limitation, and wars over water.

Westerners have long urged Congress to adopt an organic law which would spell out the rights and obligations of the users of public lands in their region. Such an act was strongly recommended by the western-dominated Public Land Law Review Commission in its lengthy 1970 report, *One Third of the Nation's Land*. Experience with government land bureaus led the commission to propose 137 specific changes in the laws and regulations. During the next six years, House and Senate committees on public lands struggled to frame a program to improve and better define the use of the 160 million acres under the Bureau of Land Management (BLM), and especially to please the grazing and mining interests in the West. In 1976 Congress finally passed the Federal Land Policy and Management Act (FLPMA). It proved quite unsatisfactory to conservationists and environmentalists, who had good reason to distrust the compromises that had been made with western representatives and who felt that the thrust of their movement had been seriously blunted. However, the economic-users group also became dissatisfied with the act, and they voiced their resentment in the "Sagebrush Rebellion" of 1979–1980. The West stood divided.[5]

In addition to passing the land policy act, Congress enacted a second recommendation of the PLLRC. In 1976 it adopted, with considerable support from eastern liberals, dubious legislation called the Payments in Lieu of Taxes

Act, which authorized payments to counties in lieu of taxes on BLM, National Forest, and National Park lands within their boundaries. The western states had previously succeeded in getting the federal government to share revenues from mineral royalties and timber licenses in the National Forest, using these monies for schools, highways, and irrigation projects. In 1978, however, the Advisory Commission on Intergovernmental Relations, which carefully studied the need for such a gratuity as grants in lieu of taxes, reported that revenue sharing already was "generally adequate to offset any adverse effect" from inability to tax federal land.[6]

In these two federal measures, western economic interests scored major victories. In addition to federal payments in lieu of taxes, the West continued to enjoy the huge payments Washington was making on a revenue-sharing basis from timber cutting, mineral leases, grazing permits, and grants for reclamation in the dry areas. Altogether, more than $800 million in federal payments flowed to the western states either for use by the counties and states or for reclamation projects.[7]

On May 4, 1981, Senator Paul Laxalt of Nevada was quoted in the *New Yorker* as saying: "Westerners should be more involved in decision making." He may have been referring to the many public-land questions that stockmen were raising about rangelands. His admonition to the people of his section was quite unnecessary, for they always have been involved in decision-making for their states and greatly profited from the results.[8]

From the first articulation of western sentiment, the section has been united in pushing the federal government to pass the public lands quickly to private ownership, even to ownership by investors (not developers), so they could be placed on the tax rolls. Gifford Pinchot's and Theodore Roosevelt's use of forestry legislation of 1891 and 1897 to lock up the forest lands and introduce scientific management of them and their forage cover displeased western users. Even when it became apparent that limiting the number of livestock on National Forest lands and imposing grazing fees to fund range improvements would raise the carrying capacity of the ranges, stockmen would not accept the same controls for the rest of the public grasslands.[9]

But when deep economic depression struck in the 1930s, a Colorado rancher-congressman began urging the government to apply similar controls to these rangelands. Edward T. Taylor represented western Colorado, where grazing, mining, and irrigated farming were the principal occupations. He saw that uncontrolled use of the public rangelands would lead to the deterioration of grasses and destruction of soil cover and reluctantly concluded that government controls similar to those in force on the forest ranges should be applied to the rest of the public grasslands. In response to Taylor's zealous efforts, the Taylor Grazing Act was passed in 1934, and the Department of Interior created a Division of Grazing with the power to grapple with the problem of uncontrolled use of the rangelands. Under Harold Ickes, the department's highly efficient secretary, the new division introduced a system of local control which allowed livestock people using the public range to elect their own representatives, set fees, and allocate the number of sheep and cattle on the lands. The division leaned over backward to appease users and keep fees below those charged by the Forest Service and by private owners of rangelands, but it was slow to reduce the stock allowed and had limited funds for making improvements. When it became necessary to increase fees and reduce livestock on the land, western stockmen became hostile. Under the leadership of Senator Pat McCarran of Nevada, they made a concerted and spiteful attack on the Division of Grazing, saw that its appropriations were sharply cut, and had it virtually stripped of authority to act.[10]

Over and over, in hearings on appropriation measures, statements were made that the division (later the BLM) had failed to accomplish what the Forest Service had in administering the forest ranges. In 1970 the Public Land Law Review Commission had declared that there were "still substantial areas of land administered by the Bureau of Land Management and some managed by the Forest Service" that were in a deteriorated state. "The objectives of public land policy," the commission added (possibly tongue-in-cheek), "should be explicit and not only place priority on the rehabilitation of deteriorated rangeland where possible but *should exclude domestic livestock grazing from frail lands where necessary to protect and conserve the natural environment.*"[11]

Six years later, the Presidential Council on Environmental Quality reported that "75 per cent of the range was producing less than half of its forage potential." In 1978, in a report on range controls, the House committees on interior and insular affairs added that the BLM had shown that 83 per cent of the rangelands were in fair, poor, or bad condition. In fact, the Land Policy and Public Management Act of 1976 was rewarding the "very people who are largely responsible for this shocking situation."[12]

In 1978 Congress finally abandoned its efforts to make range users pay for desperately needed improvements and passed the Public Range Land Improvement Act. The law commented on the effect of many years of neglect:

> . . . unsatisfactory conditions on public rangelands present a high risk of soil loss, desertification, and a resultant underproductivity for large acreages of the public lands; contribute significantly to unacceptable levels of siltation and salinity in major western watersheds including the Colorado River; negatively impact the quality and availability of scarce western water supplies; . . . prevent expansion of the forage resource

and resulting benefits to livestock and wildlife production; increase surface runoff and flood danger. . . .[13]

By 1982 the problem of grazing fees on the public rangelands became critical. These fees had been tied to livestock market prices, and when prices drastically declined that year, the fees dropped to one-fourth of those charged on privately owned land. Government fees, reported Professor Frank Busby, chairman of the Department of Range Improvement at the University of Wyoming, were difficult to explain or justify. For many years, the relatively few economic users of the public rangelands had influenced their representatives in Congress to block legislation to require user improvements on public lands. Holders of the 21,000 grazing permits virtually dictated federal policy on the BLM rangelands, including the fees they paid.[14]

The Sagebrush Rebellion in 1979–80 showed how easy it was for two western interests to fuel the fears and dislikes of the region against federal ownership and management of the public lands. Fortunately, a courageous Colorado governor punctured their charade by vetoing their bill to take over the public lands in his state. Governor Richard Lamm showed that the small appropriation proposed would be wholly inadequate for administering the lands. It was sheer folly to challenge the federal government at the time when the Rocky Mountain states were battling a move in Congress to place a limitation on their use of the severance tax. In Utah, county administrators also became concerned about the Sagebrush Rebellion. They felt it could halt the flow of federal payments in lieu of taxes to the counties which contained federal lands. State officials also might be less responsive to users of the lands than were federal agents.[15]

The Sagebrush Rebellion quickly subsided when it became apparent that the chief objectives of the westerners were being accomplished through administrative actions ordered by Secretary of the Interior James G. Watt, the secretary of agriculture and the chief of the Forest Service. Offshore mineral rights were quickly offered for leasing, segments of the BLM lands were put up for sale, and mineral development in one or more National Monuments and Wildlife Reserves was permitted. These officials curtailed or failed to use appropriations for land management and made few requests to purchase lands for National Parks and other purposes. Appointees to the federal land agencies and courts showed a readiness to relax federal controls.

Environmentalists watched these changes with horror, and their outspoken and well-funded agencies (e.g., the Sierra Club and the Wilderness Society) took the issues into the courts. In some instances they forced the Reagan administration to use funds that Congress had appropriated for specific purposes, but which the administration had declined to use. But the power of the western economic interests seemed supreme.

At no time between 1850 and 1871, when Congress rapidly pushed railroad building through the West and granted land (two railroads also received more than fifty million dollars) to aid in construction, did the federal government intend to allow the railroads to retain unsold lands permanently. To prevent the Union Pacific and Central Pacific from retaining these tracts, the charter act of July 1, 1862, required that all granted land remaining unsold three years after the completion of construction "shall be subject to settlement and pre-emption, like other lands, at a price not exceeding one dollar and twenty-five cents per acre. . . ." Nevertheless the Union Pacific-Central Pacific, Northern Pacific, Santa Fe, and Southern Pacific retained large acreages, and today are among the principal owners of great blocks of land from the Rocky Mountains to the Pacific. Much of the land the transcontinentals sold went to large corporations interested in exploiting timber and grazing areas. The most startling was the Northern Pacific's huge sale of 900,000 acres to Frederick Weyer-haeuser, who earlier had bought 212,722 acres of timberland from the same railroad in Minnesota. In Arizona, the Atlantic & Pacific and Santa Fe railroads sold 1 million acres to the Aztec Land and Cattle Company and 258,873 acres to Dr. E. B. Perrin. This railroad ownership pattern continued into the twentieth century.[16]

The speedy alienation of land suitable for agriculture, mineral production, and timber cutting pleased westerners, who regularly encouraged the transfer of public lands to private hands. But they eventually expressed displeasure with the growing speculation, concentration of ownership, and creation of land monopolies. Land monopolists combined with the railroads to keep millions of acres free of or meagerly assessed for taxes. The Union Pacific, for example, kept its assessments in Wyoming well below what settlers had to pay on their land. Wyoming, as a territory and later as a state, may not have been a satrapy of the Union Pacific, but railroad officials exercised a powerful influence in political matters. This was also true in Arizona and Montana. In Arizona, mining companies and railroads kept their assessment rates at one-thirteenth of that of other properties. As for Montana, mining companies secured a constitutional limitation on taxes in 1889, and for three-quarters of a century enjoyed low taxes compared with rates on farms and railroads.

This was not a situation that the East or the federal government imposed on the West, but was what western voters tolerated. Colorado, the best-developed of the states straddling the Rockies, "fell under the control of absentee bankers and entrepreneurs," and became "a colonial economy," a pocket borough of the "corporate oligarchy." At the insistence of western congressmen, the federal government gave the enormously rich tidelands of California and the Gulf states to the states. There was no requirement that the profits from private exploitation be shared with governments at various levels, as federal income from mineral land leasing was so shared.[17]

The questions of mineral lands had not entered into early railroad land grants in the fifties. However, in 1862, in the midst of civil war, Congress was under great pressure ("imperative military necessity") to push railroad building to the West Coast. Since the Pacific railroad had to go through the gold- and silver-mining areas of California, Nevada, and Colorado (where Congress had left control over such claims to locally organized camps and later to the state), it was essential that the railroad should encounter no friction or litigation with mine owners. Mineral lands, therefore, were reserved—not granted—in 1862. In 1864 coal- and iron-bearing land was excluded from the reservation because of the need for fuel. The Union Pacific-Central Pacific were given twenty square miles of land for each mile of the road completed, together with large financial loans. The Atlantic & Pacific (a part of which fell to the Santa Fe) and the Northern Pacific received forty square miles of land for each mile of track, but received no bond bid. For those parts built through the states, these railroads were given twenty sections per mile.[18]

Neither the railroads nor the General Land Office (GLO) had an easy way to determine which lands contained minerals other than iron and coal. The earlier experience of the GLO with legislation affecting lead-bearing land had been most unsatisfactory, and it would be more so in regard to copper and iron lands in the future. Under pressure from the railroads, the GLO made a cursory investigation and declared that the lands the companies selected were nonmineral. In turn, some of the early railroad land sales to settlers carried no mineral reservations.[19]

The Union Pacific received 18,492,000 acres for its line from Kansas City to Cheyenne, via Denver, and for its main line from Omaha to Ogden. In 1982 the railroad still held 1 million acres in full ownership and 7 million acres of mineral rights in twelve western states. In this extensive acreage, the Union Pacific owned or shared ownership in 1.8 billion tons of coal, making it one of the largest owners of mineable coal in the country. By 1980, through its lessees, the Union Pacific shared in the profits of mining thirteen million tons of low sulphur coal. The coal was sold to Japanese companies and to power companies in Indiana and Illinois. These sales assured the railroad of a long haul of 1,195 miles from Wyoming to San Pedro, California, and 640 miles to Omaha.[20]

The Northern Pacific Railroad, which had a huge grant of 39,414,000 acres, faced a serious dilemma when it began separating the mineral rights upon the sale of land for agriculture. In early sales, the company included reservations, but soon found that buyers were not content. Northern Pacific officials came to think the reservations were a deterrent to sales. By 1900, however, the railroad was making reservations, and states were taxing the severed mineral rights. In 1918, the Northern Pacific offered to pay taxes on the mineral reservations at an assessed value of $50 per section. Most counties accepted this compromise, but refused where there were valuable coal deposits on the railroad land. On land deemed to have no valuable minerals, the company sold quit claims to the minerals for a modest price, thereby ridding itself of possible litigation. By 1952, the Northern Pacific still held mineral rights to 5,040,485 acres in the West from Montana to Washington.[21]

The Northern Pacific's successor, the Burlington Northern, claims ownership to 1.5 million acres of forest land between Bozeman, Montana, and Puget Sound. Included in the acreage are the summit of Mount St. Helens and 40,000 acres within sixteen miles of the volcano, much of which has since been declared a national monument. The Burlington Northern also owns 1.2 million acres of grazing lands, mostly in North Dakota and Montana, as well as 32,000 acres of irrigated land. Yet the company, despite its mineral, forest, and gas rights remains primarily a railroad.[22]

The Central Pacific, which built the line from Ogden, Utah, to the coast (now the Southern Pacific), the Southern Pacific line down the San Joaquin Valley to the Arizona-California boundary, and another line from Sacramento north to the Oregon boundary, was entitled to some 10 million acres, the larger part being in California. With other large landowners, the Central Pacific became involved in efforts to secure government water for its 160,000 acres in the Westland district in the San Joaquin Valley—and it naturally favored the Central Valley Project. From these highly productive lands, the company's receipts from leases reached $17,400,000 in 1981 and $18,400,000 in 1982. In 1981 the Southern Pacific's holdings remaining from its land grants included 3.7 million acres of land and mineral rights to 1.5 million acres. From its rentals, its oil, gas, and mineral royalties, and its sales of industrial and commercial properties, the company derived the sum of $194,500,000.[23]

Railroad ownership of large tracts of coal lands and increasing demand for the fuel led to a scramble for acreage still in the public domain. Under the Coal Land Act of 1873, coal properties lying more than fifteen miles from railroads sold for $10.00 an acre and those within fifteen miles for $20.00. As there was no scientific procedure for classifying these lands, large acreages containing coal passed to private ownership by the homestead route. Fearful of a monopoly of coal, and to halt the misuse of homesteading, Theodore Roosevelt withdrew 66 million acres thought to have coal to allow time for examination and classification of these lands for sale or leasing. This, in turn, led to an act in 1909 that allowed homesteading of surface rights only on coal lands. Two enlarged homestead acts increased the acreage that could be acquired to 320 and 640 acres but retained mineral rights in the government. Such separation of surface and sub-soil rights proved a major deterrent to new mining efforts in Wyoming and Montana and was made more so by an act of 1977. This act stated that under certain circumstances surface owners could delay mining of federal coal underlying their land for at least three years.[24]

Railroad land-grant policies left in their wake many unresolved issues. These issues included the avoidance of the fair share of local taxes the minerals should pay, difficulties of acquiring economic land-use units, divided administration of Oregon and California revested lands and Forest Service lands, and conflicts over water rights. The taxability of railroad lands and the long delays in assessing them produced strong complaints by landowners who had no easy way to avoid taxes once title was in their name. The demand for forfeiture of railroad lands, especially those granted without required railroad construction, took up much time in Congress in the seventies and eighties and culminated in a series of acts between 1870 and 1916 that forced railroads to return nearly 37 million acres to the public domain. Included were large grants intended for the Texas & Pacific and a part of the Atlantic & Pacific railroads. The Union Pacific and most of the Northern Pacific and Southern Pacific holdings remained intact.

The movement for forfeitures was part of the anti-monopoly fervor that swept the West and led to efforts to force the breakup of large individual holdings and ban alien ownership of land. The Anti-monopoly party had its heyday in Kansas and Nebraska, but its influence was felt throughout the West. It was particularly strong in the Northern Pacific country, where members urged forfeiture of the grant along the railroad route down the Columbia. But railroad influence in the Senate safeguarded the bulk of the grant.[25]

Over the years, concerted action by the western states might have forced the speedier forfeiture and cancellations of unearned grants in the West and substantially enlarged the total acreage recovered by the United States. However, railroad influence in the state capitals and in Washington ensured that the companies remained secure in their holdings.

The breakdown of the once efficient and competitive national railway system in a technological age that judges changes on the basis of profits and losses has been sad to contemplate. Built largely with private capital plus land grants and government loans, the railroads have been heavily taxed from their construction days. In the twentieth century they have had to compete with highly subsidized waterways, subsidized airlines flying out of government-built airports, and a highway transport system utilizing thousands of miles of roads built at public expense. These competing means of transportation plus the featherbedding practices that railroad brotherhoods successfully demanded, have brought about the bankruptcy of some railroads, the abandonment of many branch lines, and absorption of the passenger business by Amtrak and some freight lines and bankrupt companies into Conrail. Whether the railroads can continue to look to income from their grant lands to rescue them from financial woes is an interesting question.

The United States has an estimated 400 billion tons of coal and continues to depend heavily on this fuel for domestic and corporate use. In the early 1960s, interest in building coal slurry pipelines made news. In one of his more imaginative moments, President John F. Kennedy, speaking at Laramie, Wyoming, on September 25, 1963, not far from the huge coal resources of the Powder River, commented on the application of technology to the mining, transportation, and burning of coal in great steam generators. The federal government, Kennedy said, was already pursuing "new opportunities in coal . . . examining the feasibility of transporting coal by water through pipelines. . . ."[26]

Seven years later, the Bechtel Corporation completed a coal slurry pipeline for the Southern Pacific Railroad that ran 273 miles from Black Mesa, near Kayenta, Arizona, to the Mohave power plant in Nevada. The successful transportation of nearly five million tons of coal yearly, at about half the cost of hauling by rail, opened the eyes of business leaders, government agencies, and environmental organizations who questioned whether coal slurry pipelines might be successful elsewhere. Here was a major railroad owning and boasting of its coal slurry pipeline. Its success frightened other railroads more heavily involved in transporting coal. The Burlington Northern and Union Pacific quickly began a race to be the first to complete a fast freight line to the Powder River coal region. A new branch of the pipeline industry was about to open.

Several extensive coal slurry pipelines were planned. The project that carried major economic and political influence was the Energy Transportation System, Inc. (ETSI), which involved Bechtel, Atlantic Richfield, Lehman Brothers, and a number of gas pipeline companies. ETSI proposed building a slurry pipeline from the Powder River of Wyoming, where huge supplies of low sulphur coal were available, to Little Rock, Arkansas, and on to Louisiana. ETSI secured the promise of 50,000 acre feet of Missouri River water from the Oahe reservoir in South Dakota, and, before gaining approval of the needed rights-of-way, it made contracts totaling at least 3.8 billion dollars.[27]

The *New York Times* on June 1, 1982, reported that the sale of Missouri River water for a coal slurry pipeline to carry Wyoming coal to Louisiana had "provoked outrage and court challenges from conservationists, Sioux Indians, and several states downstream." However, South Dakota governor William J. Janklow supported the scheme. He stated that the Oahe and five other flood control dams built in his state had flooded nearly 600,000 acres, which were removed from production and the tax rolls, and the state had gotten little in return. South Dakota would profit from the fifty-year contract to the amount of $9 million a year and still would have more water for irrigation in the western part of the state than it had in the past. The Oahe dam had benefited only the lower states, he maintained. South Dakota's secretary of the Department of Water and Natural Resources called the deal "the most politically popular act in South Dakota in the last 25 years." But a downriver representative promptly introduced a measure in Congress to block a state from diverting water from an interstate basin unless all states in the basin approved.[28]

Altogether, thirteen proposals for coal slurry pipelines were planned, said a spokesman for the Association of American Railroads, who calculated that their construction could eliminate 41,000 railroad jobs. Even more important was the fact that coal traffic was vital to the welfare of a number of railroads, notably the Burlington Northern, Union Pacific, Illinois Central Gulf, CSX-Chessie, and Norfolk-Southern systems. The slurry pipelines would only carry coal, but the railroads also carry grain, livestock, and miscellaneous products. As coal provides the bulk of the operating costs of most railroads, what would noncoal shippers do for transportation when railroads quit hauling coal and revised their schedules? It is understandable why the western states, the National Grange, and the American Farm Bureau, which frequently are on opposite sides of economic questions, in this instance united to protest adoption of the slurry pipeline bill.[29]

Strong support for Congress to grant the right of eminent domain to the coal slurry pipeline companies came from large public utilities in noncoal states in the East, South, and Midwest which feared growing public resentment at their recent rate increases. The utility companies argued that the nation's railroads, freed from the authority of the Interstate Commerce Commission by the Staggers Rail Act of 1980, had pushed their rates to almost monopoly levels. Competition with slurry pipelines could restore competition and bring transportation rates down. The common argument in support of the pipelines was their greater efficiency and lower costs. To combat the pro-pipeline forces, the Association of American Railroads marshalled all its weapons, for it feared the members might lose all they had gained by the Staggers Act.[30]

Both House and Senate committees labored long over bills to grant the power of eminent domain to coal slurry pipeline companies. Ardent conservationists representing the western states (such as Morris Udall of Arizona and John Seiberling of Ohio) apparently supported the argument that the pipelines would be more efficient than the railroads for transporting coal. But dry state leaders also had to consider whether pipeline construction would threaten the water supplies needed for irrigation and domestic use. Some members of Congress became concerned over the effect the lines would have upon the railroads and their thousands of employees. Committees responsible for action on the pipeline bills voted their support, and there seemed to be a general belief that the House, which was first to act, would approve them. Yet, to the surprise of many, on September 27, 1983, the House voted 235 against and 182 for the eminent domain bill. Water was an overwhelming issue, but the probable economic plight of the railroads if the legislation were enacted proved the critical factor.[31]

How did the western states vote? One might think that the common need for water and the heavy dependence on railroads might have led Western congressmen to unite and vote against the coal slurry pipeline—but they did not. Representatives of the twelve public-land states voted 43 for to 39 against. Two states voted yes, while Idaho, Montana, and North Dakota gave no support. California's congressional delegation upset the balance by voting for the bill 28 to 16. Most of the coal slurry plans were to start in Wyoming. Its single member of Congress voted favorably, although the Burlington Northern and the Union Pacific were major employers in the state. Republicans generally favored the idea; Democrats were more inclined to oppose. The House vote thus put a quietus on coal slurry pipelines for the time being.

Both the *New York Times* (December 27, 1981) and the *Wall Street Journal* (January 27, 1982) had favored giving the coal slurry pipelines the right of eminent domain, mostly because the pipelines would be more energy efficient than the railroads. Utility spokesmen may have been correct in assuming that the transportation of miscellaneous products, including coal, was a deficient use of energy, while unit trains operating directly from mine to consumer were energy efficient. But arguments in opposition to the pipelines were equally valid: billions of capital were required for construction; interruptions would occur; and, most important, an excessive amount of water was needed—water that the states in question could not afford to allocate for the pipelines. President Ronald Reagan's position on the matter was awkward. He was trying to turn back to the states certain powers they had lost, yet pipeline legislation would be an unacceptable intrusion into their field of constitutional power. The West cannot agree on coal slurry pipelines.[32]

Conventional taxes, such as the property tax, were designed to produce essential revenue for governments—local, state, or national. Property taxes could not be based on ability to pay and had to be applied to all property at the same rate on its valuation. However, the rise of humanitarianism and the institution of public welfare programs in western states increased the costs of government and the need for more revenue. Many turned to the severance tax to help satisfy these needs. It was admirably adapted to provide revenue without reducing profits of producers, since it could be passed on to consumers. State severance taxes came to be extensively used in the West in the output and sale of oil and gas and were extended to the mining of coal, sulphur, potash, iron ore, and other minerals.

An early use of the state severance tax was in the 1930s, when Huey Long, as governor of Louisiana, had seized upon this measure, not because it was progressive but because he could use it as an additional source of revenue to provide free textbooks to children in public schools. Furthermore, it would hit hard the Standard Oil Company, a major oil producer in Louisiana which supported Long's political opponents.[33]

Once the states possessing great quantities of minerals, coal, oil, and gas learned how to use the severance tax, it became a major source of revenue for them. The total state severance taxes in the United States increased from $19,000,000 in 1932 to $2,493,000,000 in 1978 to $4,167,000,000 in 1980, and on to $7,838,693,000 in 1982. By 1980 thirty-four states were gathering severance taxes on products beyond coal, oil, gas, and other minerals. Oregon and Washington drew large incomes from a severance tax on the cutting of timber. (Pennsylvania even considered a tax on the transfer of electric power across the state boundaries.) Three western states with high income from severance taxes—Alaska, Montana, and Oregon—had no general sales or use taxes.

Consumer states were angered at the high severance taxes placed on coal by Montana and Wyoming, levied at 30 per cent and 12 per cent respectively. A Minnesota utility company complained that the Montana rates raised its costs of operation by more than $10 million. The tax in 1980 brought Montana $94,636,000 and Wyoming $105,361,000, whereas only a few years before these states were drawing small sums. But they had the coal, it was easily mined from the surface, labor costs were low, and, although it did not give as much heat as eastern coal, it was a premium product because of its low sulphur content. When some prairie states considered striking back by levying taxes on their corn and wheat, they quickly realized that, unlike Wyoming and Montana, they had large urban populations which would have to bear the tax burden.[34]

Severance taxes by western states were soon challenged by large coal users, notably the big eastern power companies. They took the matter into the courts and to Congress. The Supreme Court found nothing wrong with the Montana tax, although it appeared that out-of-state residents were paying it, since ninety per cent of the fuel market was beyond the state borders. A strange coalition was formed to protest severance taxes on coal mined on public lands. The group included the American Association of Retired Persons, the Teamsters, several AFL-CIO groups, Edison Electrical Institute, and the National Rural Electric Cooperative Association. The coalition supporting limits on severance taxes was unsuccessful.[35]

The severance tax, as commonly used, had a very different purpose from that of ordinary tax measures. Part of the returns were to be invested in permanent trust funds to supply income after minerals and fossil fuels were exhausted. Interest from these trusts would support worthy enterprises. For example, the Montana State Constitution of 1972 authorized the allocation of fifty per cent of the income from the severance tax to the Severance Trust Fund "to correct unforeseen environmental damage" and broaden the economic base of the state. Other parts would go to alternative energy research, to study the impact of mining on communities, and for education. Colorado in 1977 created a Severance Trust Fund for the local governments in the areas where the tax was collected.[36]

The protests by eastern utilities and other business interests against the severance tax on coal, particularly that of Montana and Wyoming, may be premature. Increasing concern about acid rain could ultimately force those companies relying on eastern coal, with its heavy sulphur fumes, to draw supplies from the Powder River region, despite the high severance tax. On the other hand, Wyoming and Montana severance taxes on coal were small compared with the taxes on oil being indirectly paid by consumers. In 1982, Wyoming and Montana coal taxes were 368 and 149 million dollars, while the oil tax by Texas and Alaska reached 2.3 billions and 1.5 billions.

By the early 1980s presidential disfavor and the reluctance of many lawmakers to interfere with the taxing power of the states dampened interest in tampering with severance taxes. Furthermore, only sixteen states (principally in the West) received income from this source. By 1982 Alaska's income from severance taxes constituted 61 per cent of its entire tax collections, Louisiana 38 per cent, North Dakota 35 per cent, Wyoming 30 per cent, Montana 28 per cent, and Texas 25 per cent. The severance tax had come to stay and proposals in Congress to limit its use found little support in the climate of antifederalism of the 1980s.[37]

For over a century, Americans have struggled with the problems created by limited rainfall west of the 98th meridian. In 1877 Congress offered 640-acre desert claims for $1.25 an acre to settlers who would irrigate the land but provided no financial aid to build dams and ditches. All the act did was to make it possible for large capitalists to gain ownership of land not otherwise open to them. In 1894, in the Carey Act, the federal government offered one million acres of dry land to each western state and territory to finance water projects and start farms. Both measures failed to attract settlers because they provided no government aid to create irrigated farms.

Finally, in 1902, Congress passed the Reclamation Act, which offered the means to make the arid lands productive. It assigned 95 per cent of the income from public land sales to a fund to provide for the construction of reservoirs and irrigation works. The act also withdrew from sale all public lands suitable for irrigation, preventing them from being grabbed up by speculators and corporations. The lands were to be granted to actual homesteaders in tracts of 40 to 160 acres. No person owning more than 160 acres would be entitled to water for more than 160 acres. The limitation implied that excess lands would have to be sold. Residence on the land or in the vicinity was required. The Reclamation Act did not call for new or continuing appropriations; the funds were to be spent in the states of their origin. Its greatest boon, which was not apparent at the time, would be an abundant and low-cost supply of electric power and water, not only for irrigation but also for domestic, industrial, and urban use. The estimated acreage that might be irrigated through this act ranged as high as 60 million acres.[38]

Questions soon arose. Was the purpose of the Reclamation Act only to create small farms of 160 acres on the semi-arid lands still in the public domain? Or was it also intended "to disintegrate the monopolistic holdings of land that prevail on the Pacific coast and in the intermountain region?" These monopolistic holdings had been acquired through "improvident" laws. Senator Francis Newlands, the author of the act, stated clearly: "The purpose of the bill is to prevent the monopoly of land . . . and to prevent these great tracts of land now under private ownership from obtaining water rights from the Government which will encourage monopolistic holdings." When asked why not convey the arid lands to the states and let them reclaim them through irrigation, Newlands's response was emphatically negative: the states were too impoverished to undertake the task and the result would be that the lands would fall to monopolists. The object, he added, was "to promote the division of large tracts of land which, under the unfortunate administration of state and national land laws, have been created in the West. Under this plan the West could reclaim itself without calling upon the general taxpayer for a dollar."

Newlands made no attempt to hide his views, and they were not challenged at the time—although President Theodore Roosevelt and Republican leaders stressed lesser objectives. Senator Frank Mondell of Wyoming differed from Newlands over the record of the states in administering their land grants, but Newlands was better informed. Mondell, a conservative Republican, declared, like Newlands, that the Reclamation Act was drawn with the intent of breaking up large landholdings in excess of 160 acres.[39]

The Reclamation Act was adopted during a period of great excitement about the large concentrations of public, forest, and mineral lands and water-power sites. Both Newlands and Mondell lived through this excitement and sought to prevent further monopolization of the public lands. They wanted to reserve those susceptible of irrigation for homesteads of 160 acres and to deny commutation privileges on these reserved lands. They also wanted to break up the large holdings through the acreage limitation. Newlands was quite caught up in Theodore Roosevelt's and Gifford Pinchot's concern about conserving natural resources and retaining in government ownership certain public lands, especially forest and mineral lands.

The Department of the Interior was given charge of the new Reclamation Service. It marshalled its Geological Survey—staffed with engineers and specialists in mapping topography and soils and calculating streamflow—and prepared to launch a large construction program. Interior officials paid no heed to the so-called agrarian myth that the family farm was the basis of American democracy. They probably disliked the Army Corps of Engineers moving into their field, by acquiring control of the waters of the Kern and Kings rivers, but they accepted the decision of Herbert Hoover's secretary of the interior to ignore acreage limitation and residence requirements in the rich Imperial Valley. In six instances, interior officials failed to enforce the Reclamation Act, and by the use of thirteen "techniques for meliorating acreage" (as one authority has said) they prevented its enforcement.[40]

The first test for the 160-acre limitation and residence requirement of the Reclamation Act and invitation to dispose of excess lands was in California. And it was in California, especially in the San Joaquin Valley, that some of the largest landholdings existed. Five included over a million acres, and hundreds of others ranged from five to ten thousand acres. Here also was the stronghold of the opposition to enforcing the acreage limitation. By the 1940s, the powerful American Farm Bureau Federation, the State Chamber of Commerce, the

Los Angeles Times and other important papers, the Republican party in California, and most of the state leaders in the Democratic party openly opposed the limitation.

The strongest support for enforcing the law came from a group of Democratic senators (Wayne Morse and Richard Neuberger of Oregon, Paul Douglas of Illinois, and Gaylord Nelson of Wisconsin), from George Ball and his National Land for People, and from a mixture of liberal social-welfare workers and church groups. Intellectual leadership was provided by Paul S. Taylor, professor of economics at the University of California, who wrote carefully drafted scholarly articles on acreage limitation, its history, and its repeated endorsement by Congress between 1910 and 1940. Taylor patiently showed congressional committees how firmly Congress had committed itself to the plan and how it was being weakened by administrative neglect.[41]

Little study has been made of the progress in opening small farms on the homestead lands reserved for settlers in the dry states, or of how large speculative landholders have disposed of their excess lands. (Only large landowners in the canning industry have done so.) This absence of study is regrettable, for these were the two objectives that Newlands and Mondell stressed. Nor did the Reclamation Service provide useful information on these issues. In California, it is known that the number of small farms (less than 100 acres) increased from 41,259 in 1900 to 59,104 in 1969.

During President Jimmy Carter's administration, the first concerted effort was made to revive the acreage limitation and compel large landowners to pay a fair share of the costs of reclamation water. Carter and his secretary of the interior, Cecil D. Andrus, former governor of Idaho, failed to make any headway because of a major blunder. They attacked the one major political issue that drove supporters into the opposition—water projects already authorized and being constructed and new projects under consideration. Their object was to eliminate projects to be subsidized largely by the federal government and from which small returns upon the cost could be expected. These, it was contended, should be partly financed by local governments. Westerners rushed into the Republican camp and Ronald Reagan and his followers moved to Washington to set things "right." Two years later, with firm Republican control in the Senate, Congress was easily persuaded to consider measures to "reform" the Reclamation Act of 1902.[42]

Bitterness against the effort by the Carter administration to eliminate new water projects and reduce appropriations for those moving to completion surfaced in the hearings and reports of Senate and House committees on reclamation projects and in efforts to "reform" the act of 1902. Gone from the Senate were the giants of the 1960s—Morse, Neuberger, Douglas, and

Nelson. The skilled talent of Paul S. Taylor, the country's greatest authority on acreage limitation, was no longer to be had. The leading environmentalists in the House—Morris Udall of Arizona, chairman of the House Committee on Public Lands, and his close associate, John F. Seiberling of Ohio—were so overwhelmed by a nearly united West clamoring for change that they voted for the "reform" bill, hoping that they could improve the measure in conferences in both houses. But time was running out.

The Reclamation Reform Act was adopted on October 12, 1982. The new law abandoned the small family farm movement which had been the central purpose of the act of 1902. Small farms had flourished in California throughout its history, but in the haste for change they were neglected. The Reclamation Reform Act raised the acreage limitation from 160 acres to 960 acres for farms that could receive federal water. Other provisions abolished residence requirements, approved the Corps of Engineers's exemption from all acreage restrictions on properties in the Kings and Kern river areas, and allowed federal water for land beyond the 960 acres if owners paid the full cost of it. The *Congressional Quarterly* summed up the critical response of environmentalists. The reform measure "largely affirmed the existing pattern of massive corporate farms, which they view as unfair and wasteful of water," and provided for additional irrigation but at a low and subsidized cost. By so doing, the act generated serious problems, both economic and political.[43]

Over the years, the Reclamation Service, spending billions on dams, has transformed the West. But in the process, competing interests surfaced, all demanding more water and power—a demand that could not be satisfied. A multitude of problems also appeared: salinity on irrigated soils; unsalable crops produced on large-scale agricultural holdings; and crops that required federal price supports. These interests now vie with new industries and rapidly developing cities in demanding more water. Water also is needed for the projected slurry pipelines. Proposals have been made to divert water from one watershed to another to meet these demands, but these ideas have divided western states and created bitter hostility about water "theft." At the same time, environmentalists oppose the construction of more high dams, saying they would ruin scenic areas and the popular sport of white water boating.

Nowhere does the West appear to be more divided than in the planning and carrying out of trans-basin water projects. During the New Deal years, the Central Valley Project in California called for the transportation of water from the Sacramento River to the San Joaquin Valley to irrigate hundreds of thousands of acres of productive land. This federal project was broadened by the California State Water Project, which brought 2.3 million acre feet of

Sacramento River water to water-deficient Southern California at a cost of 2.5 billion dollars. The latest plan, the Peripheral Canal, defeated by the California legislature on June 8, 1984, would have increased the amount of water that Southern California could get from Northern California. The project was estimated by its advocates to cost two billion dollars. Opponents set the figure at 20 billion![44]

Long before these developments, Los Angeles had captured the sources of water in the Owens Valley and built the necessary canals and aqueducts to convey it to the thirsty metropolis. But this supply soon proved insufficient for the rapidly growing city, which was attracting population, industry, and government enterprises at an astounding rate. The region's leaders turned their eyes to the Colorado River and sought a major share of its water. Aggressive leadership, smart politics, and the power of the growing bloc of seats that California controlled in the House of Representatives enabled the state to gain 4.4 million–acre feet of water from the Colorado. California itself provided little of the Colorado water, yet it obtained more than half of the amount which had been divided among the three lower basin states of California, Arizona, and Nevada. But as events have shown, the Colorado basin could not provide this large quantity to California—and also the water to fulfill promises to other upper and lower basin states, plus a commitment to Mexico.[45]

Another critical situation developed on the east slope of the Rocky Mountains in Colorado. Here, in the twentieth century, thriving cities have enjoyed remarkable growth, all requiring an ever-increasing amount of water. Yet even before World War I, local communities restricted the watering of lawns, so tight were supplies. There being no unused water available on the east side of the Rockies, they sought water rights on the western side. Securing these, they breached the mountains with four tunnels (one used the route of the Moffatt railroad) and constructed the Big Thompson Project. Together, these projects not only met community needs but also provided irrigation water to the thirsty farms in the Platte Valley.

These developments sparked resentment in the region. On the west slope, people felt that their water was feeding the growth of eastern Colorado and endangering prospects of developing irrigated land in their own area. At the same time, Kansas dry land farmers became distressed at the amount of water that Coloradans were taking from the Arkansas, thereby reducing the flow of that river and damaging Kansas farms. They brought suit in the federal courts, asking for reduction in the drafts the Coloradans were making. The Supreme Court, in a most interesting case, *Kansas v. Colorado*, recognized that Kansas had been somewhat damaged, but held that the Colorado benefits were of greater importance. The equitable apportionment of the Arkansas water had not been seriously impaired.[46]

Colorado also began diverting water from the Laramie River, which flowed northward into Wyoming. Wyoming sued to halt such pilferage. The Supreme Court decided that the flow of the stream that Wyoming had been using was equitable and Colorado could have the balance of the water. When the settlers in the Uncompahgre Valley in western Colorado found their water resources inadequate, they induced the Reclamation Service to build a 5.8-mile tunnel and many miles of canals to tap the surplus water of the Gunnison River.[47]

Dissention also arose over Columbia River water. The Columbia is second only to the Mississippi in the volume of its flow and, because of its high elevation in the mountains, it has more power sites and produces more power than any other river in the nation. Its great power resources have been harnessed at Grand Coule, Chief Joseph, Priest Rapids, Rock Island, McNary, John Day, and other dams, and its low-cost power has brought aluminum, pulp and paper, aircraft, and other industries to the Pacific Northwest. In addition, since 1933 the use of Columbia River water for irrigation has gone through a phenomenal development. Today, economists are studying carefully the loss of power from the dams caused by the heavy draw-down of water for irrigation.

In 1968, however, members of Congress, upon comparing the overdrawing of water from the Colorado, thought of it as greatly overused, but pronounced the Columbia as far from the full potential of its use. Vast quantities of Columbia River water flow into the ocean, whereas little water flows from the Colorado into the Gulf of California—and it is greatly deteriorated by its saline quality. Surely, thought some, the Columbia had more than it needed and could easily spare two million or more acre feet to the exhausted Colorado. But when the Central Arizona bill emerged from conference between committees of the two houses, it contained a section banning the study for ten years "of trans-basin augmentation of water from outside the area" drained by the Colorado. The "real gut issue" had been eliminated from the bill.[48]

The battle over the control of water in the West may be just beginning. Southern California lost a big battle in 1984 with the overwhelming defeat of the Peripheral Canal by a vote of the people of 62 to 38 per cent. The failure of efforts to have the Army Corps of Engineers investigate interbasin and interstate water projects plus Arizona's success in assuring its share of Colorado water means that other western states must diminish their water demands. A severe struggle over water looms. An article in the New York Times, June 13, 1962, suggested that the governors of the Lake states were concerned about possible efforts to use the resources of the Great Lakes in other areas. Governor Robert D. Orr of Indiana stated: "Our abundance of water and our stand against sending it elsewhere should send a signal to a lot of industries who might consider moving South." Another governor thought the only "water we should send out of here ought to go out in cans with malt and barley."

The Intermountain West is troubled with many problems today. There are no obvious solutions or easy compromises between conflicting views. The growing environmentalist movement, the advocates of more careful use of National Parks, and people concerned about the purity of water and the most desirable uses of water oppose those favoring the elimination of government controls on public lands. Mining is intruding into wilderness areas and is still wide open in much of the National Forests. Some of the mining is polluting water, and the problem of safeguarding supplies needed by expanding urban centers defies solution. Graduates of professional forestry schools, stressing the advantages of clear cutting of forests to assure better and more abundant wood supplies, clash with environmentalists listening to the sweet music from the Sierra Club and the Wilderness Society, organizations that advocate the preservation not only of specific wilderness areas but also more trees in scenic and tourist areas. Must oil and gas drillers and the hand of the realtor be allowed on the edge of Yosemite, Glacier, and other National Parks? Are they already close to Yellowstone and its geysers and other rare natural phenomena? People who watched the destruction of the giant redwood trees do not want that kind of vandalism to happen again.

Political quarrels such as these suggest that the West is becoming in many ways like the older parts of the country. Yet it has produced leaders of thought like the two Udall brothers, Cecil Andrus, Richard D. Lamm of Colorado, and Scott M. Matheson of Utah. These men recognize that land policies, reclamation issues, range management, and mining leases and coal slurry pipelines transcend the region and have national significance. Parochial decision making concerning these questions is scarcely statecraft.

The West's greatest opponent is not colonialism, as commonly charged, nor a jealous East or Midwest anxious to control, regulate, or curb the use of the public lands. Its greatest enemy is its own opposition to policies that would do much to improve its ranges, conserve its water resources, resolve its land problems, and provide an equitable distribution of its waters.

Notes

1. Throughout this paper, I have borrowed heavily from Paul W. Gates and Robert W. Swenson, *History of Public Land Law Development* (Washington, D. C., 1968).

2. DeVoto's editorials on "The West Against Itself" ran in volumes 194 (January 1947) to 209 (August 1954) in *Harper's Magazine,* but are more accessible in DeVoto's *The Easy Chair* (Harvard University Press, 1955), 231–347.

3. William K. Wyant, *Westward in Eden: The Public Lands and the Conservation Movement* (University of California Press, 1982), 2; Everett Dick, *The Lure of the Land: A Social History of the Public Lands from the Articles of Confederation to the New Deal* (University of Nebraska Press, 1970).

4. Wyant, *Westward in Eden* and Dick, *Lure of the Land* document the misuse of settler laws to gain ownership of public lands.

5. *One Third of the Nation's Land: A Report to the President and the Congress of the Public Land Law Review Commission* (Washington, D. C., 1970). Act of October 21, 1976, Public Law 94-579, *United States Statutes,* LXXXX, 2743-93.

6. *One Third of the Nation's Land,* 235–41. Act of October 20, 1976, Public Law 94-565, *U. S. Stats.,* LXXXX, 2662–66. Advisory Commission on Intergovernmental Relations, *The Adequacy of Federal Compensation to Local Governments for Tax Exempt Lands* (Washington, D. C., 1978), 5, 11–13; Paul W. Gates, *Pressure Groups and Recent American Land Policies* (Ithaca, New York: Cornell University Department of History, 1980), 20–32. Unlike the West, federal payments in the East, South, and Midwest are primarily applied to National Forest and Park lands.

7. The grants in lieu of taxes are annually reported in *Public Land Statistics,* issued by the Department of the Interior, as is revenue sharing of BLM funds, but not the Bureau of Forestry funds, which are shared with the states. The latter are included in the Department of Agriculture annual *Agricultural Statistics.*

8. Elizabeth Drew, "The Interior Department," *New Yorker,* May 4, 1981, 115.

9. Phillip O. Foss, *Politics and Grass: Administration of Grazing on the Public Domain* (University of Washington Press, 1960), 8–36; Gary D. Libecap, "Bureaucratic Opposition to the Assignment of Property Rights; Overgrazing on the Western Range," *Journal of Economic History* 41 (March 1981), 151–61.

10. E. Louise Peffer, *The Closing of the Public Domain: Disposal and Reservation Policies, 1900–1950* (Stanford University Press, 1951), 214–21, 247–73.

11. *One Third of the Nation's Land,* 106-8.

12. *House Report 94:1106,* 94 Congress, 2 Session (Serial 13134-6), 40–56; Public Law 94-579, *U. S. Stats.,* LXXXX, 2743.

13. Public Law 95-514, *U. S. Stats.,* LXXXXII, 1803.

14. Lander *High Country News* (Wyoming), February 5, 1982; Robert S. Maxwell, *La Follette and the Rise of the Progressives in Wisconsin* (Madison: State Historical Society of Wisconsin, 1956); K. Ross Toole, *The Rape of the Great Plains: Northwest America, Cattle and Coal* (Boston, 1976). Similarly, mining interests in the same public land states have kept at low levels the taxes they pay, and, more significantly, have prevented the modernization of the archaic mining law of 1872. Robert Marion La Follette brought the railroads and the lumber companies in Wisconsin to pay their

fair share of taxes in the first decade of the twentieth century, but in Montana similar interests held power until the seventies.

15. Richard D. Lamm to Colorado State Senate, June 5, 1981, vetoing Senate bill 170, the Sagebrush bill. Copy in author's possession. Frank J. Popper, "The Timely End of the Sagebrush Rebellion," *The Public Interest,* No. 76 (Summer 1984), 61–73; Lander *High Country News,* February 5, 1982.

16. Section 3 of the Act of July 1, 1862, to provide for the construction of the Pacific Railway, *U. S. Stats.,* XII, 492; Ralph Hidy *et al., Timber and Men: The Weyerhaeuser Story* (New York, 1963), 106, 212; William S. Greever, *Arid Domain: The Santa Fe Railway and Its Western Land Grant* (Stanford University Press, 1954), 46–47; Sanford A. Mosk, *Land Tenure Problems in the Santa Fe Railroad Land Grant Areas* (University of California Press, 1944), 13.

17. T. A. Larson, *Wyoming: A Bicentennial History* (New York: W. W. Norton, 1977), 146 ff; J. J. Wagoner, *Arizona Territory, 1863-1912* (University of Arizona Press, 1970), 442; Robert W. Larson, "Populism in the Mountain West: A Mainstream Movement," *Western Historical Quarterly* 13 (April 1982), 211–27; Toole, *Rape of the Great Plains,* 80–125.

18. Nelson S. Trottman, *History of the Union Pacific: A Financial and Economic Survey* (New York: Ronald Press Company, 1923), 15; Charles E. Ames, *Pioneering the Union Pacific: A Reappraisal of the Builders of the Railroad* (New York, 1969), 11 ff; Robert G. Athearn, *Union Pacific Country* (Chicago: Rand, McNally & Company, 1971), 19 ff.

19. Ross R. Cotroneo, *The History of the Northern Pacific Land Grant, 1900-1952* (New York, 1979), 308–53.

20. Union Pacific Corporation, *Annual Report, 1981,* 2; Lander *High Country News,* February 5, 1980; Samuel P. Hays, *Conservatism and the Gospel of Efficiency: The Progressive Conservation Movement, 1890-1920* (Harvard University Press, 1959), 82 ff.

21. Cotroneo, *Northern Pacific Land Grant,* 308–54, describes the Northern Pacific treatment of its mineral lands.

22. The Burlington Northern states in its *Annual Report* for 1981 (p. 4) that it originated the shipment of 112 million tons of coal that year.

23. Under the Reclamation Reform Act of 1982, the Central Pacific may have to sell these tracts in sizes up to 960 acres, so they will be entitled to federal water. In its 1981 *Annual Report* (p. 8), the Southern Pacific conceded that, contrary to the objectives of the framers of the congressional grants, its primary goal "is to optimize total return through a combination of current income and long-term capital appreciation."

24. By 1916 a total of 140,533,745 acres of public land had been withdrawn for classification, of which 73,603,780 had been determined as noncoal-bearing land and had been restored to entry. Hays, *Conservation and the Gospel of Efficiency,* 93–94.

25. David M. Ellis, "The Forfeiture of the Railroad Land Grants, 1867–1894," *Mississippi Valley Historical Review* 33 (June 1946), 27–60; and the same author, "The Oregon and California Railroad Land Grant," *Pacific Northwest Quarterly* 39 (October 1948), 253–83; Leslie E. Decker, *Railroads, Lands, and Politics: The Taxation of the Railroad Land Grants, 1864-1897* (Brown University Press, 1964); and Elmo Richardson, *BLM's Billion-Dollar Checkerboard: Managing the O and C Lands* (Santa Cruz, California: Forest History Society, 1980).

26. *Public Papers of the Presidents: John F. Kennedy, 1963* (Washington, D. C., 1964), 722.

27. On ETSI, see "Organizational Conflict of Interest in Government Contracting," in *Hearings Before the Subcommittee on Energy Research and Water Resources of the Committee on Interior and Insular Affairs,* 94 Cong., 1 Sess., 48 ff, especially appendix. Also see *Annual Reports* of the Burlington Northern, Union Pacific, and Southern Pacific for 1980-1984. These reports (and others) are available on microfilm at the Graduate School of Management at Cornell and also at the Harvard Business School.

28. Lander *High Country News,* June 11, 1982; *Congressional Record,* 97 Cong., 1 Sess., 12617. ETSI also planned a second coal slurry pipeline from the Appalachian and Illinois basins to the East. It would carry fifty-four million tons of coal annually to major eastern centers. The promoters of this project (estimated at five billion dollars) maintained that they could save as much as fifty-four billion dollars over a century with this method of transporting coal.

29. Association of American Railroads, *Rail News,* Number 2344 (April 7, 1982) to 2354 (August 25, 1982), and No. 2403 (August 8, 1984).

30. *Congressional Quarterly Weekly Report,* January 16, February 20, March 13, 1982, 85, 92, 323, 564-66. *New York Times,* July 30, 1982.

31. *Congressional Quarterly Weekly Report,* October 1, 1983, 2034. Because the temporary edition will be replaced by a final edition of the *Congressional Record,* it seems best to use the *Congressional Quarterly.*

32. Despite their need for water and railroads, western representatives tended to support coal slurry pipeline legislation. Western representatives from the dry states voted 43 to 39 for it. The vote of the western-dominated committee on Interior and Insular Affairs was 27 to 13. Chairman Udall was astonished when the House vote was tabulated. *Congressional Quarterly Weekly Report,* April 9, 1983, 705; *Congressional Record,* 97 Cong., 2 Sess, E72. Arizona is not water rich, but it has allowed the Southern Pacific to use water for its pipeline from Kayenta to Mohave, Nevada, to operate the great power station there.

33. T. Harry Williams, *Huey Long* (New York, 1970), index. K. Ross Toole, in his admirable study of the incidence of taxation in Montana, *The Rape of the Great Plains,* 80-125, found that the great mining companies largely escaped paying a fair share of taxes, while their workers had no means of evading such obligations.

34. The Montana tax was not uniform for all coal. Coal with a low BTU rate was taxed 20 per cent and that over 7,000 BTU per pound was taxed 30 per cent. Senator Max Baucus stated that the tax applied to Montana users as well as those outside the state. *Congressional Record,* 96 Cong., 1 Sess., 31147.

35. *Commonwealth Edison Corp. v. Montana,* 453 U. S. Reports, 609.

36. *Session Laws of Montana,* 46th Legislature, 1979, 2:1385; *Session Laws of Wyoming,* 46th Session, 1979, 15. By 1981 the Montana permanent trust funds had grown to $85 million, and Wyoming's permanent mineral trust fund had reached $214 million. Wyoming's severance tax on coal was only 10.5 per cent of the value of coal, as compared with Montana's 30 per cent. Lander *High Country News,* July 10, 1982. These funds are reminiscent of the Heritage Savings Trust Fund of Alberta, Canada, now approximating $10 billion, and a similar fund in which Alaska is investing the bulk of its huge royalties from the Prudhoe Bay oil development.

37. Remarkably useful is *Facts and Figures on Government Finance: 21st Edition* (Washington, D. C., 1981), 222-25.

State Severance Tax Collections of Public Land States
(Three zeros omitted)

	1960	1970	1976	1980	1982
Alaska	1,448	10,780	27,978	506,469	1,571,583
Arizona	—	—	—	—	—
California	1,184	1,632	2,334	25,954	27,911
Colorado	2,811	1,058	4,375	31,121	49,184
Idaho	84	264	394	1,905	2,517
Montana	2,950	4,730	31,344	94,636	149,361
Nevada	49	50	148	23	—
New Mexico	16,482	35,398	87,485	213,643	377,802
Oregon	659	1,937	3,458	50,592	50,480
Utah	3,869	4,272	11,723	10,584	22,295
Washington	—	—	—	—	—
Wyoming	235	4,268	4,268	105,700	389,361

Compiled from *ibid.*, 1970-1983.

38. Act of June 17, 1902, *U. S. Stats.*, XXXII, 388. *House Report 1468,* 57 Cong., 1 Sess., Volume 6 (Serial 4404); *Senate Report 254,* 57 Cong., 1 Sess. (Serial 4257). Useful on irrigation is William E. Warne, *The Bureau of Reclamation* (New York, 1973); and Elmo Richardson, *Dams, Parks & Politics: Resource Development & Preservation in the Truman-Eisenhower Years* (University Press of Kentucky, 1973).

39. *Congressional Record,* 56 Cong., 2 Sess., 386, 1701; *ibid.,* 57 Cong., 1 Sess., 6674-78. Despite a clear statement of the purpose of the framers, Senators Francis G. Newlands and Frank W. Mondell, see William L. Kahrl's excellent but different interpretation in *Water and Power: The Conflict over Los Angeles' Water Supply in the Owens Valley* (University of California Press, 1982), 31-32.

40. Harry J. Hogan illustrates these techniques and methods of "meliorating the acreage limitation" in *Acreage Limitation in the Federal Reclamation Program* (Arlington, Virginia: National Water Commission, 1972), 81-102.

41. The five largest holders of San Joaquin Valley land were Boswell (183,000 acres), Chevron (261,000), Southern Pacific (197,000), Tejon Ranch (260,000), and Tenneco Co. (260,000). Ellen Liebman, *California Farmland: A History of Large Agricultural Landholdings* (Totowa, New Jersey: Rowman & Allanheld, 1983), 188-208. Paul S. Taylor's *Essays on Land, Water, and the Law in California* (New York, 1979) have never been answered except by the will of Congress.

42. The preliminary edition of the *Congressional Record* and the many hearings on Reclamation policy constitute the major sources now available, but listing takes too much space. Of the numerous hearings of House and Senate committees, the following are important: *Hearings Before the Subcommittee on Water and Power Resources of the Committee on Interior and Insular Affairs to Revise the Requirements of Federal Reclamation Law,* 96 Cong., 1 and 2 Sess. (Washington, D. C., 1981); *Hearings Before the Committee on Energy and Natural Resources United States Senate, on Reclamation*

Reform Act of 1981, 1981-1982, 96 Cong., 1 and 2 Sess. (Washington, D. C., 1982); *Congressional Record*, 97 Cong., 2 Sess., H901; and *Congressional Quarterly*, April 24, 1982, 944.

43. The question of the use of water for irrigation and for higher purposes is discussed in Diane Jones, *Water, Energy & Land. Public Resources & Irrigation Development in the Pacific Northwest; Who Benefits & Who Pays* (Boise, Idaho: Idaho Citizens Coalition, Boise, 1981); *Congressional Quarterly Weekly Report*, September 25, 1982, 2404.

44. *Facts on File* (1980), 632. Philip L. Fradkin, *A River No More: The Colorado River and the West* (New York, 1981); Norris Hundley, Jr., *Dividing the Waters: A Century of Controversy Between the United States and Mexico* (University of California Press, 1966); Kahrl, *Water and Power;* and his *California Water Atlas* (Sacramento, California: Governor's Office of Planning and Research, 1979), 31–45.

45. Kahrl, *California Water Atlas*, 46–57.

46. *Kansas v. Colorado*, 206 U. S. Reports, 117.

47. Carl Ubbelohde *et al., A Colorado History* (Boulder, Colorado: Pruett Press, 1976), 260–65; Robert G. Athearn, *The Coloradans* (University of New Mexico Press, 1976), 286; *Wyoming v. Colorado*, 259 U.S. Reports, 419.

48. *Congressional Quarterly Almanac* 24 (1968), 443–51; *Congressional Record*, 90 Cong., 2 Sess., 26670–26715; *Arizona v. California*, 373 U. S. Reports (1962–1963), 546–646, especially 592.

9

Canadian and American Land Policy Decisions, 1930*

With Lillian F. Gates

Lillian F. Gates, historian of Canadian land policy, and Paul W. Gates, historian of American land policy, wrote this joint article in 1984 for presentation at the annual meeting of the Organization of American Historians. They explain how Canada and the United States faced similar dilemmas concerning nationally owned lands in the territories at the time of state and provincial creation. Should they be retained by the central government or given to the new province or state? Both national governments retained them. The litigious aftermath of these decisions in both nations was strikingly similar up to 1930 when after a special committee review, the United States took a policy stance of continuing to hold federal lands in the western states, and Canada, putting an end to protracted disputes, opted to give such lands to the provinces. Fifty years later this land ownership issue tested the federal systems of both nations. Gates and Gates provide a broad interpretive framework for understanding the Sagebrush Rebellion, very thoughtful analysis of how riches in oil spawned Alberta's expansive political ambitions, and most particularly how provincial control of vast petroleum reserves related to the oil crises of the late 1970s in Canada, the United States, and in the world economy. Alberta's oil wealth forced constitutional changes in the federal system into the limelight during the Trudeau years. This article authored by the Gates husband-and-wife team reflects their many years of mutual professional support and intellectual stimulation extending back to Harvard graduate-school days.

*From *Western Historical Quarterly* 15 (October 1984), 389–405. Used by permission of the publisher, the Western Historical Society. All rights reserved.

Canada and the United States both stood at the crossroads in 1930 with respect to their remaining public lands in the West, the best of which had been selected by homesteaders, dry-land farmers, ranchers, lumbermen, and speculators in real estate. Scenic and forested areas had been placed in permanent reservations for public enjoyment and for the scientific management of their resources. Much of the remaining public land, particularly in the United States, was thought to be fit only for grazing, and that would require larger units of land than had been previously distributed. Other public land, too dry for ordinary farming, needed irrigation, which could be provided only by the construction of costly storage reservoirs on major streams.

Despite numerous similarities in the disposal of their public lands, both countries in 1930 made far-reaching and sharply different decisions that were to profoundly affect their future and to subject federalism to serious strains.[1]

In the western states, long-smoldering discontent with federal ownership of the public lands and federal land policies has existed. In every instance, acts for the admission of new states declared that admission placed them "on an equal footing with the original states in all respects whatever."[2] Clearly this was not the fact. The thirteen original states, plus Vermont, Kentucky, Tennessee, and Maine had kept ownership of the public lands within their borders, and Texas when annexed was permitted to retain all 178 million of its acres that had not passed into private hands. But the new states created out of the public domain were not given title to the land. We may say that in the minds of the people of the time ownership of the public lands was an attribute of state sovereignty. Also, the acts of admission denied the new states the right to tax the public lands, even those that were sold, until five years after purchase.[3] This five-year restriction on the ability of the new states to raise revenue was an impediment to their growth and did them serious harm until it was repealed in 1847. Landless states have never forgotten these discriminations in the acts of admission, despite the efforts of the federal government to pacify them. The Sagebrush Rebellion is just another in a long line of efforts on the part of the public land states to gain cession of the public lands within their borders.

Similar discontent had existed in the prairie provinces of Canada. The four eastern provinces that entered Confederation in 1867—New Brunswick, Nova Scotia, and United Canada, that is, old Ontario and Quebec—had all retained the management of, and revenues from, their public or Crown lands. Title to ungranted land was and still is in the Crown, but the beneficial use and legislative control of the land had passed to those provinces by various concessions made between 1835 and 1854.[4] At Confederation, by section 37 of the British North America Act, the four provinces retained control of the public property that "belonged" to them, except what proved to be needed by the new Dominion of Canada for fortresses and purposes of defense.[5] Yet, when the Dominion later created three new prairie provinces, like the United States it retained control of the land itself.

From the admission of the first public land state (Ohio), in 1803, the unpopularity of the decision to retain the public lands in federal ownership was made manifest. It was only the anxiety for the powers that statehood would give that brought the residents to accept this situation. Also, the framers of the various admission acts did their utmost to relieve the tensions of the moment. New states were promised millions of acres as aid to public schools, for the construction of roads, canals, public buildings, and later for railroads. Altogether 326 million acres were given or promised to the states. The percentage of their total area thus granted ranged from 3 per cent in Nevada to 68 per cent in Florida. It must be said that state administration of the school, swamp, and other land grants during the nineteenth century was exceedingly poor, with boodler and land-speculator influence dominant in hastening the transfer of the land to private owners.[6]

Revenue sharing was the second device worked out between the United States and the discontented public land states to give them a share in the revenue from the public lands. From the admission of Ohio, each public land state was promised 5 per cent of the net returns from the sale of lands for the building of roads to and through the states and for public schools. In the Newlands Act of 1902 congress assigned 95 per cent of the income from public land sales in the sixteen states west of the 95th meridian to a revolving fund for the construction of dams to make possible irrigation of arid lands.[7] From this point on the government was never to retain for itself even the cost of making surveys and sales.

Most productive of the revenue-sharing devices has been the Mineral Leasing Act of 1920. Under its terms, 52½ per cent of the revenues from the leasing of coal, oil and gas, potash, and phosphate sites on the public land flows into the reclamation fund, and an additional 37½ per cent is paid to the state of origin.[8] Receipts from mineral leasing from 1920 to 1982 alone totaled over six billion dollars. Other revenue-sharing programs assigned to the states of origin 25 per cent of the income from grazing leases and timber cutting.[9] Twenty Oregon counties get an extraordinarily generous return of $98 million annually from the forfeited Oregon and California Railroad land grant, which includes prime Douglas Fir.[10] Today, well over a billion dollars from federal management of the public lands is returned annually to the West.[11]

A third device to quiet western resentment against the continued retention of the public lands by the federal government is the Payment in Lieu of Taxes Act of October 20, 1976. The amount of $100 million is thus added to the payments to the states having public lands. Through revenue sharing and grants in lieu of taxes, the four most benefited states in 1980 were Oregon, $224 million; Wyoming, $123 million; New Mexico, $117 million; and California, $87 million.[12]

Still another grant to the states, and the most generous of all, was made by the Submerged Land Act of 1953, which gave coastal states title to the land from the high water mark to the three-mile limit, with all their mineral resources.[13] These tidelands have been valued as high as $200 billion. Principal beneficiaries have been California, Texas, and Louisiana, but no one in these states had the wit to provide through taxation and royalties for building heritage funds for future needs when the oil is gone, as Alaska and Alberta have done.

Notwithstanding these extraordinary revenue-sharing plans by which a large part of the income from public lands is returned to the public land states, these states continue to complain that arrogant bureaucrats are arbitrary and uselessly formal in applying legal restrictions to users of the lands and that these lands should be given to the states where local interests would prevail. That might mean they would soon pass to private ownership.[14]

With the great exception of Theodore Roosevelt, Republican presidents have consistently resisted the conservation movement, whose advocates have sought to retain much of the remaining public lands in federal ownership and under scientific management. From Taft, through Harding, Hoover, Eisenhower, Nixon, and Reagan they have seemed determined to blunt, if not to reject, what has been accomplished in the way of conservation. Herbert Hoover went so far as to propose to convey to the states much of the remaining lands in federal ownership, but he insisted that they should be given organized public management.

By 1930 there remained 190 million acres of public lands that were vacant, unreserved, and not withdrawn from public acquisition, referred to as BLM lands.[15] In addition, there were 21 million acres on which settlement or mining rights had been established, 210 million acres in national forests, national parks, and Indian reservations, and 70 million acres that had been withdrawn from entry for various other purposes.[16] The vacant, unreserved, and withdrawn BLM lands were mostly suitable only for grazing and spotty mining. They had been the scene of range wars between the cattlemen and sheepmen and later with homesteaders seeking the 640 acres free grants offered under the Stock Raising Homestead Act of 1916. Since the land was too dry for tillage farming without irrigation, the livestock interests had prevailed in their use. They criticized the government for its slowness in extending surveys and its invitation to homesteaders who cut up the ranges with their fences and

attempted to farm unsuitable land. It was these 190 million acres (their surface rights only) that President Hoover proposed should be conveyed to the
states. Reflecting western sentiment, he declared that "our Western states have
long since passed from their swaddling clothes and are today more competent
to manage" the lands "than is the Federal Government. Moreover, we must
seek every opportunity to retard the expansion of federal bureaucracy and to
place our communities in control of their own destinies." He proposed the
appointment of a land commission to investigate and make recommendations
respecting the remaining vacant lands.[17]

Having indicated the nature of the report he expected, Hoover appointed to
the Committee on the Conservation and Administration of the Public Domain
a number of able bureaucrats, more Republican wheelhorses, and some persons for window dressing.[18] They brought in an able report expanding on the
president's recommendations. Included were four major points:

(1) All portions of the vacant, unappropriated, and unreserved public
    lands should be given controlled management by the states or the
    federal government.
(2) Areas useful for defense, reclamation, reservoir sites, and national
    parks and forests should be reserved for these purposes.
(3) Remaining areas valuable for forage should be granted to the states
    without mineral rights.
(4) In the states not accepting administrative responsibility, the federal
    government must undertake controlled scientific management.

The rock on which the recommendations of the Hoover committee foun-
dered was its failure to deal with the known mineral lands then producing
coal, oil and gas royalties, which were providing revenue for reclamation and
for the states of origin, and Hoover's insistence on retaining the mineral rights
in the BLM lands to be granted to the states. With withdrawn mineral lands
not included and the mineral rights on BLM lands reserved to the United
States, few westerners could see any advantage in accepting only the surface
rights, whose administration costs would be high and whose returns would
be small.[19]

Why was there no effective opposition in 1930 to retaining the public lands
in federal ownership? It was partly owing to the overwhelming effects of
the countrywide depression. Western states with meager credit were driven
to ask for federal aid in meeting the agricultural crisis and in staying out of
bankruptcy. Their banks were rushing toward closing and their hopes were
centered on more federal intervention, not less. Resisting the federal jugger-
naut was not timely.[20] Furthermore, the United States had just undertaken to

finance its greatest, and indeed the world's greatest, water project by building Boulder (now Hoover) Dam on the Colorado. It was expected to save the rich Imperial Valley of California from angry flood waters, bring low-cost water to parched areas of the West, and provide cities with cheap power that would attract industries to them.[21] The timing of the Hoover proposal was bad, for when the report came before Congress, executive leadership had reached a low point and Congress was looking to Franklin Roosevelt's New Deal for a better way to handle the much-needed controls on the grazing lands. That came in 1934 with the adoption of the Taylor Grazing Act, which avoided state ownership and questions over mineral land by retaining all in federal hands.[22]

Meanwhile in Canada, a roadblock to expansion into the West was the Hudson's Bay Company. Rupert's Land—the area drained by rivers falling into Hudson's Bay—had been granted to the company by royal charter in 1670. The company had also obtained a license in 1821 that gave it a monopoly of trade but not proprietary rights in the area between Rupert's Land and the Pacific Coast. The license was not renewed in 1859 and the charter was surrendered in 1869. Canada agreed to give the company £300,000 and one-twentieth of the land in the Fertile Belt south of the Saskatchewan River.[23] The areas once controlled by the Hudson's Bay Company were added to the new Dominion of Canada by the Rupert's Land Act of 1868 and an Imperial Order in Council of 1870.

By 1871, the year she entered Confederation, British Columbia became a self-governing colony with an executive responsible to its legislature. Like the other four provinces, she kept control of her Crown lands, a power she had enjoyed for some years although it had not been specifically conceded to her legislature.[24] British Columbia had demanded the construction of a railroad that would tie the Pacific coast province to the rest of Canada as part of her terms for entering Confederation. She granted the Dominion a belt of land twenty miles wide on each side of the route, to be held in trust for the construction of the railway. Canada also needed the railway. It would enable British emigrants and landless Canadians then going to the United States to settle in the Canadian prairies instead. Unless this was accomplished quickly, the infiltration of American settlers might lead to the loss of the territory. The land grant railroads of the United States had demonstrated how the construction of railroads through undeveloped country could be financed. The Dominion government had been practically landless, but it now had land with which to subsidize a railway to the Pacific.

The British North American Act of 1867 provided for the admission of other existing British North American colonies—British Columbia, Newfoundland, and Prince Edward Island—into the Dominion, whenever both

parties requested it. A second BNA Act of 1871 empowered Canada to create new provinces out of the western territory she had recently received. The
first province to be created was Manitoba, which was given the legislative and
judicial powers the older provinces had received, but not control of the ungranted lands within her borders. Also, Manitoba was created with limited
boundaries containing but one-twentieth of its present area. These limitations
were hotly contested when the Manitoba bill was under consideration. Sir
John A. MacDonald, Canadian prime minister, explained that the new province must be confined to the more settled area. It was obviously impossible to
hand over the vast area of Rupert's Land to be legislated for by the few people
then resident there. Also, the lands had to be retained by the government of
Canada "for the purposes of the Dominion."

What were these purposes? Canada had obligations to fulfill for which
control of the land was necessary. £300,000 had to be paid to the Hudson's
Bay Company as part of the terms on which the company had surrendered its
charter. It had also been agreed that the company should retain ownership of
one-twentieth of the "Fertile Belt," the area south of the Saskatchewan River.
Canada also had to satisfy the claims of the half-breed families for land, for
which 1.4 million acres would be necessary. Most important, the Dominion
insisted on keeping control of the land to enable it to provide for building the
railway to the Pacific upon which British Columbia was insistent. For that
a land subsidy was needed. If the lands were left in the control of the new
provincial legislature, there might be difficulty in getting the railroad built.
Second, it was Canada's policy to foster immigration from the older areas and
from the mother country. Settlement was essential if the West was to remain
in British hands, yield revenue, and maintain a railway. Provincial ownership
would not necessarily assure these objectives.[25]

When Manitoba's boundaries were enlarged in 1881 and 1912, she did not
get control of the land in these new areas, although both Ontario and Quebec
did get the land when their boundaries were enlarged. When two more prairie provinces—Saskatchewan and Alberta—were created in 1905, they also
were denied control of the land. Again it was retained by the government of
Canada "for the purposes of the Dominion." This now meant getting the new
provinces settled by offering free homesteads.

The Dominion recognized that without their public lands the new provinces would need revenue. By the Manitoba Act the Dominion agreed to pay
two annual subsidies—one a fixed sum, the other to be increased with the
growth of population. Alberta and Saskatchewan were granted similar subsidies but on more generous terms, which were later applied to Manitoba
also. The Alberta and Saskatchewan subsidies were specifically stated to be

"in lieu of public lands" and because the provinces "would not have public land as a source of revenue." It was feared at the time that the phrasing of these subsidy provisions would be used (as it was) by those provinces to contend that the Dominion had clearly recognized from the start that the lands belonged to them and ought to be under provincial control.[26]

The Dominion government did not give the prairie provinces their natural resources until 1930 and then only after a long controversy.[27] Long before that date the main purpose of the Dominion in retaining the land had been achieved. When Manitoba raised the question in 1884, the Dominion government pointed out that it was pledged to reserve a portion of the land for homesteads and two sections in every township for schools by the Federal Land Act of 1872. These obligations, in the event of a transfer of the lands, would have to be assumed by Manitoba.[28] By 1912 all three provinces joined in asking for their natural resources. The provinces regarded the annual subsidies granted in lieu of lands as "compensation for lands already alienated for the benefit of Canada," and they asked that all the remaining public lands within their boundaries with all natural resources included be transferred to them. They were told that they might have their way but would lose the annual subsidies they had been receiving, partly at the expense of the other provinces of Canada. The dispute was dropped for the duration of the war, and when it was revived in 1920, the same answer was given: the resources, yes, but without the subsidies.[29] From this time forward the provinces pressed their case not on the basis of subsidies in lieu of land but by claiming a constitutional right to the lands as self-governing colonies with responsible government.

After 1925 the natural resources question became more complicated and was argued with more intense feeling on both sides. Some spokesmen for the prairie provinces questioned whether the Dominion ever had any right to the lands. Was it not an established principle of the British Empire that when a colony became self-governing and provided its own civil list it became entitled to the beneficial use and control of its natural resources?[30]

Then there were disputes over the interpretation of the BNA Act. It gave the Dominion power to create new provinces, but did it give her power to create new provinces inferior in status to the older ones, that is, without their natural resources?[31] They should be compensated for the land that went to subsidize the Canadian Pacific Railway and that was allotted to the Hudson Bay Company—arrangements that had benefited all Canada, but it was the prairie provinces that had paid. In addition, by "an autocratic act" they had been restricted from taxing C.P.R. land for twenty years.[32] For all this they should receive compensation offset by the subsidies they had received. To make matters worse, representatives of some of the eastern provinces insisted that they had an undoubted proprietary interest in every acre since they had helped to purchase them from the Hudson Bay Company and to develop them by means of the Canadian Pacific Railway.[33] One eastern representative even reinforced his argument that the four eastern provinces had a right to a share in the nation's land by referring to the American Distribution Act of 1836 and to the Morrill Act of 1862, which he said clearly upheld the right of all the states to a share in the public domain.[34]

By 1929 all political parties were agreed that the long, drawn-out dispute over the natural resources must be settled. The Dominion government announced that it was ready to place the prairie provinces "in a position of equality with the other provinces . . . with respect to the administration and control of their natural resources." The British North America Act of 1930 transferred to the provinces the interest of the Crown in all Crown lands, mines, minerals (precious and base), and royalties derived therefrom with all sums due from these resources, water and water powers, and rights of fishery, reserving to the Dominion only lands occupied by Indians, the national parks, land necessary for fortresses and defense, and certain specified public works. The subsidies paid in the past to the provinces in lieu of land were now readjusted, not terminated. It was also provided that to place the prairie provinces on a basis of equality, they should be compensated by additional sums for not having control of their natural resources from the day of their creation. Joint commissions were to be created to calculate this sum, offsetting it by the expenditures of the Dominion on their behalf. Manitoba had made her bargain with the Dominion by 1930, but it was 1947 and 1948 before the Alberta and Saskatchewan commissions concluded their work.[35]

British Columbia, also long dissatisfied with her treatment by the Dominion government, had been pressing for better terms since 1918. She got them in 1930 when the lands she had given the federal government to aid in construction of the railway were returned to her. This province also was to continue to receive an annual subsidy.

Half a century after Canada in 1930 had satisfied the demands of her prairie provinces for full equality with the older provinces and after the American West had let slip the opportunity to gain control of the public lands, serious disputes over the natural resources question have developed in both countries.

By the late 1970s economic users of the public lands had come to regret the failure of their states to gain ownership to part of the public lands as urged by President Hoover. The substantial withdrawal of outstanding areas of public lands from exploration and drilling led them to fear their best days might be ended unless they could arouse the West to strike hard against the alarming extension of the wilderness areas, the creation of new national parks, and the demands of the Sierra Club to withhold in national park and forest status a large part of the resources of Alaska.

These economic interests in the twelve western states came to believe that their representatives on the House and Senate committees having jurisdiction over the public lands had been outmaneuvered by environmentalists and old-fashioned conservationists on the Public Land Law Review Commission, whose report led to the enactment of the Federal Land Policy and Management Act of 1976.[36] Both report and act had declared that the lands under the jurisdiction of the Bureau of Land Management and the National Forest Service should remain in public ownership except for minor adjustments. These decisions plus the repeal of the Homestead Act and a host of other variations on the free land principle meant that the cattle and sheep ranchers using BLM forage lands could never gain ownership of land for which they had long been striving. Lumbermen must henceforth put up with Forest Service officials who, no matter how far they leaned in trying to satisfy representatives of Weyerhaeuser, Georgia Pacific, and Crown Zellerbach, would oppose the alienation of public forests. Could Amax and other hard rock mining companies ever hope to mine deposits on public lands they had located and explored at heavy capital cost?

Thus fanned the Sagebrush Rebellion, flaring up vigorously throughout the twelve public land states in 1979 and 1980. It began with members of the Nevada legislature who thought the time was right for a new sortie against the Bureau of Land Management and the 179 million acres over which it had jurisdiction. They pushed through the Nevada legislature an act declaring that the "purported right and ownership and control of the public lands . . . by the United States is without foundation and violates the clear intent of the Constitution. . . . This absentee ownership is a severe, continuous and debilitating hardship upon the people." Nevada has a "legal and strong moral claim upon the public lands." The sum of $250,000 was authorized for the prosecution of Nevada's claim of the lands. The act was rushed to other western states accompanied by complaints of mistreatment by the "absentee" government in Washington and quickly drew an excited response and support from all the public land states. Arizona and Colorado governors each vetoed bombastic resolutions of their legislatures, but the Arizona legislature promptly passed it over the veto. The states played out their game, with the obvious approval of President Reagan, but there was little to encourage the leaders that their scheme would get them anywhere.

Meantime, advocates of the Sagebrush Rebellion introduced measures in Congress to allow the secretary of the interior to convey to the states "federally owned unreserved, unappropriated lands," that is, the BLM lands, and to allow the secretary of the interior to reverse congressional will and permit mining in the national parks, monuments, and recreation areas.

The Sagebrush Rebellion was called by Cecil D. Andrus, Carter's secretary of the interior, "an attempt . . . to hornswoggle all Americans out of a unique land heritage which has been a bulwark of our society and the source of a special freedom that has made the West such a great place to live. . . . [It] has the potential of transforming the West from a land of open spaces into a patchwork eyesore that benefits the few and fences out the majority." [37] We may be assured it is not the last effort of the land grabbers to have the BLM lands, the national forests, and much of the national parks transferred to private ownership. President Reagan's first secretary of the interior accomplished much that the leaders of the Sagebrush Rebellion advocated by opening previously withdrawn lands to mining and drilling, allowing ranchers to control the grazing lands, reopening to public sale extensive areas, breaching the Surface Mining (strip mining controls) Act, accelerating timber cutting in the national forests, and opening large segments of the outer continental shelf to oil and gas leases.

In Canada mineral production was small in two of the three prairie provinces in the year the public lands were turned over to them. Only Alberta was showing much promise, its output of oil, natural gas, and coal in 1930 being worth $37 million. Thereafter, Alberta's income from sales and royalties from oil, gas, and coal climbed to $3,805,000,000 in 1979. Such a sum being quite beyond the needs of the province, Alberta began building a Heritage Savings Fund, which soon reached $10 billion. Twenty per cent of the heritage funds were being lent to other provinces for hydroelectric plants, a giant oil refinery, and harbor improvements. These loans remind one of the Reconstruction Finance Corporation grants or loans to public and private enterprises by the United States in the early thirties, except that the RFC funds were allocated by the federal government, whereas Alberta with its enormous wealth seemed to be playing a national role that the government of Canada was not able to play.[38] It was this lopsided development in the Canadian Confederation during the 1970s that led to another bitter dispute over control of the country's natural resources.

Alberta's booming oil and gas industry brought it low energy costs, no sales taxes, and low income taxes, while the residents of other provinces were dependent upon expensive imported oil. Could not Alberta's gas and oil be made available to them, or could not the enormous royalties of Alberta be shared with the federal government to enable it to subsidize the cost of imported oil for the industries and homes of eastern Canada and to enable the federal government to carry its other burdens? Prime Minister Trudeau maintained that Canada needed to retain ample supplies of these nonrenewable resources for herself. To restrain inflation, it was necessary to keep the price of domestic oil from rising to the level of world prices set by Opec, and it was essential for the federal government to have additional revenues from the oil and gas industry. "The government feels," said Trudeau in 1973, "that there will be a national interest to be considered and protected. We will not be prepared to acquiesce in any situation in which windfall profits accrue to private corporations. . . . Nor do we feel that it would be fair or just to have any windfall benefits accrue only to the producing provinces leaving all the rest of the people of Canada with nothing but the burdens." [39]

Alberta opposed Trudeau's policies of placing an export tax on oil and natural gas, limiting the amount of these exports, and regulating the price of oil and natural gas in the domestic market. The prime minister found that his interference with the provinces's control of their natural resources made them all, except Ontario, hostile to him and uncooperative in his efforts to control inflation and to get a new constitution for Canada.

The year 1973 saw a marked increase in Canada's proved reserves of oil and natural gas, but it also saw a dramatic rise in the domestic use of these products and in their export to the United States. To safeguard domestic supplies, Ottawa decided to restrict the export of crude oil to what Canada could safely spare, an amount that was to be set at one million barrels a day. As part of its anti-inflation measures, the government set the price of western crude oil at four dollars a barrel under the authority of the Emergency Energy Supplies Act of 1973. [40] The oil-producing provinces, particularly Alberta, resented the fact that the government had unilaterally set the price of oil and had placed an export tax of forty cents a barrel on one of her primary products without consultation and was going to use the revenue from that tax for the benefit of easterners. Her outstanding prosperity seemed endangered by Trudeau's policies. The attitude of Albertans, as expressed on their bumper stickers was, "Let the eastern bastards freeze in the dark." [41]

By the end of 1973 the energy situation was worse. Mid Eastern oil had risen to $7.50 a barrel. Ottawa had raised the export tax on crude oil to $1.90 and had terminated the export of gasoline and heating oil to the United States. There was a wider gap now between the federally fixed price of oil and the world price.

Trudeau made it plain that he did not intend to allow the domestic price to rise to the world level. He acknowledged that since 1930 the natural resources had belonged to the provinces and that "with ownership normally goes the customary right to receive a reasonable price." But, he asked, "Is the reasonable price necessarily the highest price anywhere in the world?" And is it a reasonable price if the high cost of oil will send inflation soaring and will put

Canada's manufacturing products at a price disadvantage? Is it a reasonable price if provincial taxes and royalties on the prosperous oil industry make some provinces so wealthy that it becomes impossible for the federal government to carry out the equalization policies that have been agreed on?[42] (The federal government was making grants to the poorer provinces to enable them to bring their social services and their educational facilities—in short, their quality of life—up to the level of the more fortunate parts of Canada.)

Ottawa was willing to negotiate on the energy-pricing question. In 1974 the oil-producing provinces agreed that for one year the wellhead price of oil should be fixed at $6.50 a barrel and that the revenue from the federal export tax on oil need no longer be shared with them. But this temporary agreement did not satisfy the western provinces. Saskatchewan attempted to impose a royalty surcharge on its oil, and Alberta raised its royalties on oil from 22 per cent of the wellhead price to 40.5 per cent.[43] That meant that the profits the oil industry would obtain from the increased price would be siphoned off before the federal government could get them by its corporation tax. Saskatchewan even threatened to "nationalize" its oil industry if her royalty surcharge act were to be struck down by the Supreme Court as an indirect tax she had not the right to impose. Nationalization would mean that the federal government could not tax what would then become provincial property. The Maritime Provinces, Newfoundland, and British Columbia also began to fear that they would lose control of their natural resources, particularly the offshore resources they claimed. Newfoundland asserted the right of the provinces to full control of their natural resources and a fundamental constitutional right to collect the full revenues from the sale of them on the world market.[44]

Ottawa was still not inflexible, but if agreement could not be reached, the federal government was determined to act unilaterally under the power the Petroleum Administration Act of 1974 gave it to set oil and natural gas prices in interprovincial and export trade.[45] In 1977 another temporary agreement was made under which the price of western crude oil was set at $13.70 a barrel, the price of natural gas was set in proportion to the price of oil, and in addition a federal excise tax of ten cents a gallon was imposed on gasoline.

By 1979, when the agreement of 1977 expired, negative feelings between the federal government and the provinces had intensified. The gap between the federally fixed price of oil and the world price was now more than ten dollars a barrel, and Alberta, with a big surplus of natural gas from recently discovered deposits, was pressing the government for permission to export more of it to the United States, but Trudeau wanted the gas reserved for markets in eastern Canada. Alberta was also demanding that she be allowed 90 per cent of the Chicago price for her oil, complaining that she had already subsidized the other provinces to the extent of $15 billion by providing them with oil at less than the world price. Ottawa's policies were criticized as "a clear attempt to change the basic concept of Confederation," which left the ownership of their natural resources to the provinces.[46]

On the return of the Trudeau administration to power in 1980, negotiations began anew. The federal government, determined to have a larger share of the profits from the country's resources in energy, placed an 8 per cent tax on the operating revenues of the gas and oil companies, cancelled certain deductions previously allowed them in calculating these revenues for income-tax purposes, and placed an excise tax on home heating oil and a tax on all sales of natural gas. This included exports of gas. Premier Lougheed called the export tax equivalent to "a declaration of war" that would shatter the whole concept of confederation. "It was a direct attack upon provincial proprietary rights." He would challenge it in the courts. Meanwhile, Alberta would cut back her production of oil. All the provinces except Ontario attacked the export tax.[47]

While these disputes were going on, Trudeau was trying to get the provinces to agree on a new constitution. Saskatchewan wanted a revised natural-resources section giving the provinces power to impose both direct and indirect taxes on their resources and also a role in discussions on interprovincial and also export trade that affected their natural resources.

Eventually both sides had to compromise. Alberta, Saskatchewan, and British Columbia were withholding revenues they should have sent to Ottawa, and Alberta was suffering from the punitive steps it had taken to curb the drilling and extraction of oil and gas. On September 1, 1981, Ottawa agreed to drop the export tax, Alberta agreed to end the cuts in oil production, the provinces consented to send in the revenues they had been withholding, and generous prices were set for new oil. The wellhead price of western crude was to be allowed to increase gradually unless the price of Mid Eastern oil stopped spiraling upward. In that case the domestic price was to be frozen. It was optimistically estimated that this agreement, which was to hold for five years, would assure Ottawa an addition of $2.6 billion annually, $1.6 billion to Alberta, and $2 billion to the petroleum industry.[48] With energy costs rising, consumers had little reason to welcome the change. More recently, the uncertainty of Opec prices has made the agreement of 1981 unsatisfactory to both the provinces and the Dominion government.

Clauses in the new constitution that were a part of the overall settlement with provinces gave them exclusive power to make laws relating to the management of their nonrenewable natural resources. They may also make laws relating to the export of these resources, but this is not an exclusive power, as federal laws may override. They may also tax their resources by any mode they choose, provided they do not discriminate against any part of Canada.

In the past, American governments had permitted the gigantic resources of Mesabi iron ore, Spindeltop oil, and Anaconda copper to pass to private interests that quickly exploited them, leaving behind to the home communities little from the development of their resources. One may congratulate Alaska, Alberta, Saskatchewan, and Montana and Wyoming for employing part of their resources for social welfare and for their wisdom in investing some of it for the future diversification of their economies when their nonrenewable resources will be gone. Today American states are receiving great benefits from their resources in the form of federal revenue-sharing grants and federal expenditures so that the West is truly the beneficiary of its resources. It needs emphasizing that it is through federal ownership and management of the public lands that this is accomplished.

Canada's federal government now has revenues from the country's natural resources that aid in maintaining social services, although that has been accomplished by methods that for a time placed a heavy strain on dominion provincial relations.

In the half century since Canada conveyed its public land rights to the provinces and the United States declined to take similar action in the western states, economic and political leaders in both countries began to question the wisdom of the decisions then made. Canada came close to a breakup of the Federation over the enormous revenues that its mineral-richest-province, Alberta, was receiving from its natural resources in which her federal government needed and was demanding a share. In the United States oil, mineral, lumber, and grazing interests had come to bitterly resent the absentee ownership and control of these resources. The climax of these uprisings was reached from 1978 to 1982. Prime Minister Trudeau negotiated a compromise with the western provinces over the taxing, pricing, and exporting, with higher returns to the Dominion and to the provinces. In the United States the Sagebrush Rebellion subsided quickly with the election of Ronald Reagan as president. The new administration relaxed or refused to enforce controls and regulations over mining, drilling, lumbering, and grazing on the public lands. Federalism in Canada has been advanced by the power Ottawa has gained from the broader sources of its revenues. In the American West mining, drilling, and grazing interests may have regretted the resignation of Secretary of the Interior James Watt, but a form of peace has descended upon land administration, and prayer and nonsectional budget problems have replaced conflicts over public land policies that characterized the seventies.

Federalism has survived in both countries after bitter skirmishes. Yet the talk in some provinces about "nationalizing" oil and gas industries in Canada and Alaska's proposal to amend the United States Constitution "to strengthen the role of the states" reflects continued dissatisfaction with, and deep suspicion of, what is sometimes called "creeping federalism."[49]

Notes

1. Basic studies of land policies in the two countries are Paul W. Gates and Robert W. Swenson, *History of Public Land Law Development* (Washington, 1968); Chester Martin, "Dominions Lands Policy," Arthur S. Morton, *History of Prairie Settlement* (Toronto, 1938); Lillian F. Gates, *Land Policies of Upper Canada* (Toronto, 1968).

2. Act of April 30, 1802, *United States Statutes at Large*, 2:173. For the story of the admission of new states, see Gates and Swenson, *History of Public Land Law Development*, 289-318.

3. Act of April 30, 1802, II *U.S. Statutes,* Section 4, 3rd Part, 175.

4. Gerard V. LaForest, *Natural Resources and Public Property under the Canadian Constitution* (Toronto, 1969), 12-13.

5. *Report of the Royal Commission of the Transfer of the Natural Resources of Manitoba* (Ottawa, 1920), 13; W. P. M. Kennedy, *Documents of the Canadian Constitution* (Toronto, 1916), 665.

6. The best treatment of a state's land policies is by Addison E. Sheldon, *Land Systems and Land Policies in Nebraska* (Lincoln, 1936), 210-85.

7. 32 *Stat.,* 388.

8. The apportionment of income from mineral leasing in the Act of February 25, 1920 (41 *Stat.,* 437-50), was changed in the Federal Land Policy and Management Act of October 21, 1976 (90 *Stat.,* 2743), to 50 per cent to the states of origin, except for Alaska, which was to have 90 per cent, and 40 per cent to the Reclamation Fund.

9. Department of the Interior, *Public Lands* (Washington, D.C., 1982), 186. The Public Land Law Review Commission contracted with EBS Management Inc., Consultants, of Washington, D.C., to study in detail revenue sharing procedures of the government, which published its *Revenue Sharing and Payments in Lieu of Taxes of the Public Lands* (Washington, D.C., 1970), in four gigantic volumes with the expected recommendation that grants in lieu of taxes should be substituted for the existing revenue sharing.

10. Elmo Richardson, *BLM's Billion Dollar Checkerboard: Managing the O & C Lands* (Santa Cruz, California, 1980).

11. Data on public lands granted to states and revenue sharing with them managed by the Bureau of Land Management are from the annually published Department of the Interior, *Public Land Statistics.* For revenue sharing of National Forest cutting, data is from the annual [Department of Agriculture] *Agricultural Statistics.* The National Forest Management Act of October 22, 1976 (90 *Stat.,* 2949), section 16, made possible the big increase in payments to the states. Payments increased from $109,333,000 in 1976 to $276,982,000 in 1980.

12. *90 Stat.*, 2662. Of the $103 million of payments in lieu of taxes made in 1980, approximately 80 per cent went to the public land states. Payments were to be made to counties for lands administered by the Forest Service, the National Park Service, and other reservations held for conservation purposes. U.S. Department of the Interior, *Public Land Statistics, 1980,* p. 177; Paul W. Gates, *Pressure Groups and Recent American Land Policies* (Ithaca, New York, 1980).

13. *67 Stat.*, 39.

14. One of the bitterest indictments of federal land management of the public lands is by Richard D. Lamm and Michael McCarthy, *The Angry West: A Vulnerable Land and Its Future* (Boston, 1982).

15. Actually the Bureau of Land Management was not created until 1946.

16. *Hearings before the Senate Committee on Public Lands and Surveys on Granting Remaining Unreserved Public Lands to States,* 72nd Cong., 1st sess., 1932, opposite 252.

17. *Public Papers of the Presidents of the United States: Herbert Hoover, 1929,* (Washington, D.C., 1974), vol. 1, 262–65.

18. *Hearings before the Senate Committee on Public Lands,* 334, for the makeup of the committee. Ray Lyman Wilbur, Hoover's secretary of the interior, was ex-officio member of the Garfield Committee. In his recollections he merely mentions the committee but devotes twenty pages to a wordy and uncritical account of the bureaus in his department and their functions. E. E. Robinson et al., *The Memoirs of Ray Lyman Wilbur* (Stanford, 1960), 422–40. William B. Greeley, a former chief of the Forest Service and later associated with commercial forestry, was a member of the Committee on the Conservation and Administration of the Public Domain, but he made no mention of it in William B. Greeley, *Forests and Men* (New York, 1951), and did not sign the report.

19. The income from mineral leases and royalties under the act of 1920 produced $4,739,095 in 1930, 90 per cent of which was paid into the Reclamation Fund and to the states. Department of the Interior, *Annual Report* (Washington, D.C. 1930), 52. It was brought out that three public land states—Idaho, Oregon, and Utah—preferred to have the lands left in the possession of the federal government; five—California, Arizona, New Mexico, Wyoming, and Utah—wanted no mineral reservations on ceded land; while five—Arizona, Colorado, Montana, New Mexico, and Wyoming—seemed to favor Hoover's proposal. *Hearings before the Senate Committee on Public Lands,* 14. For the unpopularity of the mineral reservation in land sales of the Northern Pacific Railroad, see Ross R. Cotroneo, "Reserving the Subsurface: The Mineral Lands Policy of the Northern Pacific Railway, 1900–1954," *North Dakota History* 40 (Summer 1973), 16–25.

20. William E. Leuchtenburg, *Franklin D. Roosevelt and the New Deal, 1932–1940* (New York, 1963), 1–17.

21. Paul L. Kleinsorge, *The Boulder Canyon Project* (Stanford, 1941); Beverley Bowen Moeller, *Phil Swing and Boulder Dam* (Berkeley, 1971).

22. Act of June 28, 1934, 48 *Stat.,* 1269.

23. George F. G. Stanley, *The Birth of Western Canada* (London, 1936), 42, 121.

24. LaForest, *Natural Resources and Public Property,* 31, n. 26; *Report of the Royal Commission on the Transfer of the Natural Resources of Manitoba* (Ottawa, 1929), 14–15.

25. Canada, *Parliamentary Debates,* 1870, pp. 1292–97, 1309, 1318.

26. Canada, *Parliamentary Debates,* 1929, vol. I, 222.

27. Chester Martin, *The Natural Resources Question* (Winnipeg, 1920), chapters 7 and 9.

28. *Sessional Papers of Canada*, 1885, no. 61, p. 5.

29. Canada, *Parliamentary Debates*, 1929, vol. I, 196.

30. Ibid., I, 220.

31. Ibid., I, 208, 220.

32. Ibid., I, 202.

33. Ibid., I, 199, 210.

34. Ibid., I, 210–11.

35. LaForest, *Natural Resources*, 41, n. 71.

36. Public Land Law Review Commission, *One Third of the Nation's Land* (Washington, 1970), I; 90 *Stat.*, 2744; Gates, *Pressure Groups*.

37. Cecil D. Andrus, "Fencing Out the Majority," E. Richard Hart, ed., *The Future of Agriculture in the Rocky Mountains* (Salt Lake City, 1980), 145.

38. *Toronto Globe and Mail*, June 15, 1981; *Alberta Public Accounts*, 1978–1979, vol. I, 4, 27.

39. *Canadian Annual Review*, 1973, p. 329.

40. *Canadian Statutes*, 21–22 Eliz. II, cap. 52.

41. *Annual Review*, 1974, p. 96.

42. Ibid., 1974, pp. 92–93, 385–86.

42. *Annual Review*, 1974, pp. 251, 103.

44. *Annual Review*, 1974, p. 74.

45. *Annual Review*, 1974, pp. 381, 383.

46. *Annual Review*, 1974, p. 92.

47. *Canadian News Facts*, 1980, p. 90.

48. *Canadian News Facts*, 1981, pp. 2563, 2573, 2589.

49. Alaska Statehood Commission, *More Perfect Union: A Plan for Action, Final Report*, 1983, p. 17 and elsewhere.

Publications of Paul W. Gates *

N.b.: Under each subheading, entries are listed chronologically by publication date.

Books

The Illinois Central Railroad and Its Colonization Work. Cambridge: Harvard University Press, 1934.

The Wisconsin Pine Lands of Cornell University: A Study in Land Policy and Absentee Ownership. Ithaca: Cornell University Press, 1943.

Frontier Landlords and Pioneer Tenants. Ithaca: Cornell University Press, 1945. Reprinted from *Journal of Illinois State Historical Society* 38 (June 1945).

Fifty Million Acres: Conflicts over Kansas Land Policy, 1854-1890. Ithaca: Cornell University Press, 1954.

The Farmer's Age: Agriculture, 1815-1860. New York: Holt, Rinehart, and Winston, 1960.

Agriculture and the Civil War. New York: Alfred A. Knopf, 1965.

Editor. *California Ranchos and Farms, 1846-1862.* Madison: State Historical Society of Wisconsin, 1967.

History of Public Land Law Development. With a chapter on legal aspects of

---

*This bibliography revises and expands Gould P. Colman, "Works by Paul Wallace Gates," in *The Frontier in American Development: Essays in Honor of Paul Wallace Gates,* ed. David M. Ellis *et al* (Ithaca: Cornell University Press, 1969), 407-10; Allan G. Bogue and Margaret B. Bogue, "Paul W. Gates," *Great Plains Journal* 18 (1979), 31-32; and Harwood Hinton, David Baird, and James Wright, "Publications of Paul W. Gates," *Western Historical Quarterly* 18 (April 1987), 135-40.

mineral exploitation by Robert W. Swenson. Washington, D.C.: Government Printing Office, 1968.

Landlords and Tenants on the Prairie Frontier: Studies in American Land Policy. Ithaca: Cornell University Press, 1973.

Editor. *The Fruits of Land Speculation.* New York: Arno Press, 1979.

Editor. *Public Land Policies: Management and Disposal.* New York: Arno Press, 1979.

Editor. *The Rape of Indian Lands.* New York: Arno Press, 1979.

Pressure Groups and Recent American Land Policies. Ithaca: Department of History, Cornell University, 1980.

Land and Law in California: Essays on Land Policies. Ames: Iowa State University Press, 1991.

Chapters and Introductions

"Introduction." In *The John Tipton Papers.* Comp. Glen A. Blackburn. Ed. Nellie Armstrong Robertson and Dorothy Riker. Indiana Historical Collections. 3 vols. Indianapolis: Indiana Historical Bureau, 1942, vol. 1, pp. 3–53.

"From Individualism to Collectivism in American Land Policy." In *Liberalism as a Force in History: Lectures on Aspects of the Liberal Tradition.* Ed. Chester McA. Destler. Henry Wells Lawrence Memorial Lectures. No. 3. New London: Connecticut College, 1953, pp. 14–35.

"Weyerhaeuser and Chippewa Logging Industry." In *The John H. Hauberg Historical Essays.* Ed. O. Fritiof Ander. Augustana Library Publications. No. 26. Rock Island, Illinois: Augustana Book Concern, 1954, pp. 50–64.

"Frontier Estate Builders and Farm Laborers." In *The Frontier in Perspective.* Ed. Walker D. Wyman and Clifton B. Kroeber. Madison: University of Wisconsin Press, 1957, pp. 144–63.

"The Homestead Act: Free Land Policy in Operation, 1862–1935." In *Land Use Policy and Problems in the United States.* Ed. Howard W. Ottoson. Lincoln: University of Nebraska Press, 1963, pp. 28–46.

"Foreword." In *History of the Public Land Policies.* Benjamin Horace Hibbard. Madison: University of Wisconsin Press, 1965, pp. v–xiii.

"Ulysses Prentiss Hedrick, Horticulturist and Historian." Introduction to *A History of Agriculture in the State of New York.* Ulysses P. Hedrick. New York: Hill and Wang, 1966. Reprinted in *New York History* 67 (July 1966), 219–47.

"Introduction." In *The Public Domain: Its History, With Statistics to June 30 and December 1, 1883.* Thomas C. Donaldson. Reprint. New York: Johnson Reprint Corporation, 1970, pp. vi–xvi.

"Indian Allotments Preceding the Dawes Act." In *The Frontier Challenge: Responses to the Trans-Mississippi West*. Ed. John G. Clark. Lawrence: University of Kansas Press, 1971, pp. 141–70.

"Corporation Farming in California." In *People of the Plains and Mountains; Essays in the History of the West. Dedicated to Everett Dick*. Ed. Ray Allen Billington. Westport, Connecticut: Greenwood Press, 1973, pp. 146–74.

"Foreword." In "Paul Schuster Taylor, California Social Scientist. . . ." An interview by Susanna R. Ries. 3 vols. Berkeley: Regional Oral History Office, 1975, vol. 2 (California Water and Agricultural Labor), typescript reproduction, iii–v.

"Public Land Disposal in California." In *Agriculture in the Development of the Far West*. Ed. James H. Shideler. Washington, D.C.: Agricultural History Society, 1975, pp. 158–78.

"Major Powell's 'Arid' Lands in Kansas." In *Kansas and the West: Bicentennial Essays in Honor of Nyle H. Miller*. Forrest Blackburn et al. Topeka: Kansas State Historical Society, 1976, pp. 123–29.

"The Nationalizing Influence of the Public Lands: Indiana." In *This Land of Ours; The Acquisition and Disposition of the Public Domain*. Indianapolis: Indiana Historical Society, 1978, pp. 103–26.

"California Land Policy and Its Historical Context: The Henry George Era." In *Four Persistent Issues: Essays on California's Land Ownership Concentration, Water Deficits, Sub-State Regionalism, and Congressional Leadership*. Berkeley: Institute of Governmental Studies, University of California, 1978, pp. 3–30.

"Foreword" to *Essays on Land, Water and the Law in California*. Paul S. Taylor. New York: Arno Press, 1979.

"The Federal Lands: Why We Retained Them." In *Rethinking the Federal Lands*. Ed. Sterling Brubaker. Washington, D.C.: Resources for the Future, Inc., 1984, pp. 35–60.

Journal Articles, Pamphlets, and Miscellaneous Publications

"The Disposal of the Public Domain in Illinois, 1848–1856." *Journal of Economic and Business History* 3 (February 1931), 216–40.

"The Promotion of Agriculture by the Illinois Central Railroad, 1855–1870." *Agricultural History* 5 (April 1931), 57–76.

"The Land Policy of the Illinois Central Railroad, 1851–1870." *Journal of Economic and Business History* 3 (August 1931), 554–73.

"The Campaign of the Illinois Central Railroad for Norwegian and Swedish Immigrants." *Norwegian-American Historical Association Studies* 6 (1931), 66–88.

"Large-Scale Farming in Illinois, 1850 to 1870." *Agricultural History* 6 (January 1932), 14–25.

"The Railroads of Missouri, 1850–1870." *Missouri Historical Review* 26 (January 1932), 126–41.

"The Struggle for the Charter of the Illinois Central Railroad." *Illinois State Historical Society Transactions for the Year 1933* 40, pp. 55–66.

"Historical Periodicals in the College Libraries of Pennsylvania." *Social Studies* 25 (January 1934), 10–11.

"Official Encouragement to Immigration by the Province of Canada." *Canadian Historical Review* 15 (March 1934), 24–38.

"American Land Policy and the Taylor Grazing Act." *Land Policy Circular* (October 1935), 15–37.

"Recent Land Policies of the Federal Government." *Certain Aspects of Land Problems and Government Land Policies.* In *Report on Land Planning,* pt. 7 (1935), 60–91.

"The Homestead Law in an Incongruous Land System." *American Historical Review* 41 (July 1936), 652–81.

"A Fragment of Kansas Land History: The Disposal of the Christian Indian Tract." *Kansas Historical Quarterly* 6 (August 1937), 227–40.

"Land Policy and Tenancy in the Prairie Counties of Indiana." *Indiana Magazine of History* 35 (March 1939), 1–26.

"Southern Investments in Northern Lands before the Civil War." *Journal of Southern History* 5 (May 1939), 155–85.

"Federal Land Policy in the South, 1866–1888." *Journal of Southern History* 6 (August 1940), 303–30.

"Land Policy and Tenancy in the Prairie States." *Journal of Economic History* 1 (May 1941), 60–82.

"Western Opposition to the Agricultural College Act." *Indiana Magazine of History* 37 (June 1941), 103–36.

"The Role of the Land Speculator in Western Development." *Pennsylvania Magazine of History and Biography* 66 (July 1942), 314–33.

"Hoosier Cattle Kings." *Indiana Magazine of History* 44 (March 1948), 1–24.

"Cattle Kings in the Prairies." *Mississippi Valley Historical Review* 35 (December 1948), 379–412.

"The Land System of the United States in the Nineteenth Century." *Proceedings of the First Congress of Historians from Mexico and the United States* (1950), 222–55.

"The Struggle for Land and the 'Irrepressible Conflict.' " *Political Science Quarterly* 66 (June 1951), 248–71.

"The Railroad Land-Grant Legend." *Journal of Economic History* 14 (Spring 1954), 143–46.

"Research in the History of American Land Tenure: A Review Article." *Agricultural History* 28 (July 1954), 121–26.

"Private Land Claims in the South." *Journal of Southern History* 22 (May 1956), 183–204.

"Adjudication of Spanish-Mexican Land Claims in California." *The Huntington Library Quarterly* 21 (May 1958), 213–36.

"Charles Lewis Fleischmann, German-American Agricultural Authority." *Agricultural History* 35 (January 1961), 13–23.

"California's Agricultural College Lands." *Pacific Historical Review* 30 (May 1961), 103–22.

"Vermont: Home of the Morgan Horse." *New England Galaxy* 3 (Fall 1961), 7–15.

"California's Embattled Settlers." *California Historical Society Quarterly* 41 (June 1962), 99–130.

"Tenants of the Log Cabin." *Mississippi Valley Historical Review* 49 (June 1962), 3–31.

"The Morrill Act and Early Agricultural Science." *Michigan History* 44 (December 1962), 189–302.

Free Homesteads for all Americans: The Homestead Act of 1862. Washington, D.C.: Civil War Centennial Commission, 1962.

"The Homestead Act in Operation." *Farm Policy Forum* 15 (3) (1962–1963), 19–23.

"Charts of Public Land Sales and Entries." *Journal of Economic History* 24 (March 1964), 22–28.

"The Homestead Law in Iowa." *Agricultural History* 38 (April 1964), 67–78.

"Land and Credit Problems in Underdeveloped Kansas." *Kansas Historical Quarterly* 31 (Spring 1965), 41–61.

"Pre-Henry George Land Warfare in California." *California Historical Society Quarterly* 46 (June 1967), 121–48.

"Changing Agriculture." *The Challenge of Local History.* Albany: University of the State of New York, 1968.

"The Frontier Land Business in Wisconsin." *Wisconsin Magazine of History* 52 (Summer 1969), 306–27.

"The Suscol Principle, Preemption and California Latifundia." *Pacific Historical Review* 39 (November 1970), 453–71.

"Public Land Issues in the United States." *Western Historical Quarterly* 2 (October 1971), 363–76.

"The California Land Act of 1851." *California Historical Quarterly* 50 (December 1971), 395–430.

"Problems of Agricultural History, 1790–1840." *Agricultural History* 46 (January 1972), 33–58.

"Research in the History of the Public Lands." *Agricultural History* 48 (January 1974), 31–50.

"The Fremont-Jones Scramble for California Land Claims." *Southern California Quarterly* 56 (Spring 1974), 13–44.

"Jonathon D. Stevenson and the New York Volunteers." *The Westerners Brand Book* (Number 14, 1974), 123–45.

"The Land Business of Thomas O. Larkin." *California Historical Quarterly* 54 (Winter 1975), 323–44.

"Public Land Disposal in California." *Agricultural History* 49 (January 1975), 158–78.

"An Overview of American Land Policy." *Agricultural History* 50 (January 1976), 213–29.

"Homesteading in the High Plains." *Agricultural History* 51 (January 1977), 109–33.

"Carpetbaggers Join the Rush for California Land." *California Historical Quarterly* 56 (Summer 1977), 98–127.

Land Policies in Kern County. Bakersfield: Kern County Historical Society, 1978.

"Two Hundred Years of Farming in Gilsum." *Historical New Hampshire* 33 (Spring 1978), 1–24.

"Federal Land Policies in the Southern Public Land States." *Agricultural History* 53 (January 1979), 206–27.

With Lillian F. Gates. "Canadian and American Land Policy Decisions, 1930." *Western Historical Quarterly* 15 (October 1984), 389–405.

"The Intermountain West Against Itself." *Arizona and the West* 27 (Autumn 1985), 205–36.